Traditional
Country House Cooking

Traditional
Country House Cooking

Tom Jaine

Annette Hope

C. Anne Wilson

Jennifer Stead

Alison Rosse

Edited by

C. Anne Wilson

Weidenfeld and Nicolson
London

Text pp. 1–11, 85–105 © C. Anne Wilson 1993
Text pp. 13–47 © Tom Jaine 1993
Text pp. 49–83 © Annette Hope 1993
Text pp. 106–120 © Jennifer Stead 1993
Text pp. 123–155 © Alison Rosse 1993

Illustrations © Weidenfeld & Nicolson Ltd 1993

First published in Great Britain in 1993 by George
Weidenfeld & Nicolson Limited, Orion House,
5 Upper St Martin's Lane, London WC2H 9EA

British Library Cataloguing in Publication Data
A catalogue for this book is available from the
British Library.

ISBN 0–297–83137–2

Designed by Atelier
Illustrations by Mette Heinz
Consultant Editor: Vicky Hayward

Typeset by Selwood Systems, Midsomer Norton
Printed and bound by Butler & Tanner, Frome,
Somerset

Contents

Introduction

Choyce Receipts was the title given to her manuscript cookery book by Dorothy Parsons, mistress of Birr Castle in the middle years of the seventeenth century. It was a good title, for the handwritten cookery book compiled by the lady of a great house, set in its own estate in any part of the British Isles, did contain carefully selected recipes, whether inherited from her mother's collection, given by friends or relatives, or newly invented through successful adaptations. She may not often have cooked them herself, but most ladies in her position liked to confer closely with the housekeeper, if not directly with the cook, to make sure that family and guests were offered tasty and interesting dishes, the sort of food that would enhance the reputation of the house.

Vicky Hayward first had the idea of seeking out four great country houses, one each in England, Scotland, Wales and Ireland, where enough cookery books, household accounts and estate books had survived to allow a detailed picture to emerge of how the household had been provisioned over a period of 300 years or more; and she had the further idea of making a book in which the domestic history of each house was complemented by a collection of recipes that actually were, or could well have been, in use there during those centuries.

The English house is Castle Hill in north Devon, the home of the Earls Fortescue. Tom Jaine has written its domestic history, and compiled a collection of recipes, known or likely to have been in use there during the seventeenth, eighteenth, and nineteenth centuries. Glamis Castle is the Scottish house, home of the Lyon (later Bowes Lyon) family, Earls of Strathmore, with links with the Stuart monarchy going back to the fourteenth century. Here Annette Hope has been the domestic historian, and she has also chosen recipes from the family's household books,

and one or two other books with local connections. Erddig Hall, Denbighshire (Clwyd), formerly the home of the Yorke family and now in the ownership of the National Trust, is the Welsh house, for which I have written the domestic history, while Jennifer Stead has selected recipes from cookery books in the Erddig archive dating from 1684 to the early 1920s. The Irish house is Birr Castle, Co. Offaly, the home of Alison Rosse, whose account of Birr begins in prehistoric times, continues through the centuries to the earlier generations of her husband's family, who rebuilt and developed the Castle, moves on to the days just before the Second World War when her mother-in-law entertained house parties there, and finishes with her own experiences of cooking and catering at Birr. Her recipes come from books in use between the seventeenth century and 1939, together with a few of her own devising.

The recipes have all been tested, and in most cases the quantities have been reduced to make them suitable for today's smaller families. They appear at the end of each chapter, duly set out so as to be easily accessible to the modern cook.

Estate accounts and other estate records have long been used by social historians, but early cookery books too are interesting, not only for what they tell us about contemporary foodstuffs and meals, but also as social indicators. The earliest cookery book in the English language is the one compiled about 1390 by the cooks of King Richard II, 'the which was accounted ye best and ryallest vyaund[er] of alle cristen kynges'. Its title is *The Forme of Cury*. Behind it lie still earlier cookery books (a few survive to this day) belonging to the time when the language of the English court was Norman French, and a new exciting cuisine with coloured foods and 'sotelties' was being introduced by the cooks of Crusader dukes and princes from the

Arab world at the eastern end of the Mediterranean. By Richard II's time cookery books were no longer written in Norman French, but many names of dishes still looked back to that earlier period, as in the case of the famous *blancmange*.

Several more English cookery books of the fourteenth and fifteenth centuries have survived, allowing us to chart the development of late medieval courtly and aristocratic cookery in Britain. Some include menus of particular great feasts, which prove that the recipes were actually used to create the dishes for such occasions. But simpler dishes are present too. Richard II's cooks claim that their book first teaches the making of common pottages and 'commune meatis for howshold as they shold be made craftly and holsomely', and then goes on to the 'curious potages & meetis & sotiltees' which were the fare of the highest in the land. The simple vegetable pottages or oatmeal gruels at the beginning contrast sharply with the fleshmeats or fish stewed with wine, spices and dried fruits, the pies with meat and spice fillings, and the 'standing' pottages thickened with ground almonds and rice flour.

Richer, more elaborate dishes are also well represented in other late medieval cookery books. They were prepared and cooked by male cooks, and were carried into the great hall and presented by male servers to diners who were also predominantly male. Even in peacetime feudal society remained close to its military origins. In a noble household the lord and his guests sat at the high table, and his retainers at the other tables in the hall in carefully ranked order. The only women who might be present were the lord's wife with her ladies-in-waiting, and the wives of principal guests. The wives of all others in the great hall stayed at home.

In peasant homes, of course, women prepared the simple stews of roots and herbs and the hearthbread that formed the staple diet, and shared them with their families. Their cookery lore was transmitted from mother to daughter orally, for they could neither read nor write.

In between, in terms of wealth, were the small manor houses, and here, especially in the late Middle Ages, a single recipe book was often maintained. It was a medical recipe book, recording the herbal medicines that the lady of the house might be called upon to prepare, for when illness struck a member of her family, a household servant, or even a poor neighbour, it was she who advised them and tried to effect a cure.

Sugar supplied the link between the medical books and the cookery books. It had a long history, having first come to the notice of Europeans after Alexander the Great's expedition to India. His admiral, Nearchos, reported back on certain reeds there that 'produce honey although there are no bees'. But its usage in India then must have been entirely medicinal, for when small amounts of sugar began to be traded through Arabia to the Graeco-Roman world, it was recognized there only as a medicine, good for the stomach and bowels, the kidneys and bladder, according to Dioscorides.

By the sixth century AD sugar cane was being grown within the Persian empire, in the Tigris and Euphrates delta and in parts of Baluchistan. When the Arabs overran Persia they extended its cultivation to the new lands they conquered in the West – Egypt, Cyprus, Rhodes, Crete, North Africa, Spain and Malta. By this time its delights as a food sweetener had been discovered, and also its value as a preservative for fruits and fruit juices. Hitherto honey had, of course, been used for both purposes.

Thus by the time sugar reached north-western Europe it was used in both a culinary and medical context. It was the sweetener for rich Arab-inspired dishes introduced by returning Crusaders, such as *blanc desire* (white food of Syria) made with pounded chicken flesh, almond milk, rice flour, sugar and spices; *saunc Sarazine* (Saracens' blood), a similar confection reddened with wine; and *egredouce*, the spicy, sweet-sour sauce, based on wine vinegar 'and the third part of sugar', in which gobbets of fish or flesh could be cooked. Meatless pottages based on sugar combined with cereal flour and the pulp of fruits or flowers were produced too. But sugar remained very expensive until well after the end of the Middle Ages, and was used only in the cuisine of the wealthy.

Sugar arrived in the West with a high reputation as a medicine. Arab physicians had followed the Greeks in recognizing it as a remedy, and in addition they used it to preserve fruits, seeds and roots, and to make syrups in which the properties of the preserved plant were combined with the virtues of sugar (itself warm in the first degree, according to the theory of the four humours). This lore and its recipes reached north-western Europe from the late eleventh century onwards, when the works of Arab writers were translated into Latin, and it brought some new medicinal usages into fashion. Aniseeds and caraway seeds coated in sugar were taken with spiced wine at the end of a great feast as digestives (they were also scattered over some of the pottages served at the feast as decoration). Royal and noble families consumed quantities of rose-sugar, violet-sugar and sugar candy in an attempt to ward off colds, chills and lung complaints, which must have been all too prevalent in draughty medieval castles.

The recipes for sugar-based medicines were translated into English in due course, and some were copied into the household books of herbal remedies. *Chardequynce*, prepared from quinces with spices and honey, and later with sugar instead of honey, was one such confection, valued as a digestive. *Penidia*, little sugar sticks resembling barley sugar and taken against the common cold, were another.

A different technique for extracting and preserving the virtues of plants was distilling. Nowadays we tend to think of early distilling in Britain as essentially a monastic activity, carried out on behalf of the monks and those people living near enough to turn to the monastery for help in times of sickness. But the practice of distilling was adopted in other large households, too – the household book of Henry Algernon Percy, 5th Earl of Northumberland, drawn up in 1512, lists twenty-nine different herbal 'waters' distilled each year for his two Yorkshire castles.

After the Dissolution of the Monasteries in 1539, even quite small gentry households acquired stills and built stillhouses or still-rooms in which to use them; and flowers, herbs and fruits were harvested from their gardens and distilled under the supervision of the lady of the house. The 'waters' created by distilling the plant material with wine had better keeping properties than simple herb- or flower-waters; nevertheless, there was considerable production of the simple flower-waters, especially rosewater, in demand not only as a cooling medicine for fevers, but also increasingly for cookery. The distilling recipes were duly copied into the household books, where they joined the herbal remedies and a growing number of fruit and sugar confections. *Chardequynce* and similar preserves made from other fruits came to be called marmalades, a name derived from the Portuguese *marmelada* (*marmelo* means quince), which was first imported into England in the fifteenth century.

The new additions to the household manual were linked with changes in the social situation of the womenfolk of noble and gentry families during Tudor times. The resources of those families, previously absorbed by the expenses of the Wars of the Roses, were now directed towards improving the quality of peacetime life. Castles and older manor houses were modernized, or else abandoned altogether in favour of a fine new country house. Families could entertain friends and kinfolk privately and with greater social ease now that the hierarchical disposition of guests practised during the later Middle Ages was going out of fashion. In fact the families themselves had been eating their meals in the great chamber for some time, apart from the rest of the household, rejoining them in the great hall only when important feasts took place; and it was during the sixteenth century that a room which did not contain a bed (as did the great chamber) was first set apart especially for the family's own meals, with the new name of dining-parlour. Here the members of the family entertained visitors of both sexes, and in due course paid return visits where the entertainment was reciprocated.

The lady of the house therefore took much more interest than before in planning meals and in choosing special dishes for her guests. William Harrison wrote in 1587 about the great ladies at court, and claimed that there were 'none of them but, when they be at home, can helpe to supplie the ordinarie want of the kitchen with a number of delicat dishes of their own devising, wherein the Portingall is their cheefe counsellor' (i.e. they followed Portuguese recipes). Harrison reported too that some of the ladies consulted regularly with the clerk of the kitchen in their own houses, and wrote down menus for particular meals to file away for future reference. The ladies of lesser gentry families followed suit, and

copied their favourite cookery recipes into their household books, along with the herbal remedies, sugared fruit conserves and distilled waters.

About this time the custom began whereby young girls copied some of their mothers' recipes into notebooks of their own, which they took with them on marriage to their new homes, and added to down the years. This practice explains why recipes appearing in manuscript cookery books can sometimes seem much too early for the date written on the title page or elsewhere. It could also happen that recipes came from someone else of an earlier generation, like those from Lady Dorothy Parsons' cookery book at Birr Castle, which can be traced back to her husband's aunt Elizabeth.

Meanwhile the tradition of the total cookery book, compiled or recopied by male cooks, was carried forward when the earliest printed versions appeared. The first known example, printed by Richard Pynson in 1500, simply reproduces a fifteenth-century manuscript, and contains many recipes in common with other contemporary collections (all the surviving manuscripts of this period have groups of recipes in common with some others, though never in quite the same arrangement).

It was to be some fifty years before a new cookery book was printed, though the possibility of a lost book issued in the interim cannot be ruled out. *A Proper Newe Booke of Cokerye* belongs to the middle years of the sixteenth century, and it was reprinted more than once. It displays a different approach from the medieval cookery books – the recipes are simpler, the instructions fuller, there is much emphasis on tarts with fillings of fresh fruits or vegetables, and some of the recipes show the influence of recent European cookery.

The next printed cookery book, *A Booke of Cookry Very Necessary for All Such as Delight Therein, Gathered by A.W.*, was published in 1584 with further editions in 1587, 1591 and 1594. Its recipes are grouped under headings – 'For stewed and boiled meat', 'For fish', 'Bake meats', 'Roast meats', and 'Tortes' are the principal ones. Nearly all the tarts are sweetened and spiced fruit tarts, and they are followed by an interesting additional group of recipes described in the table of contents as 'Divers other banquetting dishes'. They comprise the traditional spiced wine *Ipocras*, a *marchpane* (a disc of marzipan set on wafers and decorated with coloured comfits and gold leaf), and several fruit conserves; and in the later editions this section is expanded with syrup of violets and more preserved fruits.

The 'banquet' at which these sweet confections were offered had become an important feature of every feast or great dinner by the middle of Queen Elizabeth I's reign. It was a separate course served after the last main course of the meal, in another room, or even in a different building altogether. Banqueting-houses were built in turrets at rooftop level, or on raised mounds in gardens, where in summer the banqueters could enjoy both the sight and scent of the flowers and the views over distant prospects. Here they consumed a variety of sweetmeats accompanied by spiced wine or the sweetened distilled 'waters' which were the prototypes for the fruit brandies and liqueurs of our own time.

Some of this fare had first entered into household books with a medicinal reputation. But by the Tudor period it was fully accepted that sugar-sweetened confections of fruits or spices were more delectable if the eater was in good health to enjoy them. Mary, Queen of Scots, may have taken marmalade for *mal de mer*, as tradition records, but banqueters on land

found it very acceptable as part of the final course following a substantial meal. Banqueting fare was decorative as well as delicious, and came to include a wide range of sweet confections – wet and dry suckets (the wet were fruits in sugar syrup, the dry candied fruits), sugar-plate cast in a variety of shapes and colours, marmalades of different fruits, coloured jellies, gingerbreads, cakes, tarts, biscuits and wafers, and a variety of creamy dishes, such as syllabubs.

The recipes for this wide range of sweetmeats were duly copied into the household books, and the fashion for keeping such books spread to the wives of prosperous farmers and of men of the newly emerging middle class. More printed cookery books were issued too, to advise families who were rising in the world and who wished to learn how to offer hospitality in the most up-to-date ways. The books of the early seventeenth century gave great prominence to the making of sweetmeats. In Sir Hugh Plat's *Delightes for Ladies*, first published in 1605 and many times reprinted, the long first section is on 'The Art of Preserving, Conserving, Candying, &c.' (the other three are 'Secrets in Distillation', 'Cookerie and Huswiferie', and 'Sweet powders, Oyntments, Beauties, &c.', comprising recipes both for cosmetics and for cures for skin complaints). There were even little handbooks devoted entirely to sweetmeats, such as *A Closet for Ladies and Gentlewomen* (1608) and *A Daily Exercise for Ladies and Gentlewomen* (1617). The eating of the sugar-based goodies was no longer confined to the banquet course of a formal meal. A stock of them was kept at hand, so that two or three items could be offered by way of refreshment to visitors who called during the afternoon.

Within the country house the still-room became an important area for the realization of the recently acquired recipes. Garden produce gathered by the mistress of the house, her daughters and her maids, was distilled there, both for medicinal use and for 'entertaining waters'. Flowers, fruits and herbs were candied or boiled in syrups over a brazier for controlled heat, and that work too was often carried out in the still-room. Many of the sweetmeats were then set to dry in a stove, a sort of open cupboard with copper-wire mesh shelves, kept in the still-room to take advantage of the warmth of the furnace; and finally they were boxed and stored in that room. Cakes, tarts and biscuits were baked elsewhere, being set in the bread-oven after the loaves had been withdrawn. But creamy confections, if they required cooking at all, were prepared with care in a saucepan over the brazier in the still-room.

In gentry households the closer involvement of the lady of the house in kitchen affairs continued. The aristocratic family might still employ a male clerk of the kitchen to oversee male cooks and kitchen workers. But in other houses women began to be employed not only in lowly kitchen tasks (initially wives of estate workers came in to help temporarily in emergencies, thus paving the way for a more permanent female workforce) but also as cooks and housekeepers.

The household book became an important aid to both mistress and housekeeper. It now contained far more cookery recipes, and also the many preserving and confectionery recipes which were often copied into a different part of the book, beginning either half-way through or else at the end (when the book was inverted for easier reading). The conserves, cakes and sweet dishes were sometimes given a book of their own, as seems to have happened in the case of the earliest Strathmore book (Volume 243); here the three savoury recipes for sousing (pickling) a 'turkie', sousing a young pig, and making black puddings were perhaps included as they were preserving recipes.

Medical recipes still loomed large, and they often contained remarkably unpalatable ingredients. Many derived from a medieval past, yet they continued to be copied into household books until well on into the eighteenth century. Even untried remedies were not lightly discarded in those days of poor hygiene and alarming illnesses. One never knew when it might be necessary to turn to them as a last resort. In the early household books at Birr Castle, the medical recipes are nearly as numerous as the cookery ones. Elizabeth Mynne's small notebook in the Erddig archive, probably compiled around 1680 or a little earlier, includes a substantial number of medical recipes following those for cookery and preserves.

However, as the eighteenth century progressed, the number of medical recipes copied into cookery books did begin to dwindle. Sometimes they were excluded altogether, and were gathered into notebooks of their own. To compensate, some of the printed cookery books of the period began to include a section on invalid cookery. An early example is the group of light, easily digested dishes under the heading 'Directions for the sick' in Hannah Glasse's *The Art of Cookery Made Plain and Easy* (1747).

In the greatest aristocratic houses the cookery books had always been quite separate from the books containing the family's collection of medical recipes, for they belonged to two different areas within the household organization. Thus it has come about that at Castle Hill the Fortescues' family books of remedies, including the recipes for the distilling of curative 'waters', still exist and now form part of the estate archive, while the cookery books have disappeared.

Nevertheless, it is not too difficult to deduce what sort of dishes were served at the Fortescues' table from the seventeenth to the nineteenth century. There was a remarkable degree of homogeneity in the country-house cookery of aristocratic and gentry families throughout that period, except in the most remote areas. One or two traditional dishes of the region might appear on the menu, and of course the ingredients were mostly of local origin. But fashions for particular dishes prepared in a particular way had in years past originated from the court and spread downwards, and the connection with court and London fashions continued. From Tudor times members of the great landed families paid regular visits to London. They owned or rented London houses where they entertained other families of similar social standing. When back in their own country homes they invited kinfolk and friends to stay with them, sometimes for many weeks, or themselves went off to pay reciprocal visits. All this social interchange encouraged the tendency to a common cuisine.

That same cuisine formed the mainstay of the printed cookery books. Many were published only in London, and those that were printed initially in provincial towns and sold locally rarely deviated from the general pattern, for the authors hoped to republish their books in the capital (as did, for instance, Elizabeth Raffald, whose *Experienced English Housekeeper* first appeared in Manchester in 1769; the second and many later editions were issued in London – and an additional sixth edition came out in Dublin in 1778).

Elizabeth Raffald was one of many popular cookery book authors whose recipes were carefully copied into manuscript books compiled at home. Individual recipes can often be traced in such books, and the owner of the Erddig cookery book dated 1765 went further – a six-page section beginning on page 86 is headed 'receipts from Mrs Raffolds printed book'.

Thus it was that Tom Jaine was able to consult printed cookery books, published between the mid-seventeenth and late nineteenth century, to match up recipes with the foodstuffs being raised on the Castle Hill estate or bought in from outside at the time, and to assemble a collection probably differing very little from the recipes which once appeared in the lost manuscript cookery books. Also, the Fortescues' housekeepers may have owned and used contemporary printed books for day-to-day meals. The only two cookery books in the family's own library, one in French and both by Frenchmen, could have played a part in meal-planning at Castle Hill, but may have been used more often in London for fashionable entertainments at the family's house there.

The manuscript cookery books of Glamis Castle examined by Annette Hope are of the seventeenth and eighteenth centuries, and she was able to deduce the probable identities of their owners, even though there is something rather mysterious about Volume 244 of the archive. With no Glamis cookery books for the nineteenth and twentieth centuries available, she turned to the recipe collection of Lady Clerk of Tillypronie for the earlier period, and to the notebook of the Hon. Mountstuart Elphinstone, a relative by marriage of the family at Glamis, for the 1930s, and in both was able to find dishes typical of the Scottish country-house fare of their periods.

The Erddig Hall manuscript cookery books, now preserved with the vast Erddig archive at Clwyd Record Office, posed problems of identification in the case of the two earliest ones, which bear the dates 1684 and 1765 respectively. Both proved to have arrived at the Hall rather later than those dates suggest. But Jennifer Stead chose from them a selection of recipes that could certainly have been made with materials available at Erddig Hall in the years following those dates, and she made a further selection from the nineteenth- and early twentieth-century books known to have belonged to the last two mistresses of the Hall, and to the housekeeper who was responsible for the cuisine there during the First World War.

All the Birr Castle recipes, by contrast, are very closely identified with Birr. They were found in manuscripts compiled by forebears of Alison Rosse's husband, the 7th Earl of Rosse, and when she tried out recipes from the seventeenth- and eighteenth-century books she was actually cooking them in the very room in which they were originally prepared, though the former vast fireplace is now blocked up and she cooks on an Aga. Only two or three of the 1930s recipes reproduced in the Birr Castle collection came from printed cookery books. They were used or adapted at that period, and so much enjoyed that they were taken into the Castle's repertoire of recipes.

For each of these country houses there is a large collection of other records to show how the various foodstuffs were produced or acquired and assembled in the kitchen to supply the ingredients for the household's meals. The first thing that strikes anyone looking at them is how complex the food economy was, compared with that of a modern urban household. Moreover, as Tom Jaine points out, a great country house was provisioned on a long-term basis, and individual meals were the result of a choice made from several possibilities. Food was seldom procured specifically for a particular meal, except perhaps in the case of a festive meal for exceptionally large numbers.

When the food animals raised on the estate became too numerous, or there was an excess of fruit, vegetables, cheese, butter or other produce, the extra stock was sold off; and these same foodstuffs were bought in when there were losses, or perhaps at certain times of year. By-products, such as fleeces or hides, were sold to increase the income of the estate, or of the individual who received them as perks. Tenants arrived at the back door with poultry or young pigs or lambs or garden stuff, and were paid appropriate sums, duly recorded by the housekeeper. At Glamis livestock was brought in as rent, for part-payment of rents in kind still continued there throughout the eighteenth century, and, conversely, servants and estate workers were paid partly in measures of oatmeal, partly in cash.

Neighbours and kinfolk sent presents of venison to families whose estates lacked a deer-park, so such families ate venison at home several times a year. When shooting parties brought in large quantities of game-birds – as happened at each of the four houses described in this book – they were presented liberally to tenants, neighbours, and friends, and the remainder often sold through shops or market stalls in the nearest town.

That same nearest town could be the source of many imported foodstuffs, such as spices and dried fruits. At Birr the town lay close to the Castle on the south and east sides. Its original name was Parsonstown, after Sir Laurence Parsons who encouraged its growth when he acquired Birr in 1620; it was he who instituted the town's weekly markets, and in due course a wide range of shops followed. For Erddig the town of Wrexham lay within easy reach, and its shops could supply the imported foods for everyday use, procured via the seaport of Chester not far away, while Chester itself and Shrewsbury were the source of more exotic purchases. Castle Hill's nearest town was Barnstaple, and many grocery items such as dried fruits, spices and sugars were served to the household by grocers there. But citrus fruits came from Exeter, where an agent made purchases on behalf of the Fortescues, and also met part of the family's large requirement for sea-fish, while some items came direct from London. By contrast, the household at Glamis did not rely on Forfar, a few miles away, for any of its major grocery purchases until Victorian times. During the eighteenth century, tea, chocolate, sugar, almonds, spices, dried fruits, rice, sago, macaroni, and vermicelli were all purchased in bulk in London and despatched by sea to Dundee, from where they were transported to the Castle. Other foodstuffs were acquired in Dundee itself. But by the later nineteenth century the household was patronising both the Forfar Co-operative store and the Army & Navy stores in London for its groceries.

There was also an underground economy, not easy to pin down. Housekeepers superintended local purchases, and, in return for the trade of the big house, shopkeepers adjusted the accounts to make sure the housekeeper was well rewarded. This practice was said to have reached outrageous proportions in London houses in the eighteenth century, but it is surprising to find it going on at Erddig in the nineteenth on such a scale that Mary Webster left more than £1,300 in her will in 1875, far more than she had earned in some thirty years as housekeeper to the thrifty Yorkes. Another housekeeper, Miss Harrison, was less lucky, and was dismissed in 1897 for illicitly disposing of pheasants.

Opportunities also arose for gardeners to take advantage of gluts of produce. At Castle Hill in the 1770s Lord Fortescue instructed that the surplus be given to neighbours and to the steward's family, and the gardener 'may make what he can of the remainder'. At Erddig the head gardener, James Phillips, died in 1882 leaving nearly £4,000 in the bank, again far more than his lifetime's earnings, so Erddig's surplus produce must have contributed handsomely to that sum.

Another call on the income of the estate was charity, given sometimes in cash and sometimes in food. Two sheep a week were killed at Castle Hill and bread supplied to accompany the meat for local poor people in 1776 during a bad winter, and turnips were grown specially in the park to help provide for them in 1811, another dearth year. At Erddig the housekeeper's accounts from the 1790s to 1815 (when they end) show frequent payments of 2s.0d. or 2s.6d. under the head 'Charity' – though whether these went to individual families or were distributed through a parish benevolent scheme is not explained. Also in the Erddig archives is a late eighteenth-century 'receipt for making a savoury & nourishing food', which begins promisingly enough with 3 lb lean beef, plus smaller quantities of rice, parsnips, potatoes and onions, but then goes on to add 3 gallons of water, thus producing one of those temporarily warming soups which used to be so popular with philanthropists as food for the poor. Another recipe of similar proportions at Abbey Leix, not far from Birr Castle, is thought to have been used there during the potato famine of the 1840s. Today we know that such dishes supplied very few calories for a hungry person. Help of a more practical nature was offered at Birr in the 1840s, when up to 500 people at a time were given employment in building long walls and other work on the demesne. Their wages must have ensured that their families had more than just thin soup to live on in the famine years.

The servants' wages and their board had, of course, to be supplied from the resources of the estate. Within each country house there were at least two dietary regimes, one for the family and their guests, and another for the servants. In Victorian times the nursery diet of simple, plainly prepared food could form a third. The family ate a variety of different fleshmeats, and doves, chickens, ducks, rabbits, hares, venison, and woodcocks and other game-birds appeared not infrequently on their table, to supplement the roast beef, mutton, and pork. They also consumed a wide range of fish. The servants ate the coarser cuts of beef and mutton, bacon, and sometimes rabbits. In earlier times they received saltfish but, later, fish was not usually a large item in the servants' diet. They were given some vegetables, mainly root vegetables and herbs in meat stews, and plain puddings, perhaps fruit pies in summer, cheese, and plenty of household bread.

The families, when they entertained guests at their country homes, enjoyed many made-up dishes, both savoury and sweet; among the recipes at the end of each section of this book are some typical examples. Afterwards the upper servants, at least, expected to receive the leftovers, which added welcome variety to their diet. But all servants in country houses were generally well-fed, sometimes overfed, though mainly on rather stodgy food. A favourite celebration meal was beef and plum pudding. That was what Dorothy Yorke provided for the local carters who brought the tiles to re-roof the mill at Erddig in the 1760s. At Castle Hill in 1852 the New Year's supper prepared for the labourers and their wives was 'hot roast and boiled beef and plum pudding: 1 lb. of meat with $\frac{1}{2}$ lb. of pudding and $\frac{1}{2}$ lb. of bread and a portion of vegetables fully sufficed'.

It was partly because their estates supported similar food animals and crops that the families at Castle Hill, Birr and Erddig could, without difficulty, enjoy a rather similar cuisine. Glamis in the Scottish highlands came to share in it too, but the estate there was more limited in its scope, being not only much further north than the other three houses, but also on the east side of Britain, whereas Castle Hill, Birr and Erddig experienced in varying degrees the advantages of the Atlantic climate. But even in Scotland, walled

gardens and eventually cold frames and greenhouses made it possible to grow a considerable range of vegetables and fruits, though the wheat for the family's white bread could not always be raised on the estate and might have to come from further south.

The families at each of the four houses were highly distinctive in their achievements. But they all shared aspirations to improve their houses and gardens through successive centuries. At Glamis Castle expansion was initially upwards. The old great hall of fourteenth-century origin was superseded in the seventeenth century by a new vaulted great hall with a very fine plaster strapwork ceiling at a higher level in the building. At Birr Castle Sir Laurence Parsons in the seventeenth century created a Dutch-style house, recorded in a delightful drawing at the front of his daughter-in-law Dorothy's cookery book, by building onto the gatehouse of the original keep and joining it to two flanking towers. In the early nineteenth century the house was castellated and given a Gothick saloon, and later in the century a new wing with a dining-room and a huge basement kitchen was added.

At Filleigh in Devon the Fortescues remodelled the earlier manor house in about 1684, and extended it in Palladian style in the 1720s with nine-bay wings at either side of the main building, which was refaced in Portland stone. At Erddig Philip Yorke I refaced the west front of the brick-built Hall in stone in the 1770s, when he also built on the new kitchen and added other outbuildings. Refacing houses in stone was a popular improvement at that period; Philip's second wife Diana almost bankrupted herself by refacing her own house, Dyffryn Aled, in Bath stone shortly before she married him.

Gardens also underwent changes. The formal walled gardens extending in front of Glamis Castle, and the seven fine gateways decorated with stone ornaments and statues and set at intervals across the long driveway belonged to the days of Patrick, the 3rd Earl of Strathmore. They were swept away in the eighteenth century when Capability Brown redesigned the park. Later still, formal Dutch and Italian gardens were laid out close to the Castle.

The southern slope below the house at Castle Hill was terraced after 1730 down to a serpentine pool, with wooded walks at either side, all adorned with obelisks, temples in varied styles and other garden buildings, while to the north of the house the rising ground was crowned with a sham castle, whence it took its name. Even distant prospects were changed, with Filleigh church rebuilt to form a Gothick 'eyecatcher', and a sham village created towards the south-west horizon.

At Erddig the formal gardens designed by John Meller after 1718, comprising a 'Best garden' with a canal at its further end, a 'Harty Choak garden', a kitchen garden, orchards and fishpond, were only slightly modified by Philip Yorke I in the 1770s. His garden additions were the series of waterfalls along the Black Brook below the house, culminating in the unusual 'cup and saucer' – a cylindrical waterfall disappearing through a hole in the centre of a wide basin; it can be viewed only by looking up the tunnel from the verge of the stream lower down. In the nineteenth century a parterre with fountains was set out on the east side of the house.

At Birr in the seventeenth century the formal flower, artichoke and kitchen gardens were established. In the later eighteenth century Sir William Parsons dredged the lake from bogland within the park and began to landscape the surrounding area with clumps of beech trees. His son and later successors followed him in tree-planting, and during the twentieth century the 6th Earl of Rosse added many rare trees and shrubs from China and the Far East. But the garden has still more unusual features. The earliest known suspension bridge was hung across the River Camcor below the Castle walls about 1810. The 3rd Earl of Rosse, who succeeded to the title in 1841, erected the then largest telescope in the world (for the next seventy-five years) in the park. The speculum was cast in a furnace in the Castle moat, under his guidance, by local workers, and polished to reflect the light of hitherto unobserved nebulae, which he drew with the greatest accuracy. The arches of the telescope's outer casing still stand on their site, and will soon be a focal point for visitors to Ireland's first science park.

The economic structure of all four estates is still complex today. Visitors now make a modest contribution towards the upkeep of house and gardens at Glamis and Birr Castles, and a greater one at Erddig Hall, owned by the National Trust. Castle Hill lost much of its historic internal structure through a disastrous fire in 1934, and the interior was rebuilt in altered form. But the estate still flourishes, and if the greenhouses no longer produce 'pines and melons' Castle Hill tomatoes are nevertheless a byword for excellence in local shops for miles around.

In the pages that follow the reader can learn a great deal about how these four very different estates were organized, and how their households were provisioned in years gone by. Four different food historians have each contributed their own insights to the interpretation of the evidence, thus building up a remarkably comprehensive picture of the food economy of the British country house. And at the end of each section are the recipes to prove that over the past three hundred years British country-house cookery has been one of the finest cuisines in the world.

C. Anne Wilson

ENGLAND

Castle Hill, Devon

Tom Jaine

Castle Hill, Devon

'The Gardener attending, I rode through Lord Fortescue's grounds, passing before the front of the house of no extraordinary beauty. Very little taste had been displayed.' So begins a rather grudging account of a visit to Castle Hill near South Molton in Devon, written by local antiquary John Swete in 1789. There had been many other, and more appreciative, tourists since the house and park first took its present shape in the early eighteenth century. Swete himself noted the intended conversion of a small building 'for the reception of Strangers, where they may take a cold repast or drink their tea, for there is no Inn near'.

Castle Hill was the grandiloquent name accorded the mansion of Filleigh as the social, political and architectural ambitions of its owners took flight. It was the seat of Earl Fortescue, and had been in the family since the marriage of Martin Fortescue to the heiress of Filleigh and Weare Giffard in 1454. Description of genealogies is as wearisome and mind-numbing as the detailing of points and junctions in a railway marshalling yard. Fortescues trace their arrival in Britain, inevitably, to the Norman conquest, but the family first came to prominence in south Devon during Henry V's French campaigns. The next generation included Sir Henry Fortescue, Lord Chief Justice of Ireland, and Sir John Fortescue, Lord Chief Justice in Henry

VI's reign and author of *De Laudibus Legum Angliae*.

The dynasty once founded – Martin Fortescue was Sir John's second son – spread like wildfire through Devon and beyond. There were Fortescues of Ebrington (in Gloucestershire, the estate that lent its name to the cadet title of the family), Spridlestone, Fallapit, Buckland-Filleigh, Shebbear, Dromiskin (in Ireland), Punsborne, and Salden; and, indicatively, there have been more sherriffs and MPs in Devon from the Fortescue family than any other. In the single parliament of 1592, the head-count was eight. Judges, generals, Chancellors of the Exchequer, defenders of the Old Faith in the reigns of Henry VIII and Elizabeth, diplomats, conspirators, politicians and lord lieutenants: each tendril of the stem made its contribution.

As is the way of these things, there was an element of haphazard natural selection in the eventual concentration of Fortescue honour at Filleigh. It was not the most glorious line, nor immediately the richest. Perhaps it kept its nose clean the longest. At any event, from a slightly parlous condition at the end of the seventeenth century, they married and intrigued their way to considerable estates, a new mansion, a barony and an earldom by the reign of George II. Thereafter, they were content to play their role as local grandees, and aspired only periodically to strut upon a wider stage. The 2nd Earl Fortescue was Lord Lieutenant of Ireland in 1839–41; his son was a Lord of the Treasury and Secretary to the Poor Law Board in 1846–51. Throughout, they kept themselves solvent, secured the succession, and consolidated their estates.

By the end of Victoria's reign, these were among the largest in the county. Seymour Fortescue, who spent many years as aide-de-camp to King Edward VII, described his father, the 3rd Earl, thus:

After giving up political life, until old age and infirmity had limited his activities, he remained faithful to his County duties and was a most just and generous landlord. When he died at the age of eighty-seven, I believe it to be true that the only building on the estate, whether it were cottage, farm, farm building, village school, or church that was badly in need of a new roof and general repair was his own house. In fact, he was an excellent specimen of the average Victorian peer.

Only in this century has the title been separated from the house. On the death of the 5th Earl in 1958, the title passed to his brother, who took the Gloucestershire estate of Ebrington (which went back to Lord Chief Justice Sir John Fortescue, who lived there in the fifteenth century), while Castle Hill descended to the 5th Earl's daughter. The house still stands proud above the main road to Barnstaple, though a fire in 1934 destroyed much of the original interior.

It was at Castle Hill that the family's voluminous archive was preserved. Today, it is safe within the walls of the Devon Record Office at Exeter. Any student of domestic and cookery history must wonder if a private archive will yield to them the precious facts they seek. Will there be recipe books? Will the cook have left accounts? Will the lady of the house have carefully noted what meals were served, and to whom, so as not to duplicate a dish or serve a pet dislike? It is the way of things that no single collection will supply each and every thing. None the less, if at all extensive, it will offer material on a wider range of topics than can be covered in a single short essay. The Fortescue archive is like that.

There are regrettably few recipes. Those which remain are medical rather than culinary. Nor are there volumes of menus. It is therefore difficult to know exactly which dishes the Fortescues liked and consumed. Nor does their private correspondence help towards an opinion. It was ever considered bad form to discuss food at the dinner table, at least until the present day, and most people's letters show the same healthy disregard of diet and cookery. Lady Blanche may complain that her neighbour at dinner was boring, but she does not go on to excoriate the roast beef.

There are, however, accounting records in profusion. This is the particular strength of the Fortescue papers. Accounts were kept as records of income and expenditure, or as a check on the probity of various household officers. At the outset of accounting history, it was this latter function that bulked the largest. The Bishops of Winchester, whose account rolls are among the earliest private accounts of the Middle Ages, would not have been able to tell if their manors were in profit, but they would have been sure that their bailiffs were not cheating them. In the same fashion, the baker would keep a flour account, and the butler a cellar-book, so that the proprietor could see what had happened to all that money spent on grinding wheat or laying in claret. It is from such items that a picture of how the Fortescue household was managed emerges.

We talk of 'the Fortescue family' as if it were an identifiable nucleus of father, mother and offspring. However, over time, it became a sprawling cousinage, encompassing several generations, forms of household and economic situations, each with a hundred and one different interpretations of food and feeding. At the outset of the eighteenth century there was William Fortescue, an eminent lawyer who ended his career as Master of the Rolls. He was a cousin of the Castle Hill Fortescues, and had a fine house and garden at Buckland-Filleigh; he counted the poet Alexander Pope among his friends. 'Be assured', Pope wrote to him, 'that Lord Burlington is issuing orders to his gardener to attend you with pineapples.' By contrast to this easy conversance with life's luxuries, another cousin, 'cozen Dudley', had 'a lame son in so much want that after he dined here they tell me hee picked up the crums and offals upon the hall table to carry home'.

Family is also an extensible term from the point of view of consanguinity. In late classical and medieval times, *familia* referred to the servants who were fed and clothed by the master, just as the Mafia 'family' takes in more than blood relations. In the nineteenth century, 'family' could have the specific meaning of those eating in the parlour – a term which, in servants' talk, survived the conversion of that room into dining-room – or it could take in the close household. These people, too, had to be fed, and their diet occupies nearly as much space in records as the grander meals

served to their masters. In the Elizabethan era, noble households were extremely large. But a house such as Castle Hill in Victorian times continued to reveal the same imbalance between employers and employed. In 1854, a total of 266 meals were served in a single week in November. The household that consumed these was made up of five adult members of the family, with one visitor and three children. They were supported by four nursemaids, five upper man-servants, five upper women-servants, four footmen, five stablemen (who ate indoors, while the gardeners did not), nine maids, and two part-time washerwomen. In addition, three farmers, nine tradesmen, and a visiting servant were fed during the week.

Even in the relatively small London household of Lord Ebrington in the 1840s, while twenty-one dinners were served in one week to family, seventy-nine were eaten by servants. The daily allowance at Castle Hill in the 1850s of $1\frac{1}{2}$ lb of meat, 1lb of flour, 1 quart of ale, and 1 pint small beer was eloquent argument for remaining in service. Even if the wages were small, you knew whence the next meal would come, just as you knew a clothing allowance and free laundry were part of the contract. In 1775, Lord Fortescue suspended the cash allowance for livery, and had the suits made up himself:

I found the servants putting as much as they could into their own pockets without caring how they appeared ... I have already made the full dressed liveries, they are blue coats laced with yellow linings and yellow breeches, and waistcoat and a gold laced hat – these are the ancient liveries of the family.

The privileges extended to household staff were spread more widely at festive times. In 1852:

Having closed the old year with a dance to the servants, we began the new one with a 5 o'clock supper to our labourers and their wives; about 200 of whom sat down in the coach house to a repast of hot roast and boiled beef and plum pudding; 1lb of meat with $\frac{1}{2}$ lb of pudding and $\frac{1}{2}$ lb of bread and a portion of vegetables fully sufficed. The tables were then cleared and they danced till 9.

Nor were the poor forgotten. In the bad winter of 1776, two sheep were killed each week, 'for the use of those who are the most proper objects, together with a proportionable quantity of bread and this I would have continued until the weather becomes milder'. Come the next month, his Lordship comments that he would not like to put charity to bad use by 'encouraging illness, a vice as you know the parish of Filleigh are much addicted to'.

The feeding of the poor, linked in popular historical mythology to the days of the monasteries and 'good old England', was seriously undertaken here until well into the nineteenth century. Although there are no references to distributing the offal of the table in surviving documents, there is plenty of evidence of cooking specifically for the indigent. In the time of dearth in 1811, some of the park was put to turnips – for human, not animal, consumption. Soup was made in the Castle Hill kitchen during the winter of 1854, and distributed to approximately forty poor people in one week in December. In 1858–9 'African port' was given out to the poor over the winter festivities, and, if she was lucky, a 'poor woman' would get 'a little' port or brandy at the back door, according to notes in the cellar-books.

As family is susceptible to broad or close definition,

so 'home' extended to more than one house. The Fortescues of Castle Hill maintained several establishments: Weare Giffard near Bideford, which had been the principal dwelling of the original estate; Ebrington in Gloucestershire, inherited from Lord Chief Justice Fortescue, and source of the cadet title of the family; Tattershall in Lincolnshire, coming to them through the Clinton connection made by marriage in the seventeenth century; Simonsbath on Exmoor, used in the nineteenth century as a summer residence and hunting lodge; Summerville in Waterford, Ireland, owned during the Victorian period; and a succession of London houses from the beginning of the eighteenth century until modern times.

Although usually life was divided between Castle Hill and London, periodic visits to the other properties were never entirely suspended, unless for a time they were left in the hands of dowagers or younger brothers. This division of focus is an essential characteristic of modern British aristocracy. It might affect the sort of food one served in dining-room and hall. The autarchy of the country estate counted for much. Even by the seventeenth century, when the migration of country families to the capital was a matter of national political concern, people were beginning to see a distinct country style of plain cooking, served generously. At Castle Hill, there were tenants' dinners, the poor were fed regularly with soup in times of dearth, great quantities of game were eaten as they were shot, bread was baked and beer was brewed in the house itself, and parlour guests were usually members of the family or close relations.

In London, by contrast, nearly everything was shop-bought, there were fewer dependents to feed or consider, and guest lists consisted of high-flying political and social acquaintances. Cooking might be more precious and more influenced by fashion. Thus, it is possible to think of at least two dietary regimes being followed by the family in any year. In the same way, when Lord Fortescue was made Lord Lieutenant in Dublin in 1839, his kitchen establishment increased from a single cook and a couple of maids to a cook, a roasting cook, three kitchen maids, a confectioner and two assistants in the confectioner's office. It was not merely that more meals were served, but also that the style of the cooking took on more gloss.

Certainly the transfer of the household from one residence to another was a sizeable task. In 1853, the cost of transport of servants, plate and baggage to London was nearly £33, the equivalent of a week's household bills. The baggage cost in 1804 was as high as £68. About a ton and a quarter went up from Castle Hill, and more than two tons returned. Family tradition notes that the maids slept in the beds for a day or two to air them for the family's return.

Accumulation of houses like this can appear a useless encumbrance to us. A man, after all, can only sleep in one bed at a time. In the Middle Ages it was common sense. Not only could the lord progress from one house to another, thus saving the trouble of transporting food, but also by showing himself to his neighbours and tenants, he preserved his political influence. More recently, these considerations were not so important. Income in kind was replaced by money. The Fortescues did not take foodstuffs from their outlying estates, save perhaps in sport, although they did make regular deliveries to their residence in London. Political influence became focused on the polling

booth alone, rather than spread through the countryside at large. Nonetheless the building of mansion houses was still a political statement. It is significant that Castle Hill's major cycle of construction and improvement commenced in the 1730s, when the Earl of Clinton retired from metropolitan politics but wished to build up his influence in Devon.

In this sense, use of buildings as visible status confirmation and for maintenance of political and economic control went on for a long time after the Middle Ages, even if in attenuated form. Another Devonshire family, the Viscounts Courtenay of Powderham Castle, spent at least one month each year in residence at Forde Manor in Newton Abbot, a small market town an hour's ride away, where they had considerable landed interest. When at his chief mansion, Lord Courtenay maintained a sophisticated table. He hired French chefs, and held fashionable routs, buying in the works of the best pastrycooks, and indulging in architectural embellishments on the buffet. The visit to Ford, a solid Jacobean manor house, old-fashioned and unimproved, must have been akin to a camping holiday; everything was taken from Powderham, from servants to bed linen, and catering was of the simple sort. It was endured so the flag might be kept flying.

It is noticeable that families blessed with several properties tended to move from one to another rather than rebuild on the same site, as and when their fortunes improved. Thus the Fortescues' first major piece of construction, their north Devon inheritance once consolidated, was the manor of Weare Giffard. As marriage and politics pushed them towards the aristocracy in the eighteenth century, they did not rebuild this house but began a new one on more acceptable modern lines at Castle Hill. On the south coast, at Plymouth, the Parkers did the same thing, building the Tudor and Jacobean house of Boringdon Hall to begin with, but eventually letting it go to rack and ruin. Their new mansion at Saltram was more convenient and more fitting to their greater influence.

Weare Giffard and Castle Hill display the essential progress from dining-hall to dining-room. The manor house that John Fortescue built at Weare Giffard at the end of the fifteenth century has a magnificent hammerbeam roof, an ornate screen, and upper gallery in the great hall. The quality of the carving is exceptional, with nothing so grand for many a mile. This room was the visible centre of the dwelling. On formal occasions, the squire sat at one end, the dais end, facing the screen which masked the main entry to the lodging and access to the rooms necessary for the serving of food: the buttery and pantry with kitchen beyond.

Not all meals were taken in the hall. Much of late medieval domestic architecture was preoccupied by the arrangement of varying layers of privacy for the actual owners of the house, from the king down to relatively minor gentry families. Families had taken to dining, still rather formally, in the great chamber; and, by Tudor times, the family might often eat by itself in the parlour. Even so, the centrality of the hall to the dining process was preserved. The food for the lord would be paraded through the hall, where the rest of the household might be eating, on its way from the kitchen to private chamber. The ordinances of the Earl of Huntingdon in 1609 demand that all men 'be bare-headed whilst their Honnors' meat passeth through' the hall on its way to the chamber.

Many of the arrangements at Weare Giffard have been swept away by later improvements, but an inventory of the manor house of Salden in Buckinghamshire belonging to a cousin, Sir Adrian Fortescue, taken after he was executed for treason in 1539, gives some idea of the organization of rooms. There were two chambers, both used for sleeping; the hall contained two 'great side tables with standing trestles' and five benches; and the parlour was fitted out with a table and two trestles, five chairs and a bench. Dining, therefore, had its public and its private faces. Meals were provided out of the buttery, pantry and kitchen.

Ancillary rooms for food production at Salden included the larder, where meat was salted and preserved – it contained a brine tub and a 'powdering trough' where meat could be dry-salted; a boulting-house with a kneading trough for the bread dough, the name of the room referring to the preparatory sifting of various grades of flour for baking; the fish house, where salted ling, stockfish, and 'haberdens' or sun-dried cod were stored; and a brewhouse.

Neither the theory nor practice of dining in public survived into the eighteenth century, when Castle Hill was remodelled. The great hall that was part of the earlier house was converted into a saloon, used for formal receptions but not for eating, which took place entirely in the adjoining dining-room – for the family that is, the servants being confined to the servants' hall. This is the most important aspect of the re-allocation of rooms: the daily life of the family became distinct from that of the household, while the great hall had imposed a notional unity.

Medieval togetherness, expressed by sharing food

and table, could survive many centuries. In the north Devon parish of Hartland, not a dozen miles from Castle Hill, farmers today can remember how their grandparents would eat Sunday dinner together with the farm workers, who then might go to their families for Sunday tea. Sometimes, if they had guests, employers would eat apart, and other households imposed a distinction rather similar to that of the parlour and the hall, except in a Victorian farm where the family sat in the kitchen and the workers sat in the scullery. Another distinction, a parallel this time of the lord sitting on the dais and the retainers in the body of the hall, was drawn by those farmers who would lay the kitchen table with a cloth for the family end, leaving bare boards for the staff.

Entering the Fortescues' kitchen and offices at about the time of the Restoration, the visitor would have been greeted by a large open fire, flanked by an oven built into the masonry of the chimney. Cooking equipment is listed in a couple of inventories dating from the years before the family's return to Castle Hill. The fire was maintained by a shovel and there was a 'sifter for the coals' to recover as much charcoal from the ashes as possible for use the next day. Cooking revolved around the open flame: spits there were aplenty, and two dripping pans to catch the fat. There was also a 'pike' or pronged fork for toasting, and then the hangers and hooks on which to suspend kettles, boilers and crocks (which in the south-west refers to metal pots as well as pottery). Flesh and fish were grilled on a couple of gridirons, and two old and two new frying pans are noted.

It was never easy to undertake dainty dishes on a roaring fire, and sometimes there were charcoal stoves consisting of small burners set under a stone top perforated with holes to accommodate the bottom of a pan. The alternative was a chafing dish. This was a movable free-standing charcoal brazier that could be stood near the fire yet would not leave the cook fainting from heat. Two are listed, one brass, the other iron. Not much by way of kitchen hardware is mentioned: some ladles and skimmers, a shredding knife, and a cleaver; and there was a 'rasp for manchetts' jotted down in a note of 1686.

Most pictures of early kitchens make much of dressers weighed down with pewter and pottery. Lists from the seventeenth century, made perhaps as one member of staff succeeded another, show that fair storage was needed for Fortescue dishes and crockery. In 1668, pewter left in the kitchen for 'ordinary use' consisted of fourteen dishes with arms and stamps; ten dishes with arms but no stamps; eight narrow-brimmed workmen's dishes; twelve broad-brimmed workmen's dishes; two pasty plates and three pie plates. Pewterware was regularly recycled and remodelled. In 1656, 200 lb of it was melted down and taken to London for remaking. In 1682, they sent off an old chamber pot, a dish, two old plates, a platter, a basin, and two little pieces from an old still to Amos Bishop, so that he could make a new still for the preparation of all the cordial waters, one of the principal domestic responsibilities of the lady of the house. The list of kitchen pewter in 1683 was quite different to the first: twelve dishes including one for 'pottedge', and four 'little sallet dishes'; seventy-eight plates for 'ordinary use in the parlour'; twenty-four plates for 'the hall and workmen'; and five pie plates.

Metal was then the most important material at table, though another inventory (1660) of kitchen earthenware and 'chinay' serves as a reminder that porcelain would soon overtake it, and that Barnstaple and Bideford were great centres of pottery making in the seventeenth century. Pottery items listed included thirty-seven plates, nine cream dishes, five porringers (small bowls) and three custard cups. The 'chinay' included twenty dishes, a couple of flower pots, three basins, and a ewer.

The progress of kitchen technology was not just the replacement of open fires and wood-burning ovens by coal-fired ranges or even gas cookers, it took in all the smaller items of daily use as well. Comparison between the earlier inventory and the metalware listed at the Fortescue London house in 1898 is very striking. First, the saucepans were no longer of brass or iron, but of copper; second, there was a great increase in moulds, shapes, and special-purpose implements. Cookery required absolutely more equipment. Even in this relatively less important kitchen – certainly smaller than the one at Castle Hill – there was a stock pot, a fish kettle, five bain-marie pans, two saucepans and lids, five stewpans and lids, one preserving pan, one omelette pan, two copper kettles, and two copper baking sheets. Culinary realization of a colour-plate from Mrs Beeton was achieved with three large moulds, two tin border moulds, a small china mould, twelve small tin moulds, a box cutlet cutter, six cutlet moulds, eighteen small copper shell moulds, and two scallop shells.

Not that the earlier period lacked for specialist equipment, but it was for different things. A 1666 inventory of the dairy shows a bewildering range. There were two pottery bowls to hold cream, one to salt the cheese, and ten to hold butter or sour milk. Seven tubs, two with legs, were used to store flour, to make butter, to make cheese, and to salt cheese. There were three new milking buckets,

three to be used for ewes' milk, a water bucket, and one reserved for whitepot (see recipe on page 33). There was a set of scales to weigh the butter, and several vats for pressing the curds to the shape of the final cheese. Some cooking went on in the dairy; among the metal goods noted are a pair of trivets, two brass pans and 'my little preserving pan', as well as two kettles and a skillet.

The housekeeper's monthly accounts at Filleigh in the first years of the eighteenth century amplify these lists of kitchen goods. Replenishment was constant, if only because much of the equipment wore out quickly. Inventories also pay scant attention to the ephemeral cloths, brushes, and bits and pieces that were the stuff of everyday life. Some entries for items that were bought during these years include larding needles; tinder boxes; regular supplies of paper for lining tins that were to be used for pastry work; crooks to hang gammons on; straining cloths and cheese cloths; stair brushes, brooms, and many other brushes that are not, unfortunately, detailed; a tin colander; pans for potting venison; four beehives; a payment for a man who came to mend the sieves; two graters; a wooden tray; cabbage nets; custard cups and porringers; bellows; pudding bags; an oil and vinegar cruet; dripping pans; a cheesecake pan; a syllabub glass; and, finally, a payment in 1704 to the tinker for mending the chafing dish and tinning the pots.

The kitchen was the cook's province, but rarely his or her kingdom. Overall supervision rested with the housekeeper or the house-steward. Administrative details vary from household to household and over time. In general, the housekeeper was the linchpin at Castle Hill, reporting, at least in matters of finance, to the steward who had command of the indoor and outdoor servants and the home farm. In the late eighteenth-century household of Viscount Courtenay of Powderham Castle, the butler was in charge, holding the joint office of butler-steward. This chain of command disguised but did not ignore the practical importance of the cook, especially if he were a man and, even more, if he were foreign.

In a book published in 1825 describing the functions of various servants, great distinction is drawn between a woman and a man cook.

The man cook, now become a requisite member in the establishment of a man of fashion, is . . . generally a foreigner, or if an Englishman, possesses a peculiar tact in manufacturing many fashionable foreign delicacies, or of introducing certain seasonings and flavours in his dishes, which render them more inviting to the palate of his employer, than those produced by the simple healthful modes of modern English cooks. . . . His attention is chiefly directed to the stew-pan, in the manufacture of stews, fricassees, fricandeaux etc. At the same time, his situation is one of great labour and fatigue, which . . . procures him a liberal salary, frequently twice or thrice the sum given to the most experienced female English cook.

This is fair explanation of Lord Fortescue's payment of £50 to M. Peltuet the cook for a year's wages in 1792, while the housekeeper earned only £26.5s.0d. It is, however, the only indication of a foreign, male cook at Castle Hill that I have so far discovered.

The cook often gained in assurance and skill with close direction not just by the housekeeper, but

also by the employer. There is not much sign of the Fortescues themselves mixing in the kitchen and offices; unlike the fashionable diarist and letter writer Lady Mary Coke's friend Lady Holdernesse who, in 1768, 'would have taught me to boil shrimps, but as they are put to boiling water alive I could not see it, so I always left her when that operation was going to be performed; but I have learned few cooks put half salt enough into the water that boils fish. The Dutch [Lady Holdernesse was Dutch] certainly understand that part of cookery much better than we do. I have ordered the usual quantity to be doubled.' None the less, instructions were doubtless given at Castle Hill too. This may be the explanation for the existence in the library of Chapelle's *Modern Cook* (1736 edition), Beauvilliers' *L'Art du Cuisinier* (1814) and five menu books (no longer extant). A list of books, some in her ladyship's bedroom, made after the First World War included *From Kitchen to Garret: hints for young householders* by J.E. Panton, *How to Keep House* by Mrs C.S. Peel and a collection of fifty cookery books of the time.

Cooks never stay for ever, though by cossetting they may be persuaded to extend their tenure. Is this the reason for an entry in Castle Hill accounts for 1796 for the apothecary's supply of tonic, emetic, liniment and aperient to a cook who had perhaps lost all appetite for work? It may of course be necessary to sack them. Lady Ebrington's correspondence in 1849 refers to the evident falsification of the weight of meat delivered to the kitchen, to the advantage of both cook and butcher.

By the nineteenth century, there can have been few households that were able to undertake every task without some outside assistance. A current analogy might be the placing of local government responsibilities in the hands of private contractors. In the 1850s at Castle Hill, experts came to do both the baking and the brewing, and there was even a man employed just to do the mangling. In 1853, Mr Berry came up to the house to smoke hams and bacon. Extra help was also welcome in the kitchen itself if the party were large, and there are several mentions of fees paid by the Fortescues for 'dressing dinners'.

The country house was a sophisticated consumer of foodstuffs, but first it was necessary to get them. How far did the estate and house form a symbiotic unit? The most important driving force towards trade and commerce has ever been food. Salt, spices and fish are but three commodities that have underpinned empires, occasioned wars and forged trans-national exchange. No European diet has ever been self-supporting, even the humblest peasant's. Hence the correspondence of country families was filled with commissions, orders, and specifications of delicacies and necessities to buttress their own produce.

Castle Hill had its agents in Exeter and in London. At the end of the eighteenth century, the Exeter agent was William Walker. His correspondence with the estate steward survives. Commissions were various: a bit of banking, making arrangements for travel, clothes buying, book buying, notary work, and, of course, food buying, especially fish from the Exeter market, exotic fruit (i.e. oranges and lemons) and cheese.

'I will obey your commands in regards to the anchovies, capers and fish,' wrote Walker in October 1780. 'I would have sent some on Thursday had the markets produced any worth it.' 'This morning I sent out a pretty sized turbot, two pair of soles and two whiting, a crab and a 100 of oysters. I wish they come as fresh as I sent them away for I never saw finer. I shall continue to send some twice a week [Tuesday and Friday].'

Being sure that the commission was properly executed to his Lordship's liking always induced a certain insecurity: 'I hope the oysters are the sort my Lord and Lady mean, there is a sort smaller but I hope I have picked out on purpose,' he commented one day, subsequently observing that 'our best services can only be clumsy and rustic tho' sincere and hearty.' It did not always work: 'I have bought two of the best toasting cheeses I can get which will make me happy to hit the tastes of the eaters,' on one day; 'I am sorry that the last did not please the eaters,' on another. These dealings were carried on amiably: 'The carrier shall bring tomorrow a couple of salt fish and a few [cods'] tongues which I hope you will like. Shall I not incur Mrs Hilliard's [the wife of the Castle Hill steward] censure to give you a receipt of this country for watering and dressing them?'

Cheese and fish were the most regular commodities dispatched, though Castle Hill had its own dairy and was nearer the fishing fleet of Barnstaple than Exeter's market. In fact, they were drawing from Plymouth and Barnstaple at the same time, evidently unable to rely on a single source. Much of the cheese referred to in the accounts of this period was designed specifically for toasting. Lists of produce from the home farm in the 1820s include only butter, milk and cream, as if the laborious cheese making of the sixteenth and seventeenth centuries had been superseded by the tastier products of Cheddar, Cheshire and – occasionally by name – Stilton. When the house was remodelled in 1804, no dairy was included in the plans. Its room was taken by the steward's office and milk processing was relegated to the farm itself. Even then, the estate had never been able to produce sufficient butter for the stupendous requirements of the kitchen for this commodity. In 1820, Castle Hill got through about 3 pints of cream a day and about 5 lb of butter. The home farm supplied all the cream, but only about two-thirds of the butter. Similarly, in 1700, the housekeeper did not often need to buy cream, but butter was regularly served in.

If some goods were obtained through agents, by means of time-consuming correspondence, many necessities were supplied by local tradesmen. In some instances these were village people drawing on farm surpluses to maintain a country business. Such was the Dunn family, who brought meat to Castle Hill during the first half of the nineteenth century. In 1821, the estate produced 11,224 lb of mutton, beef and veal, 2,441 lb of bacon and pork as well as all the poultry, but Mrs Dunn supplied more than 3,000 lb of butcher's meat.

Some of the trade was also casual, hardly serious business: 'paid the maid that brought the pigg', 'a boy that brought quinces' and 'the man as brought articho' are items from an account of 1702. Specialists apart, in the countryside, the most important shopkeepers were the grocers. Three supplied Castle Hill during the reign of George IV: Mackrell, Roberts and Linnington, all from Barnstaple. Mr Linnington's account is instructive for the range of goods delivered: pipe macaroni, vermicelli, Carolina rice, Patna rice, pearl sago, tapioca, cocoa nuts, patent cocoa, Turkey raisins, muscatel raisins, Jordan almonds, Valentia almonds, bitter almonds, capers, Souchong tea, Turkey figs, Faro figs, best pickling vinegar,

tarragon vinegar, elder vinegar, mushroom ketchup, Harvey's Sauce, shrimp sauce, superfine mustard, salad oil, salt lemons, lemon peel, isinglass, bicarbonate of soda and cream of tartar, and various apothecary items such as alum, nux vomica, sal prunella, and saltpetre.

In addition, there were the regular supplies of spices, sugar and fruit, particularly oranges and lemons, that formed the pillars of the grocer's business. In 1821, the Castle Hill kitchen got through 17 lb of nutmeg, 7 lb of cinnamon, 8 lb of mace, 4 lb of cloves, and 19 lb of ginger. This short list, but in fair quantities, is not so very different from the spices consumed in 1706, save that at the earlier period caraway seed and oil of almonds made regular appearances, and there is mention of turmeric on one occasion.

Sugar came in far more variety than our own caster and granulated, white or brown. It was also a luxury for most of the period under discussion. In 1817, the kitchen kept brief notes of the bulk uses sugar was put to at Castle Hill, in other words when it was employed for preserving rather than mere flavouring of individual dishes. In the winter and early spring, it was used for brining bacon and hams; in July for preserving cherries and making raspberry, gooseberry and blackcurrant jelly, as well as for serving strawberries and pineapples. Come August it was time to make redcurrant jelly, and more gooseberries were dealt with as well as a pineapple and white and red raspberries. Three and a half pounds were used for pickling gherkins in this month also.

The presence of Harvey's Sauce in Linnington's account is anticipation of the change in shopping during the Victorian period. Certain commodities had always been almost exclusively brought down from London: tea, coffee, and many wines for example. With the greater ease of transport and the development of manufactured foods, particularly canned goods, London merchants were used for their specialities: Fortnum & Mason for preserved fruits; Hedges & Butler for marmalade; Gunter for turtle soup.

In 1859, Lady Ebrington returned briefly from a long sojourn in Madeira on account of her husband's ill health. A shopping list survives from her few weeks in London. 'Newspaper arrangement, postage stamps, a *Peerage* for 1860 and new reviews' are notes for the improvement of the mind; 'mutton, hams, tongues, cheese, tea, caviare, truffles, turtle soup, partridge and truffle pâté, lampreys done in claret and either celery or onions, foie gras, reindeers' tongues, venison pasty, and macaroni' were to keep the body going, canned or potted goods all.

Compare such a list with that made in 1645 when Sir Edmund Fortescue was revictualling Salcombe Castle: hogsheads of salt beef, ox-tongues, bacon and pork, oil, vinegar, dried peas, 'poor jacks' (dried hake), dried whitings, biscuit and coarse oatmeal, '20 pots with sweetmeats, and a great box of all sorts of especially good dry preserves', 200 lemons, six hundredweight of tobacco, one hundredweight of raw milk cheese, 'six pecks of fruit', and butter. Enough to withstand a siege, but all dry or pickled.

More rapid transport had abiding consequences on the relationship between London and the country estate. In the 1770s, Lord Fortescue spent quite a lot of time in town. His letters to the steward refer to the impossibility of transporting the surplus of garden produce from Devon: 'They had better be given to my neighbours, and do you and yours take what you want and after the family are served with the common things, James Bale [the gardener] may make what he can of the remainder.' In other words, sell the produce on the open market. The gardens were in full maturity by then. When Lord Fortescue died in 1785, his son countermanded orders that the establishment be reduced: 'I would not like to see the pines and melons destroyed.'

With the coming of the railways, however, a week on the road was reduced to a day, and it became feasible to supply many a town house from the wealth in the country. William Taylor, gardener to the Marquess of Bath at Longleat, had a graded set of purpose-made boxes for transport: for flowers, for peaches, nectarines and grapes, for strawberries and so on. Soft fruit would be individually wrapped in leaves, grapes in stiff cardboard cones, asparagus and beans separated by spinach leaves. There are few signs of this system being in force on the Fortescue estate, although game, butter and clotted cream were regularly dispatched.

Usually, the London house was supplied entirely by tradesmen, just as travels across England were not backed up by a supply train from the estate. One good reason for this was that the London season was generally over before the period of harvest and highest yield. In June 1769, Lady Mary Coke, living in Notting Hill, commented, 'You are much forwarder than my garden is here. I shall not be able to have one thing out of it; everything must be bought; strawberries are eight shillings a small basket and cherries half a guinea.' The tradesmen were well able to respond. The Fortescues' London greengrocery account for 1814–15 included tarragon, chervil, sorrel, 'mackerel herbs', groundsel and chickweed for birds, parsley, thyme, green mint, pennyroyal, corn salad, small salad, endives, and watercress among herbs and saladings; spinach, sea kale, asparagus, asparagus tops, globe artichokes, French beans, cucumbers, and green and white broccoli among vegetables; early potatoes, turnips, parsnips, shallots, onions and button onions, beetroot, carrots, and Spanish onions among root and bulb crops. Fruit included sweet, China and Seville oranges, lemons, apples, and pears. The poulterer in the same years was happy to oblige with widgeon, green geese, turkey, woodcocks, larks, pigeon, rabbit, pullets, duckling, and plovers' eggs.

Dealing with fruiterers and greengrocers was a necessary penance if you lived in Georgian London, or your income was too small to support hot-beds, greenhouses and walled gardens, but every effort was made by the provident landowner to grow common as well as luxury items. In the Fortescue accounts of 1702–5 there are references to cabbage, cauliflower, radish, and celery seeds; as well as purchases of Golden Pippin, Kentish Codling, and Hampden apple trees, Bergamot and Bon Chrétien pear trees, and peach and nectarine trees.

West Country gardens were as highly developed as in the rest of England. The region was always a producer of good or early vegetables. Broccoli was an important cash crop from sheltered coves along the southern coast; cabbage was a specialist harvest from Paignton and Torbay; sea kale was domesticated and grown at an earlier period than in mainland Britain. And although the damp sea air might militate against some fruits, exotics and luxuries did well here. The peach trees in the

garden at Castle Hill were famous in their time; the largest was espaliered across forty feet of wall. But landowners did not stop short at peaches, or even pineapples. At Bicton, the Rolle family interspersed their pinery with ginger plants, enough to supply 10 or 12 lb yearly; Dunster Castle sported a large lemon tree and a pomegranate tree; Luscombe Castle, in a garden laid out by the Veitch family of nurserymen of Exeter, had fruiting olive trees as well as lemons, citrons and limes; and even the King's Arms of Kingsbridge had a lemon tree, 'protected by glass in the winter, but without fire-heat, which supplies lemons enough for the use of the inn'.

Some idea of the output and range of a Devon garden is gained from an account kept during 1819 at Lord Courtenay's Powderham Castle. The gardener sold produce surplus to household requirements on the open market. The record shows both the sort of things grown, and the varied types of people who came to the garden door to buy them. The most important customers were tradesmen, taking regular and large supplies, but there were also individuals who called by, much as we stop at a roadside booth for strawberries or apples today. The range and scale of production is impressive, everything from sea kale and asparagus, cucumber and rhubarb, to peaches, nectarines, cherries, grapes, soft fruit, mulberries, apples, and pears.

The estate, if it were large enough, would also be the source of meat, poultry and game, to say nothing of the corn that was sent to the miller to make flour for the bakehouse. There was a slaughterhouse in the stable court at Castle Hill, whence the kitchen – as well as the kennels – might be supplied. However, killing your own stock –

even for a large household – was sometimes more trouble than it was worth, and the accounts make clear that butchers continued to be patronized. If an ox was killed, it would mean 450 lb of flesh to be consumed at fairly short order (there was no refrigeration). This makes sense of one eighteenth-century letter writer commenting that she had been 'fifteen days without the butcher ... but luckily we had sheep, hogs and poultry. On the fifteenth day, the butcher sent over two men with a little beef and veal.'

Although it might seem an easy matter to provide eggs and poultry from the home farm, these items also figured often in tradesmen's bills. Chickens never lay according to plan, and cookery needed eggs by the hundred. In the 1870s, during the London season, the Fortescues were consuming twelve dozen eggs, about 20 lb of butter, 3 lb of clotted cream, and 3 pints of double cream every week. In Devon, quantities would double with the larger household. Turkeys and chickens were certainly kept at Castle Hill: in the 1760s, Lady Fortescue employed a woman who tended the 'Menagerie' by the kitchen garden. In 1703, a payment is on record to 'my sister's man as brought the peacock', and peafowl were tended throughout the eighteenth century, although for ornament rather than appetite.

Game-birds were also nurtured, both to increase the sport and to supply the table. Sport became ever more important to the family, culminating in the acceptance of the mastership of the staghounds by Lord Fortescue in 1812 and by Lord Ebrington in 1881, and the purchase of the lodge at Simonsbath on Exmoor. Not for nothing was the hall at Castle Hill decorated with a thicket of antlers.

Game's value to the menu was never ignored, and many are the references to its encouragement and pursuit. In 1762, twenty-two brace of partridge were caught (not shot); in 1787, half-a-crown bounty money was paid for each fox caught on the estate; in 1789, pheasants were brought down from London; in 1793, £2.1s.0d. was paid for the destruction of crows and kites; in 1807, red-legged partridges were bred in the kitchen garden; in 1815, sixty-seven pheasant and forty-seven partridge eggs were purchased, and three years earlier there was note of payment for feeding pheasants so as to stop them straying onto the common-land where they might be killed.

The yield of birds was large enough, though never on the industrial scale of the East Anglian or Scottish sporting estates. In 1880–81, the Fortescues and their guests bagged 159 partridges, 828 pheasants, 142 hares, 39 woodcocks, and 32 'various', mostly duck and pigeon, together with 1,372 rabbits. The rabbits were obtained by the efforts of five cony-catchers. These people maintained a steady trade, here as everywhere else, in the fur and the meat. A man from the parish of Hartland remembers it from the early part of this century, when he contracted for the rabbits caught on a series of farms: 'The season lasted from September to Lady Day; I dealt with an average of five tons [of rabbit] each week, filling 40 hampers each weighing an average of one hundredweight. The end of September/early October was the time of the heaviest consignment. We used gin traps ... and ferrets and guns as well.' In 1702, there is a payment by the housekeeper at Castle Hill for the man who came with the ferrets.

This harvest was either eaten at Castle Hill, sent up to the family in London, sold, or given away as tips. The delicacies – woodcock and wild duck – were always eaten at home, too nice to let go. Game was not usually served to the staff, nor poultry for that matter. The servants' diet might be copious, but it could be boring. At Castle Hill in the 1850s, two hundredweight of potatoes, one hundredweight of turnips, and 250 lb of bread were fairly normal for a week's use. It is for sure that most of this was eaten by the hungry footmen and their colleagues.

Gifts of game to outsiders were generous: at Christmas 1899, his Lordship dished out fifty-seven pheasants to stationmasters, postmasters, railway traffic managers, tradesmen, and servants. Venison, too, might be a useful present, though to more exalted friends than the postman.

The practice of bearing plenty to hosts or neighbours is long-lived. In 1591, the Earl of Northumberland received from Sir Matthew Arundell partridges, pigeons, rabbits, herons, chickens, and trout. The catholic approach to game of the Middle Ages and Tudor years lessened somewhat by the eighteenth century. Just as early cooks were willing to roast most birds of the air, so they were prepared to handle most parts of the beasts killed on their behalf. If you have to deal with a whole carcase, you make use of all its component parts. We now read with wonder of European peasants' economical way with a winter pig, but the English gentry were no more profligate. In 1698–1700, the Fortescues were eating good quantities of tripe, tongues, lambs' 'possets', lambs' heads, calves' heads, and calves' 'moods' (possets and moods are sweetbreads or testicles).

Fifty years later, the butcher's bill included ox-tongue, bullocks' tongues and cheeks, and calves' heads. In a dinner book kept by a Northamptonshire gentleman at the end of the eighteenth century, this taste for offal is evident. At one dinner given by a friend in 1794, he noted the serving of hashed calf's head, browned ox-cheek, and stewed pigs' feet in the first course; and fried tripe and fried calves' feet in the second. The exception to the rule was liver: an infrequent sight. In similar fashion, the offal of fish, that now we would spurn, was considered a delicacy.

When we go out today to fill shopping baskets and supermarket trolleys, the expedition is made with certain meals in mind. The message from the records of Castle Hill is of a continuum of food production. Just as for the executive chef of a grand hotel, individual meals were less important than the week-by-week organization of the kitchen brigade. However much was brought in from outside sources, it had to be processed to a much greater extent than the finished or semi-finished commodities that are stocked in today's shops. Indications of self-sufficiency are everywhere.

Without the luxury of long-term storage, perishable foods needed preserving. This is the rationale of the house dairy: to convert short-term milk into medium- or long-term butter and cheese. It is the cause, too, of the constant labour of preserving, jam-making and bottling – the most significant aspect of early recipe books after medicinal matters. In 1664, the steward was noting the quantity of sugar used for storing raspberries, the apricots that had come from London, and cherries. In 1700, a peck of samphire was bought and pickled. In 1815, bulk supplies of laver, samphire, and vinegar were laid in for the same reason. Constant purchases are made of jars for holding the summer's harvest. In

1856, the family bought 15 dozen jam pots, 329 lb of preserving sugar and 2 gallons of preserving brandy.

An aspect of this same work – the conversion of raw materials into useful consumables – is seen too in the still-room and home-made medicines. The only recipe books that now survive in the Fortescue archive are from the seventeenth century, for medication and strong waters, merging into cookery as they note instructions for possets used as tonics.

The medicine cupboard governed the herb garden as much as did the kitchen in the seventeenth century. (Rhubarb first occurs in these accounts as a medicine, not a food.) There is a notebook listing plants that should be used to make strong waters in the still mentioned above. These included lettuce, endive, sorrel, colts foot, plantain, costmary, burnett, wormwood, and calaminth. Then there were ointments made with butter as their vehicle: purchase of butter for ointments is noted as late as the 1850s. As the still was used less and less (apothecaries tended to make more exciting mixtures), the still-room continued to produce flavoured drinks. Thus spirit was bought to make cherry and orange brandies in 1856.

Self-sufficiency was intermittently pursued with the staff of life: bread. The only survivor from the nineteenth-century kitchens at Castle Hill is the bread oven: a giant that was too large to dismantle. It was not invariably used, however. Perhaps there were sometimes staff difficulties. In 1858, bread and flour were being bought from a local baker. A few years later, a man was coming in each week specifically to bake household bread – in loaves of about 4 lb weight. Bread then was expected to last.

A flour account of the 1840s shows how consumption was divided. In one week of April 1847, eleven loaves were eaten in the parlour, twelve in the housekeeper's room, fourteen in the servants' hall, six by the maids, three in the laundry and one in the kitchen. The account is also interesting for its references to small quantities of imported American flour, and the regular baking of biscuits (about 10 lb per week) and seed cakes (about 4–6 lb).

As they baked their own bread, so they brewed their own beer; not invariably (there is reference to bought Stogumber ale), but mainly. North Devon was not cider country and there are few references to this drink. Even in the seventeenth century, the Pine Coffin family of Portledge near Bideford were growing hops for their brewhouse. Strong beer and small beer were brewed in the winter months, and stored in their respective cellars at Castle Hill. More than 40 hogsheads (containing 52 gallons each) were put by each year in the early nineteenth century, mainly for consumption by the staff.

Brewing might cast its heavy fumes over the courtyard on two or three days a month from August, or there would be heavy sessions in October and December when the bulk would be dealt with. In 1807, they brewed on seven days in October. It would certainly all be drunk. At rent day at Castle Hill in 1810, they polished off three hogsheads; on Lord Ebrington's birthday in 1804, a like quantity. Everyone got their beer allowance, but there are signs that it occasionally got out of hand. There is a note in 1851 stating that servants should not consume more than three-shillings-worth of beer during London dinner parties – when doubtless visiting servants and the home team caroused below stairs as their employers were conversing decorously above.

To what extent did the Fortescues eat different food because their estates were centred on the West Country? The broad truth is that their station in society was a stronger determinant of diet than their location. When the Frenchman, Faujas de St Fond, visited eighteenth-century Scotland, he found the tables of the Anglo-Scottish nobility as well furnished as any in the Home Counties; he only felt he was encountering truly northern manners when he fell among the less rich and certainly less mobile Highland gentry families. The Fortescues were part of this dietary consensus.

Even regional geography played a relatively smaller part than might be expected. When the Somerset parson William Holland complained in 1807 that 'we had salmon again for dinner today so that for a week past we'v had our fill of fish', he was giving involuntary voice to the gluts of certain commodities that might be caused by location. However, there are few signs that the Fortescues ate more fish, a regional speciality – the actor Quinn would go from Bath to Plymouth especially to feast on John Dory – than anyone in midland England. Accounts for 1822 indicate purchase of herrings, oysters, sea bass, cod, whiting, sole, salmon, and sprats, as well as red herrings and salt fish. But this list is not more impressive than the entries in a Northamptonshire dinner book at the same sort of time: turbot, lobster, salmon, salmon peel, cod, crab, sole, crayfish, prawns, eels, gurnard – always at least one substantial fish dish at every dinner – and very rarely either freshwater fish or salt fish, both of which were going out of fashion by then.

Although a sense of place would come about

because Castle Hill was in the southern half of Britain and in relatively fertile country, in a wheat and barley rather than an oat or rye zone, where sheep and never goats (then still consumed in Wales) were eaten, there were not large numbers of regional specialities. Alexander Pope wrote to his Fortescue friend in 1730, 'I forgot to mention a commission of Lady Walpole's that you will not forget her laver,' – the edible seaweed of the north Devon coast. This Lady Walpole was a Rolle of north Devon by birth, and was probably reliving her childhood memories. Laver and rock samphire were two coastal delicacies that found their way to the Fortescue table. Laver was potted in the eighteenth and nineteenth centuries, much as today we put it in cans, and distributed throughout the inland counties.

Another food specific to Devonshire was clotted cream. This had figured in cookery books since the seventeenth century as a West Country method for cooking and thickening the cream from the milk, thus preserving it for slightly longer. The Fortescues had sufficient taste to have it shipped to London when they were there.

I can still remember some of the house parties at Castle Hill. My father, like all the Whigs of the early '60s, was greatly interested in the Italian movement. Various Italian celebrities used to undertake the long journey down to Devonshire, I suppose to make the acquaintance of a specimen of an English country house and see a week of English country life. It was our great amusement as children, just before being packed off to bed, to lean over the gallery which surrounded the hall where the guests were assembling before dinner, and watch them processing into the dining-room, and I can well remember our childish delight and wonder at the behaviour of the Italians, who invariably went in to dinner, as was the custom in those days on the Continent, with their gibus hats [opera hats] under their arms.

Such were the memories of Seymour Fortescue, looking back on the 1860s. Not every meal, however, was necessarily a feast. Not every generation was hospitable. Families varied in size. Cooks had to be masters or mistresses of adaptability. As one climbed the social scale, so the eating arrangements became less malleable, more ritualized, but the scale of provision varied quite markedly even in grand houses.

Even so, by the twentieth century, the Fortescue household had contracted. The permanent indoor establishment at Castle Hill during the 1920s numbered five, with extra daily staff coming in from the estate. The kitchen's role had been transformed, both by these social changes and shifts in dining fashion. In the reign of George II, a cook needed to send ten to fifteen dishes to the table at one time. Practically speaking, cooking was then exceptionally difficult, because available technology fell far short of culinary ambitions. Delivering a cooked, hot, handsome and palatable meal of two courses, each consisting of seven or nine dishes, from an open fire, or even an enclosed kitchener, was no mean feat.

It is surprising that complaints are so few. Taken in aggregate, surviving letters and diaries make very little fuss about the food that was served their writers; even if Lady Mary Coke reflected in 1767 that:

I never saw a worse dinner: a great round of boiled beef, little mutton pyes, beans and bacon, mackerel without fennel sauce. The second course, a neck of lamb, a gooseberry pie, and two little other things, not meat. You know I am not difficult, and yet I was at a loss to make my dinner. Boiled beef is a good thing, but a dish I seldom eat, and little mutton pyes are too savoury for me; beans I hate, and mackerel without fennel sauce I can't eat.

Early dinners usually made a point of displaying several cooking techniques at once – frying, boiling, stewing, baking, roasting – as well as several types of food – fish, game, poultry, meat, vegetables, staples. In this they may be compared to a Chinese or Japanese banquet that takes people through each cookery method in turn. By the modern period, this firm structure and extensive repertoire had been confined to the most formal, most elaborate meals; affairs concocted no more than once a week, often once a season. Ally to this the decline in household size, improvements in technology, and the disappearance of the requirement for the kitchen to provide the infrastructure of bread, butchery and preservation, and the cook's lot had lightened greatly.

A modern coda may be sought in the books of Winifred, Lady Fortescue, who wrote a series of bestsellers in the 1930s and beyond, commencing with *Perfume from Provence*. She was the widow of Sir John Fortescue, younger son of the 3rd Earl, historian of the British army and librarian at Windsor Castle. On his retirement, they moved to Provence, where they were better able to support a life of gentility on a restricted income. In *Beauty for Ashes* (1948), she describes how at first they were offered Hartland Abbey, a mansion towards Westward Ho!, by their cousin's heir:

*We could never have borne to see it gradually
degenerating. In place of the army of gardeners, once
employed, we could perhaps engage one and a half
... Inside the Abbey, instead of a butler, an odd man
and a staff of female servants we should have to
manage with a married couple or a cook and a
house-parlour-maid. We should have to close the
upper floor and live in one wing. Even then, the huge
kitchen in the cloisters beneath was half a mile from
the dining room.*

It is heartening that this was not the fate of Castle
Hill itself. Although it suffered a crippling fire in
1934, it survived, prospered, and is still being
improved and embellished today, even if on a more
convenient plan.

Recipes

A Paste of Apricots 17th century

A Fortescue notebook of 1664 records: 'what sugar
I have used for sweetmeats: for the aprecokes came
from London.' The fruit harvest happened once a
year and jams, marmalades, bottled conserves,
butters, and pastes were the accepted ways of
preserving summer magic. In the seventeenth
century, sweetmeats of fruit paste were a delicacy
for the end of the meal. This recipe is based on
one from *A Queens Delight* (1655). The book was
used by the Fortescues, a quotation from it is found
in their medicinal and still-room recipes.

> 2 lb (900 g) apricots
> 2 lb (900 g) granulated sugar
> 1 tablespoon rosewater

Halve and stone the apricots. Put them to cook
gently with 5 fl oz (150 ml) water in a covered pan
until soft. Push through a sieve or the fine plate of
a food mill. Add the sugar and the rosewater to
the purée, and cook it gently, stirring constantly,
until dissolved. Raise the heat and continue to boil
until the moisture has evaporated, and the mixture
has become viscous and gloopy. It will need stirring
constantly to avoid burning.

Pour into a well-oiled tray, or one lined with baking
parchment, and leave to cool. Then allow it to dry
out further, in a very cool oven (for instance a gas
oven with the pilot light on) for twelve hours, or
an airing cupboard for a couple of days. Cut into
cubes, and toss these in caster sugar.

Whitepot 17th century

This is bread and butter pudding by another name.
The existence of a whitepot pan in a Fortescue
inventory of 1665 testifies to the regularity of its
consumption at Castle Hill. John Nott's *The
Cook's and Confectioner's Dictionary* (1726) has
nine recipes for whitepot, including two from
Devon. This recipe comes from Sir Kenelm Digby's
Closet (1669).

> Serves 4 to 6
>
> 2 oz (50 g) butter and 1 oz (25 g) more for
>   finishing
> 2 oz (50 g) raisins
> small loaf of stale white bread
> 1 clove nutmeg
> 3 eggs
> 2 oz (50 g) white sugar
> 10 fl oz (300 ml) double cream
> 10 fl oz (300 ml) milk
> brown sugar for sprinkling over the top

Pre-heat the oven to 150°C (300°F, Mark 2). Melt
the butter over a very low heat, and steep the

raisins in it for five minutes. Cut the loaf into thin slices, and remove the crusts. Butter a 10-inch (25-cm) oval pie dish, and lay a layer of slices across the bottom. Scatter half the raisins over the bread, and grate half the nutmeg over. Lay on another layer of slices, then the rest of the raisins and grated nutmeg. Keep back two slices of bread.

Break the eggs into a bowl, and whisk lightly with the sugar. Scald the cream and the milk together, and pour it over the eggs, stirring all the time. Pour this over the bread. Lay the final two slices on the top, and sprinkle them with brown sugar. Dot with butter. Bake in the pre-heated oven for about 30 minutes until the custard is set.

Custards in Cups 18th century

There are many references in the early accounts to the Fortescues buying pottery cups for baked custards. It was another way of presenting Devon's favourite ingredient, cream. This recipe comes from *The Complete Practical Cook* by C. Carter (1730).

Serves 6

1 pint (600 ml) single cream
1 oz (25 g) sugar
3 egg yolks
1 whole egg
1 tablespoon rose or orange flowerwater

Pre-heat the oven to 150°C (300°F, Mark 2). Scald the cream and sugar together, and pour over the yolks, the whole eggs, and the rose or orange flower water. Stir together and strain the mixture into six ramekins. Set these in a roasting tin containing 1 inch (2.5 cm) of hot water, and place in the pre-heated oven for about 50 minutes until the custards are set.

Green Goose Boiled 18th century

In the Castle Hill accounts of the early eighteenth century, there are many references to 'green geese'. These are young birds, up to four months old, not the Michaelmas geese of the autumn, nor the mature fattened geese of winter. Dr Kitchener, who wrote the characterful *Cook's Oracle* (1817), considered them insipid. The Fortescue MSS mention goose very much less frequently in the nineteenth century, by which time the family apparently preferred turkey.

Serves 6

1 7 lb (3 kg) goose and giblets
4 oz (100 g) green bacon
1 onion
1 stick celery
1 carrot
small bunch of parsley, chopped
bay leaf
1¼ pints (750 ml) dry white wine
salt
freshly ground black pepper
nutmeg
8 cloves
half a lemon

Sorrel sauce

2 handfuls of fresh sorrel, stripped
broth from the goose
3 oz (75 g) butter
salt
freshly ground black pepper

Sweat the feet, winglets and giblets (but not liver) from the goose with the bacon for 5 minutes without colouring. Peel and slice the onion. Slice the stick of celery. Scrape and slice the carrot. Add the vegetables, and sweat for a further 5 minutes. Add 3 pints (1.7 litres) cold water, parsley, and bay leaf. Boil gently, uncovered, for about an hour until the stock is reduced by approximately one-third. Skim at regular intervals. Strain.

Place the goose in a large saucepan. Pour round it the stock, and the wine. Season with salt, pepper, a generous grating of nutmeg, and the cloves. Add the lemon. Bring to the boil and simmer gently, covered, for about $1\frac{1}{4}$ hours, until tender. Lift out the goose and keep warm.

To make the sauce, wash and strip the sorrel leaves. Sweat them in 1 oz (25 g) butter until they are a purée. Add 5 fl oz (150 ml) of broth from the goose. Simmer to reduce by about half. Cut the remainder of the butter into the sauce, and shuffle until melted. Taste for seasoning. Serve separately.

Cherry Composte 18th century

Castle Hill's orchards may have supplied enough apples and pears, even peaches and nectarines, but the Fortescues were never sated of cherries. It is one of the fruits for which there are constant entries in the accounts, sure sign that home production was insufficient.

Serves 4

1 lb (450 g) Morello cherries
5 oz (125 g) sugar
5 fl oz (150 ml) water

Trim the cherries, leaving a short stalk. Dissolve the sugar in the water, bring to the boil, add the cherries, and simmer until they are soft. Remove them with a perforated spoon, reduce the syrup by fast boiling, pour over the cherries, and serve.

Potted Venison 18th century

Venison was a favoured meat in the seventeenth and eighteenth centuries. In the Fortescue household, thanks to Exmoor and the North Devon Staghounds, it continued to be much eaten until modern times. Potted meat is mostly found as a supper dish, and at breakfast. There are entries in the accounts for the purchase of pots in which venison was to be preserved. This recipe is from Hannah Glasse's *The Art of Cookery Made Plain and Easy* (1747).

Serves 6

1 lb (450 g) haunch of venison
6 oz (150 g) butter, plus 3 oz (75 g) clarified
   butter for sealing the pots
1 teaspoon ground mace
$\frac{1}{2}$ teaspoon ground cloves
$\frac{1}{2}$ teaspoon grated nutmeg
salt
freshly ground black pepper

Pre-heat the oven to 150°C (300°F, Mark 2). Put the venison into an ovenproof dish, and dot it with the butter. Cover closely with foil. Bake in pre-heated oven for about 2 hours. The meat must be thoroughly cooked and all moisture expelled. Remove and drain the meat, reserving and cooling the fat and juices.

Cut the meat into manageable chunks, and process in a food processor with the spices and seasoning. Add some of the cooled butter from the cooking process to make the mixture moist. Do not add meat juices, however, as they will inhibit long storage. When sufficiently processed, put into one or more pots and smooth off the top surface.

Finally, pour over a generous layer of clarified butter to seal the meat.

Quaking Bag Pudding 17th century

Puddings boiled in bags were a dominant feature of English cookery from the seventeenth century onwards, often remarked on by foreign visitors. Before potatoes were common fare, they were a good and interesting way of eating starch.

Before cloths were used, puddings were encased in animal gut or intestine: hogs' puddings are their descendants. If you generously flour and butter a napkin, the sloppy pudding will not leak out before it is set by the boiling water. There are entries in the Fortescue accounts for the purchase of pudding cloths and pudding bags, just as there were also entries for bladders and skins, presumably for varieties of sausage and meat products.

A china or plastic pudding basin used in conjunction with a generously floured tea towel is a compromise with the potential mess of filling a pudding cloth without the help of a basin at all.

Serves 4 to 6

15 fl oz (450 ml) milk
5 fl oz (150 ml) single cream
a pinch of salt
nutmeg
3 tablespoons soft white breadcrumbs
4 oz (100 g) sugar
1 oz (25 g) butter
3 eggs plus 1 extra white
1 oz (25 g) flour
2 teaspoons rosewater (optional)
1 tablespoon sweet white wine (optional)

Sweet sauce

3 oz (75 g) butter
1 tablespoon caster sugar
1 small glass sweet white wine

Lightly season the milk and cream with the salt and nutmeg, bring to the boil, and pour on to the breadcrumbs, sugar, and butter. Cover and leave to stand for 30 minutes. Beat the eggs and flour, and pour on to the milk mixture. Add the rosewater and wine. Beat well. Pour into a large greased pudding basin. Butter and flour a tea towel, and lay it over the top of the basin. Invert on to a work surface and tie the cloth tightly over the bottom of the basin. Lower into a pan of boiling water and boil continuously for $1\frac{1}{2}$ hours, refilling the pan with boiling water if necessary. Lift out, untie, and turn the pudding on to a serving dish.

Make the sauce by melting the butter with the sugar, and whisking in the white wine. Serve round the pudding.

Asparagus with Melted Butter 19th century

No vegetable was more eagerly awaited than the asparagus. Cooking of the vegetable altered over time. In the courtly recipe books of the Restoration, it was a common ingredient in complex pies and fricassees. In later years, it was valued for itself.

Serves 2 to 4

2 bundles of asparagus
salt
4 oz (100 g) butter
tarragon vinegar
cayenne pepper

Scrape the asparagus and trim the bottoms. Boil in

a wide pan, or a tall asparagus pan, in salted water for between 5 and 12 minutes. The time will depend on the size of the spears and how fresh they are – basically, the older the longer. Drain. Melt the butter, sharpen with a little vinegar and a knife-tip of cayenne pepper, pour over the cooked asparagus, and serve.

Fricassee of Tripe 18th century

At the turn of the seventeenth century, the butcher was delivering a fair quantity of tripe (along with tongues and sweetbreads) to Castle Hill. Although other offal continued to figure, tripe seems less favoured in later documents. This recipe comes from *The London Art of Cookery* by J. Fairley (1783).

Serves 4 to 6

1½ lb (700 g) cooked tripe
7 fl oz (200 ml) dry white wine
½ teaspoon freshly grated ginger, blade of mace, 7
  white peppercorns, a sprig of thyme, and a
  sprig of marjoram, all tied in a muslin bag
1 onion, peeled and halved
1 tablespoon parsley, finely chopped
juice of a small lemon
2 anchovy fillets, chopped
5 fl oz (150 ml) double cream
2 oz (50 g) butter
salt
freshly ground black pepper

The tripe you buy from the butcher is blanched and part-cooked. It needs further cooking at home in milk and water, for about an hour. Drain it, trim it and cut into 2 inch (5 cm) squares. Put in a pan with the wine, bag of spices and herbs, and

the onion. Stew gently for 15 minutes. Take out the herbs and onion, and add the chopped parsley, lemon juice, anchovy, cream, and butter. Stir well over the heat, season to taste, and serve.

Clotted Cream Traditional

Clotted cream has been a speciality of the western counties, particularly Devon, almost as long as cookery books have been written. It was evidently favoured by the Fortescues themselves, who had it shipped to London in the season. What is more surprising, perhaps, is that the technique did not spread more widely across England, for it extends the life of cream as well as being delectable in itself.

The author William Ellis, in *The Country Housewife's Family Companion* (1750), describes the making of clotted cream on an estate in south Devon. It reflects the great difficulty of working over live embers when making something relatively temperature-sensitive:

The morning's milk is commonly set over the embers about four o'clock in the afternoon; but this varies according as they have more or less of their embers in a right heat, for many will set their milk over them as soon as they have done dinner, as there is then commonly a good quantity of them free of smoke, and are ready without the trouble of making them on purpose: the evening's milk is commonly set over them about eight o'clock next morning, sooner or later; however, care must be taken not to do it before the cream is well settled on the milk, which will be in the before-mentioned time. And as to the quantity of milk we scald at once, it is very different: from one gallon in a pan to three or more;

and the measure of each pan of the biggest size is three gallons, or three and a half. There are pans of several sizes less, but the most common quantity is about two gallons, or two and a half in each brass pan; and brass pans are commonly used for this purpose, as they are certainly the best of all other inventions, because the milk will both heat and cool sooner, and far more safe than in the earthen sort; for these (especially in the Summer time), are too long in cooling; and as the cream cannot be used before it is cold, these earthen pans are in disuse. I never saw any of them used in this manner but at Sir John Roger's: their reason was, that they are something sweeter than brass pans, and I must confess they are so, if the brass ones are not kept in the nicest order possible. As to the height of the pans standing above the embers, it is according to the height of the iron trevit, which is commonly about six inches, with this difference; if on a stove six inches, if on a hearth eight inches, the latter being most in use. As to the exact time of scalding the milk, to have a full clouted cream on it, it is about one hour; yet this varies according to the heat of the embers, and therefore it is sometimes two or more hours, but seldom less than one.

There are two methods of making clotted cream in current usage: the Cornish and the Devonian. The first skims the fresh cream off the top of the milk, and scalds it separately; the second sets the whole milk over heat, and clots the cream on the milk. The disadvantage of the latter is the danger of mess, and the resulting quantities of cooked skimmed milk, which do not taste especially attractive. By following the Cornish method, you can save up the cream until you have sufficient to work with, and drink the skimmed milk in the normal course of events. You can, of course, clot double cream bought from the supermarket. However, because it has been pasteurized, it will never develop the varied flavours of cream clotted from milk straight from the cow.

Fill a large and wide bowl with whole milk. Leave it in the refrigerator or a cool larder overnight. Skim the cream off the top, put it into a second bowl, and refrigerate. Repeat this over the next few days until you have, say, 1 pint (600 ml) of fresh cream. Heat a wide pan of water to 82°C (180°F) on the top of the stove. Place the bowl of cream in the water bath and hold it at that temperature for about 1½ hours until a bright yellow crust has formed. Cool quickly.

Pigeon Pie 18th century

In 1707, Hugh Fortescue was in London on legal business, renting bachelor chambers in the Temple. In his accounts are entries for the purchase of pigeon pies, custards, and cheesecakes, as well as immense quantities of asparagus. Pies have ever been an ideal take-away food.

The recipe given here is based on that of Hannah Glasse (1747). Her instructions end: 'This is the best Way to make a Pigeon-pye; but the *French* fill the Pigeons with a very high Force-meat round the Inside with Ball [cardoons?], Asparagus-tops, and Artichoke-bottoms, and Mushrooms, Truffles and Morells, and season high; but that is according to different Palates.'

This points up the difference between culinary high fashion, influenced by France and the court, and the plainer style put forward by many mid-eighteenth-century writers, often women.

Serves 4

4 pigeons, plus giblets
1 carrot, sliced
1 onion, chopped
1 stick celery, sliced
bay leaf
small bunch of parsley, chopped
8 oz (225 g) rump steak
3 oz (75 g) butter
salt
4 hard-boiled eggs
8 oz (225 g) puff pastry
1 egg, beaten

Make a stock by sweating the giblets (but not liver), winglets, and feet of the pigeons for 5 minutes without colouring. Add the carrot, onion, and celery, and sweat for a further 5 minutes. Add $1\frac{3}{4}$ pints, (1 litre) cold water, bay leaf, and parsley. Bring to the boil, and simmer gently until reduced by about one-third. Skim at regular intervals. Strain, cool, and reserve.

Pre-heat the oven to 200°C (400°F, Mark 6). Cut the pigeons into four, and the steak into 2 inch (5cm) squares. Place a layer of steak around a funnel in the bottom of a 2-pint (1.2-litre) pie dish. Dot with half the butter, and season well. Put in the pigeon, with the rest of the butter and seasoning. Cut the yolks of the hard-boiled eggs in half, and dispose them between the pigeon pieces. Cover with the stock.

Roll out the pastry and cover the dish with it. Brush the pastry lightly with beaten egg. Bake in the pre-heated over for 25 minutes until the pastry is golden, then cover the pastry with butter papers, and reduce the heat to 130°C (275°F, Mark 1) for a further $1\frac{1}{2}$ hours.

Pickled Samphire 18th century

There were two seaside plants that the inhabitants of Devon, the Fortescues among them, were able to gather: samphire and laver. The samphire was rock samphire, rather than the marsh samphire (which is glasswort) found more commonly in eastern England. Its young shoots are quite strong in salt and iodine, and it makes an excellent accompaniment to fish. The period of gathering is fairly short (afterwards it becomes too woody), and it would be gathered in the early summer to make a pickle.

John Evelyn, in *Acetaria* (1699), talks of gathering samphire from around the cliffs of Dover as well as growing it in gardens, when it will be good all year round. At Castle Hill, however, enough of it was purchased to make it unlikely that the Fortescues grew it themselves. The close proximity of the entries of laver, samphire, and vinegar in some of the accounts make it very likely that the former two were pickled.

Although we are only now ridding ourselves of the tyranny of industrial malt vinegar, the Fortescues were no strangers to a variety of flavoured wine vinegars: for instance tarragon or elder. Wine vinegar should be used in preference to anything too strong. The recipe is based on Elizabeth Raffald's in *The Experienced English Housekeeper* (1769).

samphire, enough to fill a $1\frac{3}{4}$-pint (1-litre) glass
    preserving jar
about $1\frac{1}{2}$ pints (900 ml) dry farmhouse cider
salt
about $1\frac{1}{2}$ pints (900 ml) white wine or cider
    vinegar
1 teaspoon black peppercorns

1 inch (2.5cm) length of root ginger

Pick over and wash carefully young shoots of samphire. Place in a pan with the cider and a little salt. Bring to the boil, then simmer until bright green and tender, about 5 minutes. Drain and place in a 1¾-pint (1-litre) glass preserving jar. Bring the vinegar to the boil with the peppercorns and the root ginger cut into four pieces. Pour over the samphire, and seal the preserving jar tight. Leave to mature for three or four weeks, before using.

Lemon Biscuits 18th century

In 1847, the kitchen at Castle Hill was using about 6 lb of flour to make biscuits every week, sometimes as much as 12 lb. Some were doubtless simple drop biscuits, as in this recipe. Much cake and sweet baking was done at the end of the morning's baking, as the oven temperature dropped away from the fierce heat needed for bread. These biscuits (based on a recipe of Elizabeth Raffald), however, were meant to be cooked 'in a quick oven, but do not stop up the mouth at first for fear it should scorch'.

Makes about 24

2 whole eggs plus 2 egg yolks
1 teaspoon orange flowerwater (optional)
6 oz (150 g) sugar
1 lemon
4 oz (100 g) flour
sugar for dusting

Pre-heat the oven to 200°C (400°F, Mark 6). Beat the eggs and the orange flowerwater (if used) until frothy. Add the sugar and beat very well. The original recipe says to 'beat it one way for half an hour or more'; machinery solves this problem for us. Grate the rind off the lemon, and extract the

pulp from half the fruit. Add these, together with the flour, to the mixture, and stir in gently.

Drop and spread a heaped teaspoonful of the mixture for each biscuit on a well greased or non-stick baking tray. Dust with sugar, and bake in the pre-heated oven for about 8 to 10 minutes until golden.

Grilled Mackerel with Fennel, and Gooseberry Sauce 18th century

In 1814 the Fortescues' London greengrocer was supplying them 'gooseberries and mackrel herbs': a coincidence that serves to emphasize the popularity of the fruit with the oily, rich fish. Though not to gainsay it, when back at home, the Fortescues seemed to eat far more herring than mackerel; the north coast of Devon was an important herring fishery.

'Mackrel herbs' most probably meant fennel – certainly the most frequently encountered flavouring other than gooseberry with this fish. This recipe from John Nott for serving mackerel employs both flavours. The author of *Fish, How to Choose and How to Dress* (1843), apparently well versed in the ways of Cornwall, observed: 'Mackerel should be eaten with either plain melted butter, or which may be accompanied with anchovy, soy or cornubian sauce [a patent sauce from a chemist in Launceston]. But the proper sauce is fennel chopped fine, and mixed up in melted butter. Boiled gooseberries are considered an agreeable accompaniment to boiled mackerel; and sliced cucumber seems to be even still more highly esteemed.'

Serves 4

4 large mackerel
4 tablespoons olive oil
salt
freshly ground black pepper
1 tablespoon fennel, chopped

Sauce

8 oz (225 g) gooseberries
1 teaspoon each of chopped parsley, fennel, thyme
    and marjoram
2 teaspoons vinegar
1 teaspoon capers
salt
nutmeg
2 oz (50 g) butter

Gut the mackerel and make four diagonal slashes on each side of the fish. Rub them with oil, salt, pepper, and the chopped fennel. Grill them until the skin is crisp, turning once, about 5 minutes on each side. Do not handle too frequently as the flesh becomes soft once cooked.

For the sauce, top and tail the gooseberries and place them in a covered pan with two tablespoons of water. Cook gently, until tender, about 5 minutes. Mash with a fork, add the herbs, vinegar, capers, a generous grating of nutmeg, and salt to taste, and cook gently for 3 minutes. Slice in the cold butter, and shuffle until melted. Serve separately.

Notice that John Nott does not make this a sweet-sour sauce – no sugar is added, as it often is today – indeed, he accentuates the sharpness of the fruit with vinegar and capers.

Posset 17th century

The finest products of the Barnstaple potteries of the seventeenth and early eighteenth centuries were ornamented posset pots, often made to celebrate particular events, such as marriage or betrothal. Possets are an amalgamation of alcohol and cream, sometimes enriched with eggs and thickened with crumbs, always sweetened and spiced. They bear many resemblances to *zabaglione*, even if that dish has no dairy product in it.

Possets were both enjoyed as food and used for medicinal purposes in the seventeenth century. Thus they may appear in the centre of a grand table, especially if the container makes a good show, or they might be prepared as a tonic for someone who is ailing. Small wonder, therefore, that they figure in early recipe books as instructions that span the divide between the medicine chest and the kitchen.

The only recipes that survive in the Castle Hill archive are medicinal. Mostly they are potent mixtures that would heal the king's evil or cure breast cancer; or they are recipes for strong waters – the distilling that went on at home was for medical reasons, not inebriation. However, there are some for possets such as this preparation, endorsed: 'I know not for whom this is put down.'

A quart of ale or beer. Boil it in a skillet and put thereto a good handful of fennel and six or seven figs scraped and cut in pieces, two good spoonfuls of aniseed and a little saffron. Put all these to the drink and let them boil together until the liquor be more than half consumed and in the boiling scum it clean and strain into a basin and when cold, make a posset of the same drink and drink this often warm.

These are instructions for the preparation of the alcoholic content of the posset. Some of it would be put in a posset pot, and then the boiling cream or custard would be poured onto it from a great height, stirring all the while. It should froth up; sometimes it separates out – depending on whether the cream has been thickened or not.

The following recipe is for a 'sack posset', made with sherry. It is based on the instructions given by Sir Kenelm Digby (1669), and uses less alarming flavourings than some of those designed to do you good.

Serves 2 to 4

5 fl oz (150 ml) milk
5 fl oz (150 ml) double cream
1 tablespoon white breadcrumbs
$\frac{1}{4}$ teaspoon ground nutmeg
$\frac{1}{4}$ teaspoon ground cinnamon
2 egg yolks
1 tablespoon sugar
4 fl oz (125 ml) medium sherry

Mix the milk, cream, breadcrumbs, and spices, and bring to a simmering boil in an uncovered pan. Leave to simmer for 10 to 15 minutes, making sure it does not boil over.

Put the yolks, sugar, and a tablespoon of the sherry into a blender, and blend for 15 seconds. Put into a bowl, pour in the milk and cream mixture, then return to the saucepan, and cook very gently indeed until it has thickened slightly. Do not boil. This can be done in a double boiler if you wish to guarantee that the custard does not overcook.

Put the rest of the sherry into the blender, and pour on the custard while blending so that a nice froth is achieved. Decant into a bowl. Eat warm or cold.

Stewed Oysters 18th century

The variety of shellfish eaten at Castle Hill was, as might be expected, as wide as that caught on the south-western peninsular. Crabs, scallops, and mussels, however, do not get the references accorded oysters, lobsters, and, occasionally, prawns. Of all the molluscs, oysters were those that kept the best, recommending themselves to inland households as well as those nearer the coasts.

This is a recipe given to Richard Bradley, author of *The Country Housewife and Lady's Director* (1727). It was sent him by a friend living in Exeter, together with advice on serving oysters in scallop shells and roasting them, egged and crumbed, on spits.

Take large oysters, open them, and save their Liquor; then when the Liquor is settled, pour off the Clear, and put it in a Stew-pan, with some blades of Mace, a little grated Nutmeg, and some whole Pepper, to boil gently, till it is strong enough of the Spices: then take out the Spices, and put in the Oysters to stew gently, that they be not hard; and when they are near enough, add a piece of Butter, and as much grated Bread as will thicken the Liquor of the Oysters; and just before you take them from the Fire, stir in a Glass of White-wine.

This is adequate instruction, but the danger of overcooking the oysters will be avoided if the order of assemblage is changed.

Serves 4

24 oysters (6 oysters for each person)
1 teaspoon of blade mace
grated nutmeg

8 black peppercorns
1 glass dry white wine
1 tablespoon fine soft white breadcrumbs
2 oz (50 g) butter

Open the oysters, save the liquor, and remove them from their shells. Strain the liquor to remove any grit or shell, and place in a small pan with the spices. Simmer gently for 10 minutes. Remove the whole spices. Add the white wine. Reduce by one-third to a half by boiling hard in an uncovered pan. Add the breadcrumbs and simmer for another 5 minutes until somewhat thickened. Add the butter in thin slices, and shuffle in until melted. Add the oysters for just as long as they take to warm through, about 30 seconds. There is no need to boil the sauce.

Arrange the bottoms of the shells on plates – support them with sea salt. Put an oyster into each shell and divide the sauce between them. Serve warm.

Lobster Patties 18th century

Patty pans were an item of kitchen hardware that figures regularly in the Fortescue accounts. Patties were tiny pies, sometimes suggested as a trimming to a big set-piece in the centre of the table or, more often, as a flavoursome side-dish or supper dish. We have come to know them as vol-au-vents, a staple of the buffet, but at first they were small round pies, as we make mince pies.

I have suggested a lobster filling, suitable for the Fortescues' table, but it is a useful way to use prawns, or offal, such as brains, liver, or kidneys. I have also presumed that you will use small vol-au-vent cases, but you can also make patties as if they were small pasties – cutting a circle of pastry and folding it over the filling into a half-moon, before crimping the edges.

Makes 24

cooked flesh picked from $1\frac{1}{2}$ lb (750 g) lobster
2 tablespoons brandy
ground mace, nutmeg, cayenne, salt, and black
    pepper
4 oz (100 g) mushrooms, diced
1 oz (25 g) butter
10 fl oz (300 ml) double cream
2 egg yolks
lemon juice
1 lb (450 g) puff pastry, baked as 24 small
    vol-au-vent cases

Pre-heat the oven to 180°C (350°F, Mark 4). Cut the lobster flesh into small dice. Put into a pan, and flame with the brandy. Season quite highly with the spices, salt, and pepper. Reserve. Fry the mushrooms in butter. Add to the lobster. Mix the yolks with the cream and add to the rest of the ingredients. Heat gently, taking care never to boil. Cook until the mixture thickens. Check the seasoning and add lemon juice.

Warm the prepared vol-au-vent cases in the pre-heated oven for 5 minutes. Spoon the mixture into them, replace their tops, and replace in the oven if necessary to warm.

A White Fricassee of Rabbit Early 18th century

Mention has been made in the text of the vast number of rabbits trapped or hunted at Castle Hill. Not all would have been served to the family – good cheap meat for servants, and doubtless the dogs as well – but rabbit was popularly thought to be good eating, especially in the seventeenth and eighteenth centuries.

This recipe is for a light stew; it is 'white' rather than 'brown' because the meat is not fried as a preliminary, and the seasonings are less 'chutneyfied' than the darker, stronger alternative.

Serves 4

1 oz (25 g) butter
½ oz (15 g) flour
¼ teaspoon pounded blade mace
¼ teaspoon grated nutmeg
salt
cayenne pepper
12 fl oz (375 ml) good chicken or veal stock
grated rind of ½ lemon
4 anchovy fillets, chopped fine
1 rabbit, cut in joints
2 egg yolks
5 fl oz (150 ml) double cream
3 slices of white bread, cut in quarters and fried
3 tablespoons chopped parsley

Pre-heat the oven to 150°C (300°F, Mark 2). In a casserole, melt butter over a gentle heat, and add the flour. Do not brown. Add the spices and seasoning, then the stock to make a roux. Add the grated lemon rind and the anchovies, then the joints of rabbit. Bring to a simmer, cover the casserole and cook in the pre-heated oven for about 45 minutes, until tender.

Mix egg yolks with the cream. With the casserole over a very gentle heat, shuffle in the cream liaison, and let it cook until it thickens. Do not allow to boil. Check the seasoning.

Serve this on an open dish surrounded by sippets

of fried bread that have been dipped first in the sauce, then in chopped parsley. This dish would often have been garnished with slices of lemon.

Turnip Soup 18th century

Soup was an almost inevitable prelude to a proper dinner. It could be based on every sort of vegetable, or be some decoction of oxtail, other meat trimmings, or shellfish; it could be a clear broth, or perhaps a 'white soup' – a thickened stock with herbs and spices, finished with milk and cream. Soups of the seventeenth century seemed to include every possible ingredient – as elaborate as their pies and fricassees – but later recipes could be simplicity itself.

Turnips, as mentioned in the text, were being consumed at Castle Hill in increasing quantities during the Regency period.

Serves 6

1½ lb (700 g) young turnips
1 large onion
3 oz (75 g) butter
2 pints (1.2 litres) chicken or veal stock
2 tablespoons soft breadcrumbs
salt and pepper
sugar (optional)
4 fl oz (125 ml) double cream

Top and tail the turnips and cut into dice. Peel and slice the onion. Stew the turnips and onion gently in the melted butter for 15 minutes, without colouring. Add the stock and the breadcrumbs, and simmer until vegetables are tender, about 25 minutes. Pass through the fine plate of a food mill. Return to the saucepan and season. The sugar is optional. Heat until serving temperature, then stir in the cream. Do not allow to boil.

Serve with fried croûtons. John Nott, in his *Cook's & Confectioner's Dictionary* (1726), suggests that 'you may lay a roasted duck in the middle of your soup'.

Squab Pie as in Devon or Cornwall
Traditional

In this instance, 'squab' denoted not young pigeon but a spiced meat and fruit mixture. Dr Johnson defines the words as 'a pie made of many ingredients'. It carries much of the high, sweet flavour enjoyed in meat cookery from medieval times until late in the eighteenth century in Britain.

Serves 6

2 lb (900 g) lean mutton, cut in 1 inch (2.5 cm) cubes
1 tablespoon dripping
2 teaspoons black peppercorns, 1 teaspoon blade mace, 1 teaspoon allspice, 1 cinnamon stick (2 inches/5 cm), 2 teaspoons coriander – ground together
1 lb (450 g) onions, thinly sliced
1 tablespoon flour
10 fl oz (300 ml) beef stock (more if required)
1 lb (450 g) cooking apples, peeled and cut in eighths
5 oz (125 g) prunes, stoned
4 oz (100 g) raisins
rind and juice of 1 Seville orange
salt
8 oz (225 g) puff pastry
beaten egg for gilding pastry

Pre-heat the oven to 150°C (300°F, Mark 2). Season the prepared meat with salt, and brown in the dripping on top of the stove. Add the ground spices, and fry a minute more. Add the onion, and fry until transparent. Sprinkle on the flour, then stir in the stock to make a roux. Simmer, stirring, to get rid of any lumps. Add the fruit, and the grated rind and juice of the orange. Use sweet oranges if Sevilles are no longer in season. Check the seasoning, and cook in a covered casserole in the pre-heated oven for about 1½ hours, until the meat is tender. Remove from the oven, and place in a pie dish.

Turn the oven up to 200°C (400°F, Mark 6). Roll out the pastry, and place on top of the meat. Brush the pastry lightly with the beaten egg, and bake in the oven for 25 minutes.

Golden Gratin of White Fish Early 18th century

This is an adaptation of an early eighteenth-century recipe for a fish pie, using either cod or haddock fillets. It is also suitable for saltfish, a staple then but more of a luxury today. It reflects the tastes enjoyed when fish might have been stronger (older) than thought best in our time.

Serves 4

2 lb (900 g) cod or haddock fillets
court bouillon (made of ½ pint/300 ml white wine, ½ pint/300 ml water, a small peeled onion, 1 stick sliced celery, 1 sliced carrot, a bay leaf, 6 peppercorns, and a small bunch of parsley stalks)
1 oz (25 g) butter
1 oz (25 g) flour
2 anchovy fillets

1 inch (2.5 cm) green ginger
3 cloves
1 teaspoon blade mace
pinch of saffron (i.e. 1 small packet)
salt and freshly ground black pepper
double cream
soft breadcrumbs
parsley sprigs and lemon slices, to garnish

Poach the fish gently in the court bouillon. When it is cooked, lift it out carefully onto a wide fireproof dish. Strain and reserve the court bouillon.

Melt the butter, and make a roux with the flour and $\frac{3}{4}$ pint (450 ml) of the court bouillon. Pound the anchovies and spices together in a mortar, and add them to the sauce. Cook very gently for 10 minutes. Taste for seasoning, and finish with double cream, to taste.

Pour the sauce over the fish, sprinkle generously with breadcrumbs, and brown under the grill. Serve garnished with lemon slices and parsley sprigs.

A Compote of Peaches 19th century

The peach tree at Castle Hill was famed for its size. Walled gardens and glass-houses were devoted to producing tender fruits suitable to more southerly climes, in remarkable quantity. Although the elaborate dessert course of fruit and nuts gained favour in Victorian times, there had previously been doubt of the consequences of eating too much uncooked produce – memories here of infantile collywobbles and too many apples. This is a simple method for dealing with peaches.

Serves 4 to 8

8 ripe peaches
12 oz (325 g) sugar
1 pint (600 ml) water
juice of 1 lemon

Scald the peaches with boiling water and peel them. Make a syrup of the sugar and water, and cook gently for 10 minutes. Gently poach the fruit for about 20 minutes in the syrup, until just tender. Remove with a slotted spoon. Reduce the syrup by boiling, then sharpen with the lemon juice. Pour over the fruit. Serve cool, with almond biscuits.

Seed Cake 18th century

The Castle Hill flour accounts make clear that one of the constants of baking was seed cake – well into the Victorian period. It was a staple that appears rarely on our own tea-tables, even though the taste of caraway is still much appreciated in Eastern Europe. This cake, based on a recipe given by J. Fairley in *The London Art of Cookery* (1783), carries more spice (and perfume and alcohol) than most modern versions.

Makes a 2lb (900 g) cake

6 oz (150 g) butter
6 oz (150 g) caster sugar
3 eggs
$\frac{1}{2}$ teaspoon each of ground mace and nutmeg
3 teaspoons caraway seeds
8 oz (225 g) self-raising flour, sifted
1 tablespoon brandy
1 tablespoon rosewater

Pre-heat the oven to 180°C (350°F, Mark 4). Beat

the butter and sugar until light. Beat in the eggs, spices, and caraway seeds. Fold in the flour, brandy, and rosewater, and mix well.

Prepare a 2lb (900 g) loaf tin, either by greasing really well, or by lining with silicone paper. Drop in the cake mixture and bake in the pre-heated oven for about 1 hour, until a knife or skewer comes out clean. Leave to rest in the tin for 10 minutes, then turn onto a rack to cool.

SCOTLAND

Glamis Castle, Angus
Annette Hope

Glamis Castle, Angus

Glamis Castle stands in good farming land in the pleasant, broad valley which lies between the Sidlaw Hills and the Grampians, a little way off the road running north from Dundee to Kirriemuir. The first view is of weathered towers and turrets of pink sandstone rising up at the end of a long tree-lined avenue, but this tall slender section is actually flanked by two shallow wings built at a later date. Solid and severe, unpretentious yet commanding, it is a suitable home for a family which has been part of the mainstream of Scottish history since 1372, when Sir John Lyon of Forteviot was created Thane of Glamis by King Robert II. Sir John married the King's daughter, Princess Joanna, four years after his ennoblement; thus was founded the dynasty in whose possession the Castle has remained up to the present day.

The family's affairs have been at times very much in the public eye. In 1537 the widow of the 6th Lord was burnt alive on Castle Hill in Edinburgh for conspiring by poison or witchcraft against the life of James V. Her young son, also condemned to death, had his execution deferred until he reached his majority. Fortunately a year or two later his accuser confessed that the whole tale was a fabrication. Title and estates were restored, and the boy became the 7th Lord Glamis in 1543. His grandson Patrick, the 9th Lord, was created 1st

Earl of Kinghorne in the peerage of Scotland in 1606, and it was he who began the renovation of the old castle. However, his son, caught in the struggle between Royalists and Covenanters, had no time for such pursuits, and in fact all but bankrupted the estate; as says the *Scots Peerage*, 'Coming to his inheritance the wealthiest Peer in Scotland, he left it the poorest.' In consequence when the 3rd Earl, another Patrick, came of age he inherited a debt of £400,000 and two castles – Glamis and Castle Lyon – in serious disrepair. A prudent young man with a deep sense of responsibility and a good business head, by the time he died he had not only paid off most of the debt but had improved and enlarged both his homes. Moreover, in recompense for his services to the Scottish Crown he had secured a charter providing that he and each successive inheritor should be styled Lord Glamis, Tannadyce, Sidlaw and Strathdichtie, Viscount Lyon, and Earl of Strathmore and Kinghorne.

It is to this Lord Strathmore's lifetime that our first set of recipes, Volume 243 in the Strathmore Papers, belongs. The fragile volume bound in brown calf is embossed on the cover with the letters LIM. On the flyleaf, faded brown ink records a date: 4 Oct 1666. The bulk of the recipes is consistent with this date, but a second, much smaller group, which begins after an interval of several blank pages, is of later origin. Despite the initials on the cover, it is likely that the first writer was Lady Helen Middleton, second daughter of the Earl of Middleton, who married Earl Patrick in 1662. The young couple's first home was Castle Lyon, where Lord Kinghorne (as he then was – the Strathmore title came later) had lived since attaining his majority. It was only just habitable. Years afterwards the Earl wrote in his autobiographical *Book of Record* that he and his sister, the Lady Elizabeth, had spent the two previous years collecting 'as much of cours furniture as in a verie mean and sober way filled all the rowms of my house, some on [one] way some another'. In the kitchen, old pots and pans salvaged from the near ruin that was Glamis were the only equipment.

That castle, its fabric threatened by neglect, its furniture appropriated by the Dowager Countess and her second husband, its home-farm occupied by a wadsetter or mortgagee, was left untouched for another eight years. But in 1671 restoration and improvement began, and by 1689 the place was fit for family occupation. Many of its ornaments and articles of furniture had been bought on visits to London, and in the *Book of Record* the Earl compares these shopping sprees with his first penny-pinched journey south in 1660, when he went to swear allegiance to Charles II. 'Had I been as moderate in all my severall jorneys to that place since, from which I have brought things of great value for the furniture of my houses, I had saved many a pond and pennie, but I acknowledge a great dale of weakness in my humour that way, inclining to be very profuse upon all things of ornament for my houses as I have been upon building.'

Travelling from Scotland to London or vice versa must have been a strange experience in the closing years of the seventeenth century. With the end of the Dutch Wars and the establishment of English naval power, stability and wealth were returning to England. London, after suffering the plague and the Great Fire, was rebuilding and expanding, its elegant new streets adorned with fine classical buildings and Wren's lovely churches. Some of its inhabitants enjoyed great wealth, but others lived in urban poverty, and the hedonism of the court was constantly confronted by the modest sobriety of a Puritan middle class. Nevertheless the general atmosphere was one of vigour and lively prosperity. The city was crammed with theatres, gaming-houses, taverns, and coffee-houses. Samuel Pepys could go from a meeting of the Royal Society to a performance at Drury Lane by 'pretty, witty Nelly', and thence to one of the new 'ordinaries' or restaurants, which were being set up by the Huguenot refugees from France. To a visitor from Scotland the city must have seemed quite astonishing.

The tenor of country life in seventeenth-century Scotland, even more than in England, was determined largely by poor communications and a primitive system of agriculture. While it is true that landlords lived better than their tenants, the diets of both were closely linked. Uncertain harvests were affected not only by unpredictable weather, poor soil, and crop disease, but also by religious and political events. Bad roads and a shortage of wheeled vehicles meant also that little help could be sought from outside in bad times. In the few areas where wheat was grown, for example, it was traditionally the cereal of the upper classes. But if the wheat crop failed, the nobility, like the working people, lived on oats or barley; and if drought, flood, or the ferocity of war ruined all the crops, the entire rural population suffered. The first aim for a great house, especially one in a remote country district, was to be as far as possible self-sufficient in a diversity of foods. In the *Book of Record* (written from 1684 to 1689 but covering a much longer period), we read of the measures taken to achieve this. Agricultural development was in its infancy, but some of its fundamental ideas were already formulated, and the Earl was aware of them. Thus, it was according to latest opinion as expressed in the first book on gardening in Scotland, *The Scots Gard'ner*, written by John Reid in 1683, that the castle was surrounded with a symmetrical planting of trees, 'the ground on both sydes being of a like bigness, and the figure the same with a way upon either syd of the utter [outer] court to the back court'. Scotland had been denuded of trees, but their value as windbreaks and preventers of erosion was beginning to be recognized. Livestock was another point of concern, and the Earl restocked the home-farm with sheep and young cattle, and bought 100 oxen to be used as draught animals, both for the plough and for construction work at the castle, where among other things a new dairy and still-house were being built.

All this was genuine improvement. A few years before, when Cromwell's soldiers had been quartered around Glamis, their needs could not be supplied by the estate, and the inhabitants of the little town of Forfar nearby had found themselves required to provide 'fower dussen of wheate bread' daily, and beef, mutton, or lamb each Monday and Wednesday. This was what the English soldiers were used to eating, but it cannot have been easy for the Forfar burghers to assemble the supplies.

A measure of the difficulty may be gained from the fact that even in the middle of the next century no meat was sold in Forfar by weight, and 'very seldom was an ox killed till the greater part of the carcase had been bespoke ... a man who had bought a shilling's worth of beef or an ounce of tea would have concealed it from his neighbours like murder' (*Statistical Account for the County of Forfar*, 1790–91).

In the seventeenth century the region's two predominant cereals were bere (or bear), closely related to modern barley, and oats. Bere was hardier, and therefore more generally used. It was commonly eaten as pottage or made into bannocks, and it was also the base for the ale which everybody drank. Its flour, if made from the husked grain, was said to be whiter than wheat flour and was by some preferred. Oats, far more versatile, were also more popular, but the grey oat which was then cultivated was low-yielding and disease-prone. Oatmeal could be eaten cooked as porridge or raw with a little water as *drammach*, or mixed with hot water or milk to make *brose*, or blended with a little fat and water and cooked on a girdle in the form of oatcakes. It kept better than beremeal. No part of the grain was wasted. Even the husks, soaked several days in water, gave up their residual starch when squeezed through a fine wire sieve or linen cloth. The product thus obtained was raw *sowens*, which might be eaten as they were but more frequently were taken a stage further and boiled until they thickened. When cool, the resultant jelly-like mass, slightly acid, was valued for its health-giving properties. Taken with milk or raw sowens ('sowens and sowens to them'), it was a favourite food, eaten regularly even by such people as the Duke and Duchess of Hamilton.

Both oats and bere were essential to human life, for the poorer people ate almost nothing else. Both were also vital foods for animals in the winter when grazing was poor. It is scarcely surprising therefore that they were used as currency, and made up a good proportion of most men's wages. The sixteenth-century French traveller Etienne Perlin had declared of Scotland 'Nothing is scarce here except money', and while the first part of the statement was no longer true, there was still a great dearth of coin. Landlords received their rent and paid their servants' wages in terms of bolls of oats (a boll of oats was equivalent to six imperial bushels in English measurement), bere, or meal (usually oatmeal). The rent roll of the Strathmore estates during the 3rd Earl's lifetime shows that the farm of Templebank of Thorntoun paid annually 8 bolls of bere, 8 bolls of meal, and 12 poultry. Some farms also provided Glamis with butter and cheese. As regards wages, the regular workers on the estate – farm labourers, gardeners, foremen, schoolteachers, even ministers of the Church – were paid largely or entirely in kind.

Lady Helen's recipe book (Volume 243), begun in the 1660s while she was bringing up a young family and helping her husband to restore his estates, reflects her situation. What is most striking about it is how few of the 160 recipes are actually for food – not because she had no interest in it, but because few permutations were possible. Wood and peat were still the principal fuel, roasting jack and iron pot (standing three-legged on the hearth or suspended over the fire on a mobile arm or 'swee') the main equipment. There was no equivalent to the modern gas or electric stove, and the huge oven in the bakehouse was designed for breadmaking, although it was now sometimes used for pies.

Ingredients had not changed in centuries. Compilers of recipes rarely write down the dishes they eat every day; what interests them more is the unfamiliar ones they would like to try.

If food could offer few surprises, what was far more uncertain and less within man's power was health. One hundred and twenty-two of Lady Helen's recipes are unequivocally medicinal or cosmetic. Some of the ills they attempt to treat are commonplace: toothache, constipation, wind in the stomach. Others reveal the terrible vulnerability of the seventeenth-century Scot: there are remedies for the 'bloody flux', for the King's Evil, for eyes 'that have received impediment of sight by the small pox', and, most moving of all, 'to delyver a woman of travaill in 2 hours be the child dead or alive a receipt so sure that non is surer'. Life was a sinister and dangerous journey, during which you might encounter 'worms crept into the ear', and 'worms that eat the eyelids'. The remedies too are dramatic: oil of toads, snail broth, oil of swallows (surely not often made, since it involved catching live swallows and pounding them in a mortar with herbs and butter). To 'confirm memorie' one should once a month anoint the arteries of the head with the gall of a partridge; for forgetfulness, a mixture of rue, red mint, salad oil and strong vinegar should be sniffed up into the nostrils. The cosmetic recipes also reveal eternal preoccupations: pimples, greying hair ('to colour hair black or browne ... taught by Mrs Gib. and never failing'), or roughened hands. And in addition to these are other recipes, giving instructions for marmalades, jellies, candied fruit or flowers, preserves, and distilled waters. Such things were regarded not as foods but as medicines. Sugar, imported from the East, expensive and sometimes difficult to get, was thought to be a valuable aid to health, especially for children. (Nor was this so absurd as appears to our twentieth-century eyes; in an age when many people suffered from dietary deficiencies its property of giving instant energy must have seemed curative.) The distillations too had a medical (usually restorative) purpose.

Once these preserves and cordials have been removed from the list, Lady Helen's food recipes appear pretty limited in scope. Only three are for meat: of these, two are methods to keep it a little longer ('to souse a turkie' and 'to souse an pig' – see page 68), and the third mixes the blood of an animal with oatmeal and herbs to make black puddings. It would be wrong to infer that meat was rarely eaten at Glamis. A more correct interpretation is that what were called in England 'made dishes' had not yet travelled north. If in the south meat was often part-cooked and then enriched by the addition of a sauce or a garnish, on the fringes of the Highlands it was still most often boiled or roasted, or occasionally fried.

Most of Volume 243's remaining recipes are for puddings and desserts; these do reflect outside influence. Seventeenth-century Britain had a passion for 'creams', for which our manuscript has eight recipes. One remembers that Pepys in the same period recorded his passion for 'a dish of very goode cream'. He especially liked it with brown bread, and trying out some of Lady Helen's recipes gives one an understanding of this apparently curious combination; the cream, boiled until thick and flavoured with fruit and sugar, develops a smooth, almost dry texture, which makes it spread easily while it keeps its shape. A different texture was achieved in 'snow cream' – again a great seventeenth-century favourite – where beaten egg

whites were combined and beaten again with thick flavoured cream, and the resulting froth was eaten.

But if some recipes follow fashion, others reflect little change. Much use is still made of almonds and grated bread as thickening agents. There are no recipes for biscuits or small cakes, unless one counts cheesecakes, which were probably eaten as part of a meal. The only cake recipe, called simply 'To mak a Cake', is really for an enriched bread made from spiced flour, eggs, butter, cream, sugar, and yeast. This reminds us that at this stage the words 'cake' and 'bread' were virtually interchangeable, and certainly had no connection with the sweetness or otherwise of the article, as the words 'shortbread' and 'oatcake' demonstrate. There are some pies, and a 'ryce florentine' which turns out to be rice boiled in milk then mixed with an equal quantity of butter and currants, eggs, spices, and sugar, and baked in a puff pastry case (see page 69 for recipe). 'Spinage puddings' are a sweetened breadcrumb/spice/egg mixture coloured green with spinach juice.

What is particularly interesting is that none of the recipes displays French influence in type, method, or vocabulary. This of course does not disprove the theory held by many, that Scottish cooking has strong French connections. It does, however, lend support to the view that these connections were made later than is generally assumed, and simultaneously with their appearance in England, from the beginning of the eighteenth century onwards. They were then reinforced, in a way that did not happen south of the Border, by the rebellion of 1745 and the subsequent expulsion of many Scots to France.

Lady Helen died in 1708. As is the way with such

things, her recipe book lived after her, and was added to by later hands. First come four recipes, decidedly old-fashioned and written in unbeautiful but very legible italic: 'To preserve broom buds', 'A Sallet of Jelliflowers', 'A componed egg for a sellet', 'To candie marigolds roses borage or rosmarie flours'. The 'componed egg' has a very medieval feel to it:

Take 20 eggs pairt [separate] the yolks from the whits and beat them well with a spoon in severall dishes then pour the yolks in a bladder and tye it fast as round as a ball put in a pot with watter and boyll it very hard then have the whittes in ane other bledder and put in the yolk with the whitt round about it then bind it as the other and boill it hard you may if you pleas put to the yolks muske or ambergreece beatten with suger and beatten bisket bread and to the whitts almond pest [paste] muske beatten with sugar joyce of orange and a litle brayed ginger when it is cold serve it with almond milk sugar and joyce of orange.

The last group of recipes is again mainly medicinal. One called evocatively 'The melancholie water' is cheering merely to read:

Tak violets cowslips wallflowers rosemarie flowers burrag, buglose pinks, sageflowers, marigold flowers, clove gellieflowrs, the right proper hartsease woodbine flowers red rose and damask rose leaves of dark [roses] six handfulls [?] leaves 3 handfulls cynamone half ane unce nutmegs 2 unces annyce seeds and more beat the spyce a little safron the weight of a sixpennie in figs [put] these the space of two days in a potle of Canarie Sack and then distill them in a glase still put in to the liquor six unces of whyt sugar candie fynlie batten and hang a little musk and amber at the nose of the still in a little tiffanie that the water may drop throw [through] it tak of this 3 tymes a week two spoonfulls fasting and at any other tyme when you are sad.

One of the very last recipes, 'To dress a hare' (see page 68), probably dates from the first decade of the eighteenth century. Only young hare, or leveret, is really tender enough to stand roasting, and the common method of dealing with older animals was to jug them, stewing the meat very slowly in a double container. To this, the recipe at the end of Volume 243 provides an alternative, and although there seems nothing new about the rather high seasoning of spices and the use of currants, the double cooking of the meat, the use of orange juice, and the garnish of forcemeat balls, indicate that the era of the 'made dish' was arriving in Scotland.

Lady Helen outlived her husband by thirteen years, and before his father's death, John, the new Earl of Strathmore, had married Elizabeth Stanhope, daughter of the 2nd Earl of Chesterfield. Her household book (Volume 238 in the archives) opens after the death of her mother-in-law, and finishes shortly before her own death in 1723. It is specific and methodical, and while it contains no recipes or descriptions of food, it makes it possible for us to reconstruct daily life at Glamis and Castle Lyon in a certain amount of detail.

In essence, the book records payments to servants and tenants, with a complicated system of accounting for which there were two reasons. In 1707 an Act uniting the Scottish and English Parliaments had made it possible for a single currency to be used throughout Britain. It was inevitable, nevertheless, that for many years Scots should go on thinking in terms of their own coinage, and Lady Elizabeth almost always entered her expenses in both currencies. The entry for 6 February 1714, for example, reads: 'This day the new Porter John Martin came to my service and is obliged to stay in it a year hee is to have thirty pound Scotch a year is of English money two pound ten.'

The second complication was that a changeover had now begun from payment in kind ('kain') to payment in cash. The mixed system which was operating had many permutations. At one level the old method survived, as we see from an entry for 16 November 1714: 'This day John Barney is entered to bee my Postilion and I am only to give him cloaths and lenen [linen] no money.' But when a new gardener came to work on 12 August 1716 he was promised 'five pounds sterling a year and after Martinmas two Pecks of Meale in the weke for himself and hee is to keep two men and have twenty shelings for each of them and this is all that hee is to get for himself and his men'. Cristy Wattson the dairymaid got twelve pounds Scotch a year, a pair of shoes, and 'what lening [linen] I please to give her'. Even important servants were paid in this way: 'November 26 1719: This day my new Grunter [steward, or grieve] at Castle Lyon Alexander Leach entered to my service and is to have a hundred Marks by year and three Pecks of Meal a weke while I am at Glamis and hee is to have his meat in the house in summer when I am at Castle Lyon.' However, some servants were engaged for a cash wage with no mention of any supplement. On such terms was Sanders [Alexander] Adam taken on as cook at Glamis in 1712; he was to receive four pounds sterling a year. If an employer was short of cash, or an employee ran out of his staple oatmeal, an accommodation

could often be reached. It was still possible to barter work for food, and Lady Elizabeth's entries frequently record making out a chit which could be taken to the factor and exchanged for a bag of meal. Even Sanders Adam sometimes chose to be paid in this way: 'Aug. 14 1719: Delivered to Sanders Adam my Coke three pound sterling which with the Meal and Peas hee got an order for exceeds his wages.'

The way in which farm rentals were paid was also in transition. While they continued for some time to include 'kain' in the form of a set number of chickens, capons, or even sheep where the farm was especially productive, it now appears that sometimes the tenant's produce was bought for cash: 'August 8 1722: payd ... to Marget Shaw for ... Butter, ten stone, and two Butter Baras [barrels] more the same day ...' The entry is the more surprising because the Glamis dairy was regularly producing butter, as we know by the occasional purchase of butter barrels.

There are many references in the household book to the manufacture or purchase of barm, or yeast, showing that, like the dairy, bakehouse and brewhouse were in constant use. Sanders Adam, in supplement to his wages, received eighteen pounds Scotch for supplying barm for baking and brewing. In common with everyone else the family drank home-brewed ale, although the household book notes occasionally the purchase of claret, canary, or muscat, usually from merchants in Montrose or Dundee. (Only the poor drank water, which in rural Scotland was unpolluted and safe to drink.) When the family was in residence both white bread and oaten or bere bannocks were baked almost daily. The white bread was for the family, the other for the servants.

When the 4th Earl died in 1712 he was succeeded by his third son John, still a very young man. Lady Elizabeth continued to manage the estate while he completed his education. She was an efficient farmer, selling wheat to her neighbours, and buying from them oxen, wethers, and sometimes a fat sow. She also sold wool to local spinners and linen to merchants in Perth or Dundee, for Scots linen was much in demand since a tax had been imposed on calico imported from India.

But the habits of the aristocracy were changing. City life was in fashion, and Edinburgh, rapidly developing into a sophisticated capital, drew the nobility from their country seats. The Strathmores were there from September 1713 to May 1714, lodging in the house of a Mr Seaton, to whom they paid £4 a fortnight; in fact, compared with life at Glamis and Castle Lyon, that Edinburgh winter was both busy and expensive. Everything had to be bought; there was no meat from the home-farm, no home-baked bread or home-brewed ale, and no tenants brought poultry or butter to the back door. 'Oct. 12. 1713: Given to Sanders Adam since my comeing to Ed. to bye meat more rots [roots] eggs and Earbs £01.03.1. ... Nov. 2 1713: Payd to Mrs Legorn for Ale £01.02.02. Payd to Mr Johnstone the same day for ale £01.08.08.' Another commodity makes its first appearance in the Strathmore papers: 'Dec. 10 1713: Payd for three quarters of a pound of bohee tea £00.16.6.' There is a rather curious entry for 26 December: 'Payd to Donailt my footman for his expences and bringing the geese and turkeyes £00.13.09.' Since no payment to a farmer or butcher is entered, it rather looks as if Donald put the birds in crates at Glamis or Castle Lyon, and travelled by carrier with them all the way to Edinburgh in time for the New Year celebrations. (Christmas Day had no status in Scotland, being considered a papist festival.)

It was a busy season. The younger boys, Charles, James, and Thomas, were at school, but John, the new Earl, was with his mother and sisters, and preparing to become a student at St Andrews University. The younger girl, Mary, had a full educational programme mapped out: writing lessons ('Payd to Mr Bates for learning Mary to writ ... 0.03.00'), dancing tuition, and a music master to teach her the spinet. But the true reason for the visit emerges in March, when there is heavy expenditure on 'wedding mantows', petticoats, nightgowns, and other garments. The Countess's elder daughter Nelly was about to be married. Catering preparations began in earnest on 17 March: 'Payd to Mr Stuart for five dozen of Muchkins of Sherrey Bottles and corks include.' By 1 April the affair was over, and the bills were pouring in: 'Payd to John Rudworth for meat bought for the wedding night super [supper] and the next dayes dinner is £2.00.00. Payd this same day for sweetmeats bought from Mrs Fanton for the super the marage night and the dinner next day £02.09.08', and – a modern touch – '... given her for the lend of her glases £00.10.00.'

Family happiness at this event, alas, was not long to remain unclouded. Scotland was still going through troubled times, and in 1715 the young Earl was killed leading a contingent of rebels against the Union, at the Battle of Sheriffmuir. Something of his mother's pain is evident in the bald entry made a full year after his death: 'My now eldest son Charles Earle of Strathmore set out this day for Oxford and I gave him ten Gennyes [guineas] is £10.15.00.'

For several more years Lady Elizabeth held the reins in her capable hands. Now the Castle was regularly visited by a carrier from Dundee, bringing in supplies. 'Oct. 9 1721 Payd this day to Danle Crocket ... his account for Fish Herring letters beefe and the fraight of my stamped lining [linen].' The fish would have been freshly caught: salmon from the Tay perhaps, for that river was already famous for the abundance and excellent quality of its fish. Sometimes Crocket or another merchant brought out 'hard', that is, dried fish. In the Middle Ages this had been a basic food, cheap and nearly always available, a standby when meat was scarce or on the many fast days ordained by the Roman Catholic church. By the eighteenth century it was less in demand, but its usefulness in rural areas continued for some time. If the purchase of beef seems odd, it must be remembered that because of a lack of winter pasturage only a small number of the cattle raised locally could be brought to maturity. Most were exported to England, where they fattened well on the richer pastures of the south. An entry in June 1722 again refers to 'butchermeat' bought for the Countess by Daniel Crocket.

Two years after Lady Elizabeth's death in 1723 her son Charles, the 6th Earl, married Susan Cochrane. Of this lady's housekeeping activities we know nothing. The estate accounts were handed over to a steward, and in 1728 when the Earl was accidentally killed, the title passed to his younger brother James. Lady Susan retires from the scene. James married in May 1731, but his wife died four months later, and he himself lived only until 1735, to be succeeded in turn by the youngest of Lady Elizabeth's sons, Thomas.

The account-book kept by the steward during these difficult times comprises the first part of Volume 241 of the Strathmore Papers. Here we can see an exact record of the use made of all estate produce from 1725 to 1733, with sporadic later entries taking the story to 1736. The same volume contains a 'pultrie' record running from March 1731 to September 1736, noting all birds received in payment of rent plus the occasional purchase of chickens (presumably live). Towards the end of the volume a few pages headed *A Charge of Wines* list wines bought and bottled.

The grain record is neatly set out in six columns: wheat, malt, meal (i.e. oatmeal), beare, pease, oats. The measurements used are bolls, firlots, pecks, and pounds. At the left-hand side of each page is a blank space in which is written the purpose for which the grain was dispensed. The opening entry is typical:

The Earle and Countess of Strathmore came from Edinburgh to Glamis the 7 August 1725.

Broun [brewing] of malt before	
My Lord and Lady came	*9 bolls meal.*
Ground in flour	*1 boll wheat*
Bakon [baking] of meal	*1 boll 2 firlots*

From other entries we learn that bread was baked about every ten days, always of oatmeal for the servants, and wheat for the family, and that regular brewing ensured that ale never ran short. Malt was bought either locally or from Montrose. 'Malt brued in table ale ... in strong ale ... for the ous [use] of the harvest ...' are frequent entries.

By now bere was the least used cereal. Between 1725 and 1736 only five dispenses are recorded, two for animal feeding, one to make barley groats, and two separate bolls sent to the barley mill for an unspecified purpose. The column for pease is also mainly left blank. Like meal, pease were probably still a form of currency, but at Glamis their only culinary use seems to have been 'for the servants broth.' Clearly oats were by now the dominant grain. Even though much of the oatmeal went to the servants, the family ate groats frequently, and probably sowens as well.

The columns of the livestock record are headed oxen and cows, calves, sheep, lambs, turkeys, geese, ducks, capons, poultry (i.e. hens) and chickens, the' largest number of entries coming under 'Pultrie'. In August and September 1725, hens were killed on 41 out of a possible 43 days, as opposed to chickens on 14 days (but sometimes ten or twelve a day), sheep fourteen days (usually a single animal), ducks twelve days (four each time), geese eleven days (two or three each time), lambs nine days, calves three days, cows three days, and turkeys twice (three each time). It is noticeable that from November to June few cows or sheep were slaughtered; on such occasions they were often described as 'faulty', indicating that they would not have lasted through the winter. Between January and July the main diet seems to have been chickens and sheep, but without doubt game and pigeons from the dovecote – although not listed in the record because they were not farm produce – were a valuable supplement. We know that nearby at Ochtertyre, another great estate, partridge, plover, pigeons and grouse were frequently on the winter menu. The Glamis record stops in November 1728, but resumes on 12 March 1731 with some interesting changes. There is a column now for pigs, and calves are henceforth designated veal. In place of

the word 'killed' we usually find 'spent', i.e. dispensed, although occasionally the entry is 'spent and killed'. 'Dressed in the kitchen' is another interesting new entry, for a slightly smaller room adjacent to the great stone-flagged fourteenth-century kitchen is still known as the preparation room, and may have been designated for this purpose in the 1730s. (This kitchen was gutted in Victorian times and the enormous fireplace filled with a central heating boiler, but that has now been removed and the room stands empty awaiting a new use.) Also for the first time, we read that two swine have been killed and made into hams. 'Faulty' animals, as in the entry 'killed ane faulty wedder and dressed' are still prominent during the winter months, but by 1736 it is evident that agricultural experimentation is taking place: 'killed a hilland [highland] koon' is the entry for 7 January. The Earl, like so many of his contemporaries, had become interested in the movement known as Improvement. Besides introducing Highland cattle he was also experimenting with goats. Whether that particular enterprise was successful we have no means of knowing, for the record ends shortly thereafter.

The 'pultrie record', covering the years 1731–36, throws some light on tenant-landlord transactions. 'Kain', or rent in kind, did not die out in Scotland until well into the eighteenth century. The first entry is 'Delyvered by Mrs Shaw [the housekeeper] to Alexander Adam for which she gave the tenants receipts: 7 capons, 10 pultrie'. The columns here are for capons, poultry (i.e. hens), and chickens,· but pigs are often mentioned, and it is clear that some type of *in lieu* payment or barter transaction often occurred from entries such as: '[Received from] ... John Johnson 2 pigs for 4 pultrie ... 9

chickens for 3 pultrie ... 6 ducks for 4 pultrie.'
More typical entries simply acknowledge receipt:
'March 17 1731: Received from James Honorie in
Brydestoun 4 capons; March 18, received from
James Jack in Glamis 3 pultrie.' Very rarely, the
purchase of poultry is recorded: 'Bought in
Longforgan 20 chickens.'

Finally in this steward's book (241) we have the
wine record, hardly worth dignifying by the name
of cellar-book. The first section runs from 1731 to
1737, the second from 1739 to 1762 with a few
intermissions. A variety of hands has been at work
here, some clear and legible with fairly consistent
spelling, others less well educated. The columns list
brandy, sherry (or 'Cherrie', or 'Chereay'), white
wine, claret, 'frontinack', and orange wine. Had
Glamis been an English castle, sack and port would
have been on the list, but Scottish shippers had
always had closer rapport with France than with
Spain or Portugal. It is not surprising to find a
Dundee man, John Strachan, supplying the Castle
with claret, and Peter Sloan, from the much smaller
port of Kinghorn in Fife, also sent 'strong claret
wine'. That this claret has no other designation is
not unusual; Pepys, enthusiastically recording his
introduction to 'Ho Bryan' in 1664, is the first
Briton to name a château wine, and it was to be a
long time before the provenance of a claret was
considered important. But useful as were the
Dundee and Kinghorn merchants, it is evident that
when the Earl visited Edinburgh or London he
took advantage of the wider choice available: 'Ther
came from Lieth (Leith) before the family came to
Glammis twenty one dozen and nyn chopen bottles
of Claret ...' Bottles were measured in chopins
(about an English quart) and mutchkins (about
three-quarters of an English pint). Often wine was

bought in hogsheads or barrels, and bottled at the
Castle.

I have said that we know nothing of the 6th
Countess's (Lady Susan's) housekeeping. In fact a
rather puzzling recipe book in the archive, Volume
244, is thought to date from 1692–1746, and so
covers Lady Elizabeth's and perhaps Lady Susan's
period. It is clearly an amalgam, for the pages at
the front have been neatly trimmed and glued in,
replacing some that have been as neatly cut away.
These pages hold fifty-six recipes written in the
most perfectly formed calligraphic writing
complete with flourishes. Paper and style date it to
the early eighteenth century, yet the first recipe,
for 'My admirable Dropps', is dated and signed:
[Lord] Chesterfield, White Hall 1662 (it will be
remembered that Lord Chesterfield was Lady
Elizabeth's father). This is followed by 'A rare
reseate of Sr. Kellem Digbis for the stone', also
dated White Hall 1662, and interesting because Sir
Kenelm Digby's classic of early English cookery,
*The Closet of the Eminently Learned Sir Kenelme
Digby Opened*, was not published until 1669, after
the author's death. Most, but not all, of the
succeeding recipes in the same beautiful writing are
medicinal; the exceptions are 'blanchmange',
'jumballs' (see page 74), and one for cherry beer.
Given the old-fashioned nature of the text – the
blancmange is definitely medieval in type – and the
perfection of the writing, it is possible that this
first section of Volume 244 represents a series of
writing exercises or exemplars. This theory is
supported by the fact that the rest of the volume,
written in a much less controlled but still ornate
hand, contains many but not all of the same recipes,
as well as a number of others. Again Lord
Chesterfield's 'Admirable Dropps' head the list, but

now, although the words White Hall appear at the bottom, the date given is 1694. Just possibly then, this is Lady Elizabeth's recipe book at least in part. All the second group of recipes are to be found, confusingly, in the next and most important compilation to be looked at, Volume 245.

The fact that this volume is indexed signals an altogether more methodical approach, an impression confirmed by the number of recipes whose sources are named (among the contributors are Lord Linlithgow, Sir Edward Stafford, Sir Walter Raleigh, and the Countesses of Chesterfield, Kent, and Northumberland). When trying to identify the compiler, the efficient Lady Elizabeth immediately comes to mind, and indeed the last few recipes, for a number of dishes done 'my Father's way', have her name attached. But the handwriting differs both from that in which the bulk of the recipes is written, and that of Lady Elizabeth's household book, Volume 238. It is difficult too to believe that Lady Elizabeth, energetic though she was, could have found time, with all her other activities, to compile this large collection. The writer may perhaps be Jean Nicholson, whom Thomas the 8th Earl married in 1736, but all that can be said with confidence is that the volume dates from the eighteenth century.

A few recipes copied from Volume 243 suggest that the family still enjoyed carrot puddings (see page 73 for recipe), egg pie (see page 72 for recipe), and jumballs; the old recipes for cracknells and cheesecakes (see page 73) are next to newer, simpler versions. Over 100 of the first group of 142 recipes (the following group is mainly medicinal) are for preserves, 'marmalets' (see recipe for quince marmalet on page 75) and jellies, fruit pastes, or dried fruit. While this suggests that such things

were being eaten now for pleasure as well as health, it also indicates that the gardens and orchards at Glamis could grow pears, apples, raspberries, and gooseberries in abundance, and that possibly, on sheltered south-facing walls, there were quinces, peaches, cherries, and apricots.

The meat recipes, though few, are reasonably up-to-date: an *olea* (a thick stew of various meats, game-birds, cabbage, and potatoes) was mentioned as a new dish by Pepys, and a *bisque* (not, as now, a puree of shellfish served as a thick soup, but rather a broth thickened with dried breadcrumbs or croûtons, and served with slices of the meat from which it is made) seems to have been a recent import from France. There are two recipes for 'sauciges' – one without skins – which suggest that at least at Glamis the general Scottish prejudice against pork was not shared. 'A Sheep's Pudding' is a herb-flavoured mixture of blood, oatmeal, bread, and eggs. Most interesting of all is the recipe for Scots collops (see page 71): the slices of veal served with forcemeat balls and a delicately flavoured sauce are much superior to later dishes of the same name. Not a single fish recipe is to be found in the main body of the volume, but one of those near the end, signed Elizabeth Stanhope, is 'To stew Carp my Father's Way'.

In 1753 the title passed to Thomas's son John, whose wife, a wealthy young Englishwoman, brought to the family her surname and her estates of Streatlam Castle and Gibside, in County Durham. The marriage was unhappy, and no document survives to suggest that Mary Bowes had any interest in domestic concerns. Her housekeeper's book of expenditure (1766–1771) merely summarizes annual consumption of estate produce: in one year 17 cattle, 39 sheep, 10 calves,

9 swine, and 459 poultry were eaten, together with 43 st 11½ lb of butter, 48 st 10 lb of cheese, 166 pints of cream, and 100 pints of fresh milk. Even allowing for the fact that a Scots pint was almost three times as much as an imperial pint, the milk figure seems absurdly low until we remember that the usual beverages were still home-brewed ale and, in summer, buttermilk. When tea was drunk it was taken without milk.

Four London grocers' accounts slipped loose into this book yield more fascinating information. J. Blackwell was a tea merchant: he sold Best Mysore at 20 shillings (£1) a pound, Best Green at 16 shillings, and Fine Green at 12 shillings. Six pounds of chocolate from the same firm cost £1.10s. Another grocer, Richard Gwynne, supplied Glamis with sugar in all its different forms: treble, double, and single loaves, Finest Powdered, Finest Lisbon, and ordinary Lisbon. Gwynne's bills remind us that a grocer was still a merchant 'in gross': he also sent up to Scotland 1 st of Jordan almonds; 2 st of prunes; 1 st of black pepper; 1 st of pimento (allspice); 4 lb each of white pepper, nutmegs, cloves, and mace; large quantities of raisins, 'sun raisins', currants, rice, and sago; and 8 lb of macaroni and 6 lb of vermicelli (showing the growing influence of things Italian). Everything was packed into hogsheads and sent by sea to Dundee; cartage and wharfage cost the surprisingly low sum of 3s.6d.

While the 9th Earl was yet a bachelor, someone made a brief attempt to keep a cellar-book. Although some entries refer to the year 1763 its full title is *An Account Book of the different sorts of Wines and other Liquors in the Cellar of Glammiss and what quantity of each have been used from June 1764*. A greater variety of wines than before was

being drunk. They were categorized as 'Burgundy, Claret, Hermitage, Coteroty (Côte Rôtie), Port, Mountain, Lisbon, Madeira, and Frontiniac'. Glamis had at last caught up with English tastes; the most popular wine by far appears to have been port. Between 20 September and 21 November 1763, forty-six bottles of Côte Rôtie came up from the cellar, but in the same period a staggering (literally, perhaps) 204 bottles of port were drunk (by how many mouths is unfortunately not recorded).

The 9th Earl (1753–1776) seems to have been devoted to Glamis, despite prolonged absences due to ill-health. Like many of his contemporaries he was keen on agricultural improvement, enclosing fields, enriching them with shell marl (the latest thing in fertilizers), and planting trees. He also encouraged cattle-breeding. During his lifetime the Castle was kept in good repair, and the poet Gray, who visited it in 1765, found it 'rising proudly out of what seems a great and thick wood of tall trees, with a cluster of hanging towers on the top; the house from the height of it, the greatness of its mass, the many towers atop, and the spread of its wings has really a very singular and striking appearance'. However, after the Earl's death in 1776, Glamis was neglected for a time. One writer speaks of grass growing in the driveway right up to the front door. In the 1790s it was visited by Sir Walter Scott, who was impressed by its eerie atmosphere. Although the owner was away, Scott was invited to spend the night in the Castle, and according to custom drank his host's health from the Lion, a great beaker of double-gilt silver moulded into the shape of a lion, which held about an English pint of wine. Scott managed to drain it at one draught, and used the incident in his novel

Waverley, transforming the Lion of Glamis into the Blessed Bear of Bradwardine.

The 10th Earl was succeeded in 1820 by his brother Thomas, also an improver: the *New Statistical Account for Scotland* (1836) speaks of his introduction of short-horned cattle to the estate, and his use of turnips as winter fodder for sheep. The title passed in 1846 to Thomas's grandson Thomas George. But throughout this period the archive has preserved nothing of 'the affairs of the kitchen', as John Knox once called them. It is only when Thomas George's brother becomes the 13th Earl in 1865 that we have a further opportunity to observe life at Glamis, for under the benign and hospitable stewardship of Earl Claude and his wife Frances Dora the estate and its people prospered, and from this happy time many records have survived.

An early menu book compiled by the Countess still exists. Written in her own hand (it is interesting to note that in the mid-nineteenth century she was still using -fs- where we would put -ss-), it covers six weeks in the summer of 1866: 15 July to 23 August. Why it was begun is easy to understand: anyone who constantly entertains finds a record of menus invaluable, in order to avoid repeating a dish too often or giving the same dish twice to the same people, and also to work out a balance of meals which may be usefully referred to in the future. The book's brevity is regrettable, but short as it is, it gives some insight into upper-class eating in Victorian Scotland.

Those six weeks were a sociable period. There were house-guests nearly all the time; on only three evenings did the Earl and Countess (having had four or more people to luncheon) dine alone in the evening. Luncheon parties were commoner than dinner parties, probably because travelling in a horse-drawn carriage at night, even in the light nights of the Scottish summer, was somewhat hazardous. It was the hospitable custom that, if you knew your neighbour had people staying, you invited the entire party. Especially during the shooting season this could result in a fairly large gathering, and at Glamis that summer twenty-two people for luncheon was not unusual.

On such occasions, the meal could be a formal affair with as many as eleven dishes. Normally, when not more than ten sat down to table, it consisted of two or three meat dishes and two sweets. There was little demarcation between what was offered at midday and what one might have at dinner. Roasts were not unusual at either meal. But anything which might be made from leftovers, for example hashed hare, minced mutton and eggs, and Don Pedro (cottage pie) of lamb or chicken, seems to have been reserved for luncheon.

Dinners were made up of three courses with a minimum of five dishes and a maximum of eleven. The first course was always soup: clear soup or mutton broth if the diners were family and/or close friends; mulligatawny, green pea, purée of carrots, or hare soup for larger parties. Once there was oxtail soup, and on a grand occasion mock turtle. Usually fish came next: trout, eels, or salmon (the latter on three consecutive days, suggesting that there had been an angling expedition). The entrée or 'made dish' was often, but not always, of beef or mutton. Beefsteak pudding, mutton croquettes, kromeskies of chicken (see recipe on page 77) or beef, and boiled beef or chicken were favourites. They were followed by a roast, very often of domestic duck, although twice at least there was roast wild duck. Rabbit, leveret, or roast lamb were also often on the menu. Mutton or lamb was in fact eaten every day. Sometimes it was served in three forms at the same meal, as on 2 August, when the menu was: mutton broth, perch, chicken patties, mutton cutlets, shoulder of lamb, roast duck, cheese ramequins, and ice soufflé. Roast beef was only offered at big dinner parties. Game was confined (since Glamis had no deer-forest) to hare, leveret, and rabbit, with some snipe and grouse appearing immediately after the 'Glorious Twelfth'.

The vegetables served are never specified. What probably happened was that the cook and the gardener worked out the vegetables between them.

The sweets which followed the roast are very much in the Victorian tradition. Water- or cream-based ices flavoured with lemon or soft fruit were served almost every day, together with an alternative such as jam fritters, fruit tarts, or a sweet omelette. 'Porcupine pudding' figures once, so do meringues and a trifle. Finally came the savoury, which could be cheese straws, ramequins, or marrowbone toasts, but was sometimes more substantial: macaroni cheese, a savoury omelette, even once 'cheese fondu' (actually tiny cheese soufflés – see recipe on page 80).

The menu book also specifies what the servants were to eat. Usually they had mutton, boiled and/or roasted, and another dish like Irish stew, boiled beef, or rabbit. Occasionally they were given roast beef (left over from the dining-room?). The sweet, when specified at all, was invariably a fruit tart. Perhaps here also 'downstairs' was expected to finish whatever 'upstairs' had left, and if nothing came back from the dining-room a fruit tart would have been quick and easy to prepare.

Throughout their long marriage, the Strathmores led an active social life. Earl Claude and Lady Frances, with their seven sons and three daughters, divided their time between Glamis, London, and Streatlam in Co. Durham, but tried each year to be in Scotland from July to January or February. The cellar-books running from 1863 to 1894 are almost social diaries: faithful records of events as well as of the cellar contents. They also chronicle changing taste, particularly the rising popularity of champagne and a shift from traditional brandy-and-soda to whisky. The quality of the latter (described in 1788 by Robert Burns as 'a most rascally liquor') had by this time greatly improved, and its status altered accordingly. We read now of weddings and garden parties (champagne), cricket lunches (champagne and Château Margaux), and balls (champagne and whisky). The shooting season brought many guests, to be entertained with picnics (tea and claret), private theatricals (sherry, claret, and whisky), or dances (champagne and claret). There was the Perth Ball which began the Scottish season each September; a party was usually made up to dine at Glamis (claret) and travel afterwards to Perth by special train, returning by another at 4.30 next morning. There were also estate occasions: a tenants' Christmas tree party and a servants' ball at New Year made inroads on the port and the sherry; for tenants' lunches, employees' dinners, and schoolteachers' dinners, sherry and whisky came up. The cattle sale lunch was an important occasion (Earl Claude, like his forebears, was a keen farmer and cattle-breeder), consuming 32 bottles of sherry and eight of light claret. For house-parties at Christmas, brandy was needed when the guests played the traditional game of snapdragon, snatching raisins from the burning spirit. Even the more routine entries tell a tale:

'Sent to the billiard room: brandy, whisky, and "dinner sherry"; For the curling-house: whisky.' Shooting parties took with them amontillado (for the ladies?), and a prudently small quantity of whisky. Naturally the Communion wine used in the chapel was port, but a bottle of the same wine was sent occasionally to a sick parishioner, for it was believed to be strengthening and restorative. This belief about red wine may explain too the frequent despatch of a bottle of claret (usually Esse Ludon, but sometimes Pauillac, Bages '64, or even Margaux) to the nursery. Victorian doctors often prescribed a daily glass of wine or ale after a childish illness. Finally came the demands of the kitchen: cooking sherry, amontillado, light claret, and brandy. Mincemeat called for a bottle each of sherry and brandy, Christmas cakes absorbed half a bottle of brandy.

In Lord Frederic Hamilton's *The Days before Yesterday*, published in the 1920s, there is a charming account of life at Glamis in the 1880s. Lord Frederic was a great friend of the family, and admired, among other things, their musical ability. 'I have never heard such perfect and finished part-singing as that of the Lyon family, and they were always singing: on the way to a cricket-match; on the road home from shooting; in the middle of dinner, even, this irrepressible family could not help bursting into harmony, and such exquisite harmony, too! ... Next evening Mr Gladstone asked for a part-song in the middle of dinner, and as the singing was continued in the drawing-room afterwards, he ... asked whether the young people would allow an old man to sing bass in the glees with them ... It was curious to see the Prime Minister reading off the same copy as an Eton boy of sixteen, who was singing alto. Being Sunday night, they went on singing hymns and anthems till nearly midnight; there was no getting Mr Gladstone away. Mrs Gladstone told me next day that he had not enjoyed himself so much for many months.'

The house-steward from 1891 until the 13th Earl's death in 1904 was Charles R. Collingwood. Never can the Strathmore family have had a more devoted and loyal servant, and his Consumption Books are models of meticulous account-keeping. Each week he recorded on facing pages what came in and what was dispensed. He could say at any time what meat hung in cold store and larder, how many hares had been shot on the hill, what game had been sent in presents or received from friends, or what was maturing in the kitchen garden. At every meal he recorded the numbers in the dining-room and servants' hall: family, guests, resident servants and guests' servants, and he never forgot to count too the 'casuals' – pipers, drivers, additional waiters and footmen, kitchen assistants, extra laundrywomen. To him each meal eaten represented a person, so that a guest staying for three days counted as six persons (breakfast not being reckoned a meal). Conscientiously he worked out how much a child might consume. 'It must be noticed,' he writes on one occasion, in the red ink he reserved for remarks, 'that there have been 12 children the past three weeks, but I enter them as 8.' Yet he was the least detached of men, taking enormous pride and interest in the family, as is seen by his entry for Sunday, 8 September 1901: '15 Grandchildren were at Chapel service and 2 ditto Babies [he means grandchildren too young to attend service] upstairs.' One of the 'ditto babies', incidentally, was probably the Queen Mother.

He also chronicles events: a journey to London for

the Coronation of King Edward VII, meetings of
the Primrose League, family weddings. 'There will
be found some mistakes etc.,' he writes at the end
of one book, 'but it must be leniently dealt with,
as it has many a time been written amid much
other work, demanding thought and attention ...
it will show how accounts, costs of foodstuffs, and
numbers of people fed, upstairs and down, vary
year by year, and yet a close study of the book
will show a certain equilibrium in cost and quantity,
year after year, which cannot be found out unless
in such a book as this.'

What the books show most of all is the difficulty
of looking after a large establishment with
fluctuating numbers and irregular routines. Each
week Collingwood divided the total quantity of
meat used by the number of persons there to eat it,
which gave him the amount of meat consumed per
person. Sometimes things did not go according to
plan. An entry for 10 July 1892 reads: 'Carried
over, 65 lbs of mutton – all used.' Below, in red
ink, is the remark: 'This is excessive but as we had
whole sheep could not keep it.' This was a problem
which, indeed, caused Collingwood many a
headache (see Lady Clerk of Tillypronie's solution
on page 75). He usually travelled with the family
to its various houses, and forwarded his instructions
to the permanent staff in each establishment. A
gloss in the customary red ink for the week 15
August 1897, reads: '... with regard to mutton, we
had to destroy 80 lbs which were sent in too soon
before our arrival and contrary to orders given.'
On another occasion, 144 lbs of mutton 'were
delivered unfit for food and destroyed'.

Mutton was still the daily fare – the household ate
almost twice as much mutton as beef, which
because of its larger carcase presented even greater

problems of conservation. The solution in summer
was to put it in mild brine for a short period, and
salt beef does appear, albeit infrequently, in
Collingwood's records. Someone in the family was
clearly very fond of sweetbreads, for they were
sent to the kitchen at least once a week, and oxtail
crops up quite frequently. Lamb was not popular
with the Victorians, who found it on the whole
insipid. Fresh beef was a rather festive meat. At
the three-day Golden Wedding celebrations of Earl
Claude and Lady Frances in 1903, 467 lb of beef
were eaten as against 177 lb of mutton. Also
consumed were three salmon, eight grouse, twenty-
two hares, ninety-nine rabbits, sixteen pigeons, and
fifteen dozen eggs.

Game was not costed, but the quantity brought in
and used or sent away was noted. In August and
September, with large shoots almost every day,
birds and hares were generously distributed to
family and friends. Any surplus was sold to a
dealer.

Fish was bought in fairly large quantities, especially
during the summer. A typical week was the one
ending 24 July 1892: the household got through 8
lb of soles, ten flounders, $3\frac{1}{4}$ (lb?) lobsters, five
salmon, six red mullet, and about 5 lb whiting.
That week the fishmonger also supplied the Castle
with one and a half hundredweight of ice.

Poultry and eggs are rarely mentioned. Collingwood
does record, however, that at a ball supper on 4
January 1893 three geese, two turkeys, and six
pheasants were consumed, as well as 146 lb of beef
and 47 lb of pork. We also know that he gave out
three dozen eggs for the Christmas puddings that
season.

Garden produce was costed every week, but not

detailed. Bread is never mentioned. Almost certainly it was baked on the premises, as it had been for centuries. As for groceries, all we know is that from London the Army & Navy Stores presented weekly bills; so did the Co-op in Forfar.

In 1904 the Earl died at his villa at Bordighera, in Italy. His body was brought back to Glamis and there buried on Wednesday, 24 February, at 12 noon. Charles Collingwood recorded the event in his usual precise hand, and then closed his book for good.

As the twentieth century developed, Glamis, like other historic houses, was caught up by the events which have homogenized life all over Britain. Some attributes of country-house life survived, of course, until the last war. Food was modified, perhaps for the better, by the fact that fast transport brought delicacies to the country more quickly and in better condition. Keen travellers who were also gastronomes were able to enlarge their cook's repertoires. The brother-in-law of the 14th Earl's daughter, Lady Mary Bowes Lyon, was such a man. The Hon. Mountstuart Elphinstone's notebook, with its meticulously typed recipes, shows the adventurous spirit abroad in the 1930s, while it reflects also a determination not to let the old dishes disappear. The soup section has recipes for Consommé Vesiga and Barszoz (bortsch), but also for Sheep's Head Broth and Barley Broth (see page 80). Crab Soufflé (see page 80) is followed by Partan Pie, and Truite Saumonée Reine-Marie (from the Ritz Hotel) by instructions for smoking a salmon, while among the entrées can be found not only Volaille Tout-Paris and four or five curries, but also Mince Collops (see page 81) and Venison Pie (see page 81). Where Mr Elphinstone parts company with Scottish tradition is in his collection of no

less than twenty-eight recipes for vegetables, from Russian Cabbage Pie to French Spinach to Fried Artichokes. All in all these recipes are those of an enthusiast, who appreciated what he found on his travels, but never lost touch with the dishes of home.

Recipes

Dressed Hare 17th century

Roast hare, unless very young, is apt to be tough. This method makes a change from the most common method of dealing with hare, which is to stew or jug it. The hash which is the end result is what I would describe as a family dish, but it can be put into a pastry case made from puff pastry, and covered with a close lattice of the same pastry, then baked in a moderate oven for about 35 minutes, to make a most attractive and delicious pie, worthy of any guest.

Serves 4 to 6

1 hare, jointed
2 oz (50 g) melted butter
juice of 1 orange
3 oz (75 g) currants
1 glass red wine
$\frac{1}{4}$ pint (150 ml) water
1 tablespoonful vinegar
3 sprigs fresh thyme
$\frac{1}{2}$ teaspoon ground cinnamon
yolks of 2 hard-boiled eggs, mashed
salt
freshly ground black pepper

Pre-heat the oven to 220°C (425°F, Mark 7). Put the hare in a roasting pan, and cook it for about half an hour in the pre-heated oven, basting every 10 minutes with melted butter. When it is cool, cut the meat from the bones, removing the sinews and any tough membranes. Discard the liver or not, as you wish. Mince the meat, or put it through the food processor.

Put the orange juice into a small saucepan, bring it to the boil, and add the currants. Cover and remove from the heat.

In another pan put the minced hare, wine, water, vinegar, thyme and cinnamon, and simmer for about 20 minutes, stirring occasionally. Then add the currants and orange juice, mashed egg yolks, and seasoning to taste.

This is good served with rice and sweet-and-sour red cabbage.

Soused Pork 17th century

'Take two great fat piggs,' says the recipe, 'first cut of[f] the heads then cut them in halfes, then take out all the bons and lay the four syds in water to suck out the blood, then dry them weel upon a cloath.' How fortunate we are in having butchers to do these jobs for us. A variation of the following recipe, also very good, consists in stopping the process after the meat is cooked, and serving it hot instead of proceeding to souse it.

Serves 4 to 5

1½-2 lb (700–900 g) boned shoulder of pork

2 teaspoons coarse salt

1 teaspoon grated nutmeg

½ teaspoon ground cloves

½ teaspoon ground mace

1 sprig of rosemary

10 fl oz (300 ml) milk

10 fl oz (300 ml) water

1¼ pints (750 ml) dry white wine

2 bay leaves

1 lemon, cut in quarters, each quarter cut in half
   crossways

Ask the butcher not to tie up the meat. Open it out and with a sharp knife slit it to make it open a little more. Mix 1 teaspoon of salt with the spices and rosemary, and press this into the meat. Roll the meat up, and tie it firmly with string. Put it into a heavy pan with the milk and water, bring to the boil, and simmer for 1½ to 2 hours, turning it occasionally. Have the lid half on the pan, but watch that the liquid does not boil over.

Turn off the heat, and leave the meat in the pan to cool. Then put it into a glazed pot, and cover it with the 'souse drink' made from the wine, bay leaves, remaining salt, and lemon pieces. Cover with a lid or a plate, and keep in the refrigerator for two or three days before serving.

Rice Florentine 17th century

This seems to have been a popular dish; Lady Castlehill, whose manuscript collection of recipes is in the Mitchell Library in Glasgow, has a similar recipe, although she uses more eggs and less rice, and omits the currants. The original recipe stressed that the rice must be 'picked verie clean'; we tend to forget how much work was involved in seventeenth-century cooking – the currants too would have had to be cleaned, the cloves and mace pounded, and the nutmeg grated.

Serves 8

4 oz (100 g) short grain rice

1 pint (600 ml) milk

4 oz (100 g) butter

4 oz (100 g) currants

1 egg, or 2 yolks and one white

1 teaspoon ground cinnamon

½ teaspoon grated nutmeg

¼ teaspoon ground cloves

¼ teaspoon ground mace

2 tablespoons sugar

10 oz (275 g) puff pastry

Pre-heat the oven to 200°C (400°F, Mark 6). Boil the rice in the milk until thick, then remove the pan from the heat, and add the butter cut into pieces, stirring until it is melted. Add all the remaining ingredients, except the pastry, and mix them well in.

Roll out the pastry thinly to line the bottom of an 8-inch (20-cm) pie dish, leaving enough to cut strips for a lattice top. Pour the rice mixture into the pastry case, and make a lattice across the top out of the strips of remaining pastry. Bake in the pre-heated oven for 40 to 50 minutes. Serve hot or cold.

Lemon Cream 17th century

This is thick and very rich. It was probably served in little glass dishes, perhaps with thin biscuits, and eaten with a spoon. You can serve it in tiny ramekin dishes with squares of thin brown bread, or it can be used as a garnish, piped over apple pie or fruit purées.

Serves 4

1 pint (600 ml) cream (double or whipping)
½ lemon (unsprayed)
1 tablespoon of sugar

Pare the lemon as thinly as possible, trying not to remove too much white with the peel. Squeeze out the juice, and reserve. Bring the cream gently to boil, then add the lemon peel, and let it boil for 10 to 15 minutes until it has thickened. Remove from the heat. Dissolve the sugar in the lemon juice, and gradually add this to the cream, stirring gently but thoroughly. Divide the mixture into individual ramekin dishes.

If you are serving the cream with bread, remove the lemon peel, and cut it into fine strips. Then sprinkle these over each serving.

Stewed Mushrooms 18th century

The writer of this recipe had trouble with her spelling. She began the title with the words 'To stew Champigions', inserted an 'n' after the 'gi', crossed it out, and finished despairingly 'other wayes called Mushrooms'. If her spelling was rocky, her cooking was not. This makes a lovely starter, served not on toast, but with Melba toast at the side.

Serves 2 as a starter

8 oz (225 g) mushrooms
1 glass dry white wine
1 sprig of thyme
1 onion

2 cloves
5 black peppercorns
1 tablespoon juice of a Seville orange (grapefruit juice will do)
½ teaspoon salt
1 oz (25 g) butter
2 tablespoons mutton gravy (optional)
1 tablespoon lemon juice
¼ teaspoon grated nutmeg

Wipe the mushrooms, and remove the stalks. Put them into a bowl, and pour the wine over them, then leave for about half an hour, turning occasionally. Drain, and put into a heavy saucepan with a lid (the recipe says 'between two silver dishes') over a very low heat for about 10 minutes.

Pour away the liquor that has formed, and put the mushrooms into a clean pan with the thyme, onion (peeled but left whole), cloves, peppercorns, orange juice, salt, and butter. If you have any 'pure Gravy of Mutton', you could add it, but it is not at all necessary. Cover the pan, and place on a gentle heat to stew for about 20 minutes. Then remove the sprig of thyme, cloves, peppercorns, and onion. Sprinkle the mushrooms with lemon juice and nutmeg, and serve very hot.

Chicken Fricassee 18th century

This is a tasty way of dealing with chicken that you suspect will be of indifferent quality. I prefer to use white wine rather than claret, as in the original recipe, because claret spoils the colour of the dish.

Serves 4

4 chicken joints
2 oz (50 g) butter

10 fl oz (300 ml) chicken stock

5 fl oz (150 ml) dry white wine

1 teaspoon grated nutmeg

salt and freshly ground black pepper

$\frac{1}{2}$ onion, chopped finely

2 tablespoons chopped herbs (I like to use thyme, tarragon, and lovage)

2 egg yolks

1 teaspoon lemon juice

Fry the chicken joints gently in the butter, for 15 minutes on each side, then remove them from the pan, and let them cool. Remove the meat from bones, and cut into small pieces. Put these into a heavy-bottomed pan with the stock, all but 1 tablespoon of the wine, nutmeg, salt and pepper, and onion. Cover the pan, and cook gently for 15 minutes.

In a bowl mix the herbs, egg yolks, lemon juice, and the remaining wine. Just before you are ready to eat pour this into the pan of chicken, and stir over a low heat until the mixture thickens a little, and the chicken pieces are nicely coated. Serve at once.

Collared Beef 18th century

This is an excellent and trouble-free dish for a buffet lunch party. Ask your butcher to bone the piece of brisket, and lay it in a mild brine for 48 hours. (When you collect the meat, check whether it should be soaked overnight in fresh water. 'Mild' means different things to different butchers.)

Serves 10 to 12

4–5 lb (2 kg) brisket of beef, boned and soaked in mild brine for 48 hours (see above)

$\frac{1}{2}$ teaspoon ground cloves

2 teaspoons grated nutmeg

1 teaspoon ground mace

$\frac{1}{2}$ teaspoon ground black pepper

$\frac{1}{2}$ teaspoon salt

sprigs of thyme, marjoram, rosemary, and winter savory (if available)

2–3 small bay leaves, broken into pieces

2 anchovy fillets

1 pint (600 ml) red wine

Pre-heat the oven to 150°C (300°F, Mark 2). Open out the meat. Mix together the spices and salt, and rub this mixture into the meat. Chop the fresh herbs together, and sprinkle over the meat. Scatter the pieces of bay leaf over the meat, then lay the anchovies on top. Roll the meat up tightly, and tie it firmly with string.

Place the rolled meat in a heavy casserole. Pour over the red wine, cover with a close-fitting lid, and place in the pre-heated oven for 5 hours.

Allow to cool for at least 6 hours before slicing and serving.

Scotch Collops 18th century

It seems likely that Scotch collops (cutlets) have nothing to do with Scotland at all, but were originally scotched, or scutched, collops. To scutch is to beat flax once it has been soaked in water, to get rid of unwanted non-fibrous matter; early recipes all recommend as a first step beating the meat. This is a dish which changed out of all recognition within a century. By the 1930s a recipe like the one on page 81 could be considered traditional, but here is one of the early and authentic versions. It takes time, but is worth the trouble.

Serves 4

4 veal cutlets or cutlets from a leg of lamb
$\frac{1}{2}$ teaspoon ground mace
a pinch of ground cloves
$\frac{1}{2}$ teaspoon grated nutmeg
salt and freshly ground black pepper
4 slices streaky bacon

Forcemeat balls

8 oz (250 g) minced beef
$\frac{1}{2}$ onion, finely chopped
1 sprig of thyme
1 sprig of marjoram
1 anchovy fillet
1 oz (25 g) butter
1 pint (600 ml) stock or water

To finish

$\frac{1}{2}$ onion, finely chopped
1 sprig of thyme
1 sprig of marjoram
1 anchovy fillet
1 oz (25 g) butter
2 teaspoons lemon or orange juice.

Begin by making the forcemeat balls. Chop the onion, herbs, and anchovy together very fine, then mix them with the mince, egg, and spices. With floured hands shape this mixture into small balls about the size of a table-tennis ball. Heat the stock or water, and put the balls into it. Lower the heat, and poach them very gently for about 20 minutes. Remove from the pan, and keep warm.

Beat the cutlets with the back of a knife, then sprinkle on the spices, salt and pepper. Put a frying pan on a low heat, and fry the bacon until the fat begins to run, then add the cutlets. Fry them for

about 20 minutes, turning frequently, until they are brown on both sides. Remove, and keep warm.

Take about a cupful of the stock or water used to cook the forcemeat balls, and put it into the frying pan with the finely chopped onion, sprigs of thyme and marjoram, the anchovy, and the butter. Turn up the heat, and add the cutlets and the forcemeat balls. Shake the pan, then sprinkle over the lemon or orange juice, and serve.

Egg Pie 17th to 18th century

'Take 15 Eggs and boyl them till they be hard take their full weight in beef Suet ...' Here, as so often, the twentieth-century cook must take eighteenth-century quantities as a guideline only. The following quantities produced an unexpectedly delicious result, the eggs seeming to disappear into the spicy mass of fruit and sauce. This is particularly good as a winter pudding.

Serves 6

12 oz (325 g) shortcrust pastry
5 eggs, size 3, hard-boiled and very finely chopped
8 oz (225 g) currants
4 oz (100 g) suet
$\frac{1}{2}$ teaspoon each of mace, cinnamon, and nutmeg
a pinch of salt
4 oz (100 g) sugar
egg white to brush the pastry

Cawdle (sauce)

2 eggs yolks
2 tablespoons of sugar
$3\frac{1}{2}$ fl oz (100 ml) white wine

Pre-heat the oven to 200°C (400°F, Mark 6). Roll out the pastry, and use half of it to line an 8-inch

(20-cm) quiche tin. Cut a lid for the pie from the remaining pastry, and put this in the fridge to rest for 10 minutes.

Mix together the chopped hard-boiled eggs, the currants, the suet, and the spices, salt, and sugar to make a filling. Put this into the pastry case, and cover with the pastry lid. The pie will be quite full. Brush the top with egg white, and bake in the pre-heated oven for about 45 minutes, reducing the heat if it seems to be getting too brown.

Turn the oven off, and take out the pie. With a knife carefully prise off the lid. Beat the cawdle ingredients well together, put this mixture into a saucepan, heat until almost boiling, then pour into the pie. Replace the lid, and put the pie back in the oven for a few minutes. Eat hot or cold.

Cheesecakes 18th century

These cheesecakes have a pleasing flavour and texture, and should be served warm or quite cold, with cream.

The original recipe begins at the absolute beginning. 'Take 7 quarts of Milk,' it says, 'set it as for a Cheese, when it is come break it a little, then put it in a Canvas strainer, drain ye Whey clean from the Curds.' Buying the cheese makes things easier. The bread used, if not homemade, should come from a good baker.

Makes 12

2 oz (50 g) fresh white breadcrumbs
5 fl oz (150 ml) milk
1 lb (450 g) curd cheese
3 eggs, size 3
2 oz (50 g) double cream
2 teaspoons rosewater
3 oz (75 g) granulated sugar
3 oz (75 g) currants
2 teaspoons ground cinnamon
1 teaspoon grated nutmeg
12 oz (325 g) shortcrust pastry

Pre-heat the oven to 180°C (350°F, Mark 4). Put the breadcrumbs in a pan with the milk, and bring to the boil, stirring well for a few minutes, until the mixture is thick and sticky-looking. Allow it to cool, then put it in a bowl or food processor with the curd cheese, eggs, cream, rosewater, sugar, currants, and spices, and mix very well.

Grease 12 small patty or pie tins. Roll out the pastry, and cut out rounds to fit your patty or pie tins. Press these into the tins, and pour in the cheese mixture. It does not rise much, so you can fill the pastry cases to the top without fear. Bake for about 30 minutes in the pre-heated oven, lowering the heat if the cheesecakes seem to be getting too brown.

Carrot Pudding 17th to 18th century

This simple recipe makes a deliciously light, spicy pudding, very attractive with its shades of cream, coral pink, and brown. I use bread made at home from strong unbleached flour.

Serves 4 to 5

3 eggs, size 3
10 fl oz (300 ml) milk
3 oz (75 g) sugar
4 tablespoons dry white wine or sherry
$\frac{1}{2}$ nutmeg, grated, or $\frac{1}{4}$ teaspoon grated nutmeg
   and $\frac{1}{4}$ teaspoon ground cinnamon
4 oz (100 g) white breadcrumbs

1½ lb (700 g) old carrots, grated
3 oz (75 g) butter

Pre-heat the oven to 180°C (350°F, Mark 4). Beat the eggs in a large bowl, then beat in the milk, sugar, wine or sherry, and the spices. Stir in the breadcrumbs and half the grated carrot. Wrap the remaining carrot in a clean cloth, and squeeze this tightly to extract the carrot juice. Add the juice to the mixture in the bowl, and mix well. Melt the butter over a low heat, and stir into the mixture. Pour this into a greased deep baking dish, and bake in the pre-heated oven until the pudding looks set and crisp on top, about 30 minutes. Serve hot.

Jumballs 17th to 18th century

Jumballs were to the eighteenth-century cook what scones are to the present-day cook – everyone had her favourite recipe, each slightly different from the others. They resemble Italian *amaretto* biscuits, and go better with tea than with coffee, but are best of all with a glass of dessert wine after dinner. They should be eaten the day they are made.

Makes 15

8 oz (225 g) flour
4 oz (100 g) sugar
1 tablespoon aniseed
1 whole egg
1 egg yolk
2 teaspoons rosewater
3–4 tablespoons cream

Pre-heat the oven to 180°C (350°F, Mark 4). Mix the flour and sugar in a bowl, then stir in the aniseed. Beat together the eggs, rosewater, and cream, and pour into the dry ingredients to make

a stiff paste. Mix very well, then refrigerate for 3 to 4 hours.

Roll out on a well-floured board, then take strips of the dough and between floured hands roll them to about 12 inches (30 cm) long, the thickness of your little finger. Bring one end to the middle and let it extend about an inch below. Do the same with the other end to get a bow, or pretzel shape. Put the jumbles on an oven tray, and bake in the pre-heated oven for 20 minutes.

Lemon Brandy 17th to 18th century

This makes a pleasant drink, lighter and less sweet than a liqueur, and less alcoholic than neat brandy. The clarifying process with egg whites has been omitted, sugar today being much more efficiently refined than in the eighteenth century. The recipe calls for 'the best french brandy you can get', fountain water, and the finest sugar. It also requires the finished liquor to be strained through a 'swan skin bagg', but coffee filter paper will do just as well. The lemons, of course, must be organically grown, and not sprayed or waxed, since it is the peel that is used.

Makes 1 pint (600 ml)

3 lemons
10 fl oz (300 ml) brandy
10 fl oz (300 ml) water
4 oz (100 g) granulated sugar

Peel the lemons very thinly 'that as litle of the white be at your parings as possible', then pour the brandy into a well-stoppered glass jar and add the peel. Let it stand for eight days.

Pour off the brandy into a clean jug. Add the water

to the peel, re-stopper the jar, and leave for 48 hours. Then pour the water off into a pan, add the sugar, and place over a gentle heat until the sugar is dissolved. (This is where you would clarify the liquid with egg white.) Let the syrup boil up in the original recipe for a couple of minutes, then allow it to get quite cold.

Mix the cold syrup with the brandy in the jug, and filter into a clean 1½-pint (900 ml) bottle.

Allow it to stand for 2 or 3 days for any sediment to settle, before drinking.

Quince Marmalet (Marmalade) 17th to 18th century

It was Sydney Smith who said that in Scotland, in remarkably warm summers, he had tasted peaches that made excellent pickles. The same is probably true of quinces. The following recipe is from Volume 245 of the Glamis archive.

> quinces, peeled, quartered, and cored
> sugar (half the weight of the prepared fruit)
> $\frac{1}{4}$-$\frac{1}{2}$ teaspoon ground ginger (optional)

Put the prepared fruit and the sugar into a thick-bottomed pan over very low heat. Add sufficient water to cover the bottom of the pan. Now stand by the stove and stir continuously to prevent burning. As the juice leaves the fruit this becomes easier, and the sugar dissolves.

When the fruit softens bruise it as you stir until it forms a pap. Keep stirring while the mixture cooks very gently until it forms a thick gooey mass. Then add the ginger if you wish.

Pour into heated glass jars and leave uncovered until cold.

How to use a whole sheep or lamb
19th century

This is Lady Clerk of Tillypronie's solution to one of Charles Collingwood's (house-steward at Glamis, 1891–1904) major problems:

The blood makes Black puddings ... with sieved oatmeal, or groats, or rice, and the fat under the loin round the kidney can be used in the way 'fleed' is used with pig's blood in making ordinary Black Puddings.

The head, trotters, and breast of mutton, with some of the superfluous fat on this last cut off, make, with vegetables, the best broth, and afterwards all the meat is useful in other ways.

The sheep's head, whole, is served with the feet ('trotters') round as garnish, and with broth as sauce; or cut up in squares in dressed sauce as an entree, vegetables in centre and fried brains as garnish; or can be boiled and turned out of a mould solid. The trotters require long boiling, and after removing the bones, you can make fritters of the meat for breakfast as if they were pettitoes.

For Sheep's Trotters, see also Sheep's Head recipes

The boiled breast of mutton ... can be crumbed, with mixed herbs, and broiled or baked a nice brown to eat hot. If for upstairs, serve a sharp sauce in a boat with chopped gherkins or capers in it.

Kidneys can be sliced for breakfast, with bacon, or in an omelet, and the liver sliced and fried, and served with bacon and fried potatoes.

The sheep's heart is hard if roasted; it is better stuffed and braised – but must be eaten at once – it chills so immediately. A sheep's sweetbread is not worth cooking though in the lamb it is excellent.

A lamb's head can be served upon a 'fugie', a mince of heart, sweetbread, liver, &c., but no kidneys. Make it savoury.

Much of the rest is used for Haggis. Any bits not otherwise wanted are very welcome additions to the scraps set aside for the keeper's dogs.

Carrot Soup 19th century

Carrots in the nineteenth century were not the vegetables we know today. They were sweeter, more strongly flavoured, and alas, more prone to disease and being eaten by maggots. They also had a marked core of a paler, harder texture, which is why Lady Clerk of Tillypronie writes in so many of her recipes, as in this one, 'take the red part of carrots'. This soup is undoubtedly best made with home-grown vegetables straight from the garden; failing that, add about a tablespoon of sugar just before serving. While using those invaluable cook's aids, the pressure cooker and the food processor, spare a thought for the poor skivvy whose job it would have been to press the vegetables through a tammy (strainer).

Serves 8

10 large carrots
2 turnips
1 large leek
2 sticks of celery
2 onions
1 oz (25 g) butter
a slice of lean ham or a ham bone
2 pints (1.2 litres) chicken or veal stock, or the same quantity of water with 1 chicken stock cube
½ white bread roll
salt and freshly ground black pepper
freshly grated nutmeg (optional)
1 tablespoon sugar (optional)

Peel the carrots and turnips, wash the leek and celery, and cut them all into pieces. Peel and slice the onions. Put the butter in a heavy pan over a low heat, then add the prepared vegetables and the ham or ham bone. Turn the vegetables in the melting butter until they are coated, then pour in the stock, and add the bread roll. Bring up to the boil, then leave to simmer over a low heat for about 35 to 40 minutes. Remove from the heat, and leave to cool slightly.

Remove the ham bone if used, then purée the soup in a blender or food processor. If you want a really smooth soup, it is best to also put the processed purée through a tammy or fine sieve. Then return it to the pan, and reheat. Season to taste; I like to add some freshly grated nutmeg (and a tablespoon of sugar if using shop-bought vegetables) just before serving. Lady Clerk suggests adding also a little scalded cream.

Cockie Leekie 19th century

This most popular of Scottish soups is eaten chiefly during the winter when leeks are at their best. I feel sure it was often served at Glamis in the nineteenth century. This recipe comes from Isa Emslie, who cooked for Lady Clerk of Tillypronie for many years. It calls for good chicken stock from 'luncheon chickens which have been boiled with vegetables and a little ham and trimmings of rabbit'; it is worth boiling a chicken or two, and using some of the meat as well as the liquid in this excellent soup.

Serves 8

12 prunes
1 dessertspoon sugar (optional)
4 pints (2.2 litres) good chicken stock
12 leeks
salt and freshly ground black pepper

Cook the prunes in about $\frac{1}{4}$ pint (150 ml) of the stock until tender, with or without the sugar. Remove them from the stock, and, when they are cold, stone them but keep their shape. Clean the leeks, and slice the white part and as much of the green as is tender, into 1-inch (2.5 cm) pieces. Stew these in the remaining stock until tender. Season with salt and pepper to taste. Then add the prunes and the stock in which they were cooked, and bring to the boil. Serve very hot.

Creamed Fresh Haddocks 19th century

'For breakfast,' says Lady Clerk of Tillypronie. Not nowadays, perhaps, but this dish is so simple, so quick, and so good for lunch or dinner.

Serves 4

1 oz (25 g) butter (more if the fillets are large)
4 haddock fillets
1–2 tablespoons flour
salt and freshly ground black pepper
$\frac{1}{4}$ pint (150 ml) single cream
$\frac{1}{4}$ pint (150 ml) milk
2 sprigs of fresh tarragon (optional)
1 teaspoon made English mustard (optional)

Melt the butter in a large pan. Flour the fish, and season them to taste. Next roll them in the butter,

and turn them about until well saturated. Then add the cream and milk. Let it just boil for a minute, then simmer very gently until the fish is tender.

When cooked, take the fish out and put on a heated serving dish. Keep warm. Mix in the tarragon and mustard with the sauce if you like. Reduce the sauce in the pan over a high heat till it thickens, scrape it out, and put it over the fish. Serve immediately.

Chicken Kromeskies 19th century

Although the family at Glamis was obviously fond of these, the recipe is not common in English cookbooks. This version from Lady Clerk of Tillypronie is a good one.

Serves 4 to 5

3 tablespoons flour
1 oz (25 g) butter, melted
salt
freshly ground black pepper
4 breasts of chicken, filleted
2 egg whites
fat or oil, for deep-frying

Several hours before the meal, make a batter 'the thickness of double cream' by blending together the flour, butter, a pinch of salt, a sprinkling of pepper, and a few drops of tepid water. Beat this well, and leave it in a cool place. Season the chicken, and cook it (your preferred method) for twenty minutes. Leave that also to cool.

To cook the kromeskies, whisk the egg whites to a stiff froth, and mix with the prepared batter. Cut the chicken into neat pieces (one for each kromesky), and coat each one well with batter.

Heat the oil or fat, and when a drop of the batter sizzles immediately it is dropped into it, put in the Kromeskies to deep-fry. As soon as they are a nice golden brown, remove them, and drain on kitchen paper. Serve them very hot, with a good tomato salad, or fresh young green peas.

Rabbit Posada 19th century

Lady Clerk of Tillypronie's recipe book gives sixteen recipes for rabbit. This one is noted as 'a Spanish dish', and 'the only way to make rabbit good'. It came via Lady Clerk's cook, Mrs Ford, and shows that a dim perception of countries other than those on the Grand Tour was now reaching Britain.

Serves 4

1 rabbit
2 oz (50 g) butter
2 small onions, chopped
1 pint (600 ml) brown stock
a bunch of sweet herbs: plenty of parsley, some
    thyme, marjoram, and lovage if available
salt and cayenne pepper, to taste
1 small glass of port

Joint the rabbit, and fry the pieces gently in the butter. Remove them from the pan, and fry the chopped onion until brown. Put all the ingredients into a heavy pan with a lid, and stew for 1½ hours. Take out the herbs before serving. Mashed potato is a perfect accompaniment.

Price Albert Pudding 19th century

At the beginning of her section on puddings in her book of recipes, Lady Clerk of Tillypronie has a memo on how to turn them out: 'Be sure all the pudding moulds are dry in the first instance, then well greased inside with well-clarified butter or beef suet, as otherwise the puddings will look ragged when turned out.' Also, she says, if cooked too fast, they will not turn out unbroken. She recommends turning over the mould, with the pudding in it, onto the dish it is to be served from, and leaving the mould on for a minute or two before taking it off the pudding.

Serves 4 to 6

butter or suet, to grease the mould
8 oz (225 g) cooked prunes, stoned
    (reserve the cooking syrup to make a sauce)
6 oz (150 g) butter
6 oz (150 g) sugar
6 oz (150 g) brown breadcrumbs
3 eggs, yolks separated from whites
1 glass sherry
grated peel from half a lemon or half an orange
2 tablespoons chopped candied peel or sultanas

Prune sauce
syrup in which prunes were cooked
1 glass sweet sherry

Grease a 2-pint (1.2-litre) pudding mould, and line it with the prunes. Cream the butter and sugar together, then blend in the breadcrumbs. Stir in the egg yolks beaten in the sherry, the grated peel, and the candied peel or sultanas. Finally, beat the egg whites stiffly, and fold them in. Fill the pudding mould with this mixture, and steam over a low heat for 2 hours.

Turn the pudding out of the mould carefully, and serve with a prune sauce, made by reducing the syrup of the stewed prunes till it is half the quantity, and adding a glass of sweet sherry. Strain this onto the serving dish around the pudding.

Diet-bread Cake 19th century

Most recipes call this type of light sponge a 'Diet Loaf'. Lady Clerk of Tillypronie's name illustrates the confusion between 'bread' and 'cake', which existed late into the nineteenth century. The 'diet' element presumably refers to the fact that it uses no butter.

Serves 10 to 12

9 egg whites
3 egg yolks
$1\frac{1}{4}$ lb (600 g) caster sugar
13 oz (350 g) plain flour, sifted
1 tablespoon caraway seeds
grated rind of 1 lemon

Pre-heat the oven to 190°C (375°F, Mark 5). Grease a 9-inch (22-cm) loose-bottomed cake tin (if you do not have a loose-bottomed tin, line your cake tin with greased greaseproof paper).

Beat the egg whites until stiff, then blend in the egg yolks. Whisk in the caster sugar, until thoroughly blended and the mixture is light and creamy. Now work quickly. Gently, without beating, fold in the flour, then the caraway seeds and lemon rind. Immediately turn this mixture into the prepared tin, and bake in the pre-heated oven for about $1\frac{1}{2}$ hours. Leave the cake to rest in the tin for 10 minutes, then turn out onto a rack to cool.

When cool, slice in two across, and sandwich the two halves together with raspberry jam, or simply ice the top with a lemon water icing.

Potato Scones 19th century

To make these you need a griddle or a large heavy frying pan with a perfectly flat bottom. They look like very thin pancakes well browned, but soft, not crisp. The original recipe by Lady Clerk of Tillypronie adds 'if you wish these scones to be good and light, you must boil the potatoes expressly for them and *not let them get cold after boiling, but use as soon as passed through a sieve*'. They are good at any meal, but served hot, rolled up with thin slices of cold smoked salmon inside, they make a wonderful starter for a dinner party.

Makes 8

8 oz (225 g) potatoes, boiled and mashed
1 oz (25 g) butter
$\frac{1}{2}$ teaspoon salt
3 oz (75 g) flour

Mix the mashed potato while it is still very hot with the butter. Add the salt and flour, kneading them in by hand, until the mixture holds together and looks as if it will not break when rolled out.

Roll half the dough out on a floured surface to a thickness of about $\frac{1}{16}$-inch (1 mm), and cut into a 10-inch (25-cm) round (try not to handle the dough too much). Do the same thing with the rest of the dough. Have ready a lightly greased griddle or frying pan. Cut each round of dough into quarters, and when the pan is hot lift these with a spatula and put them in, four at a time. Cook them for 3 to 4 minutes each side, until they are firm and speckled with brown.

If you wish to serve the scones with smoked salmon, make sure it is thinly sliced and very cold. The contrast between the hot potato scone and the cold fish is very pleasing.

Cheese Fondu 19th century

This popular savoury had several versions. It is really a soufflé, not a fondue, but Lady Clerk of Tillypronie seems to have used that term only of sweet soufflés. Cooked in individual ramekin dishes for only 15 minutes, it makes a very good starter as well.

Serves 4

2 oz (50 g) butter
$\frac{1}{4}$ pint (150 ml) single cream
4 oz (100 g) grated Cheshire cheese
4 egg yolks
4 egg whites
salt, pepper, and nutmeg (optional) to taste

Pre-heat the oven to 200°C (400°F, Mark 6). Grease a small (6-inch, 15-cm) soufflé dish.

Melt the butter and add the cream. Bring to the boil, and allow to cook for about 5 minutes. Take off the heat, and add the cheese, then the egg yolks, one by one. Whip up the egg whites 'to a strong froth', and fold in lightly. Put the mixture into the prepared soufflé dish, and bake in the pre-heated oven for about 20 minutes, until golden brown and well risen.

Barley Broth 20th century

Most people are unlikely ever to make sheep's head broth, but barley broth is another traditional Scottish soup too good to be allowed to disappear. This is the Hon. Mountstuart Elphinstone's recipe, although I like to add herbs, and only put the vegetables in half-way through instead of at the beginning.

Serves 6

3 lb (1.25 kg) runner of beef
2 tablespoons coarse salt
12 oz (325 g) pot (pearl) barley
a sprig or two each of marjoram, parsley, and thyme (all optional)
2 carrots
3 turnips
3 medium leeks
salt and pepper to taste

Make sure the butcher cuts the meat so it will fit your largest pan. Rub coarse salt over the meat, and leave it overnight. Next day rinse the meat well under the tap. Put it in a large pan with the barley, plenty of water, and the herbs if desired. Bring to the boil, skim thoroughly, and turn the heat down until the liquid is just simmering. Leave to simmer for two hours.

Peel and slice the carrots and turnips, wash and cut up the white part of the leeks, and add them to the soup. Simmer for two hours more. Remove the meat, and season the soup to taste just before serving.

Crab Soufflé (cold) 20th century

By the 1930s, it was possible to get fresh shellfish even if one lived some distance from the Scottish coast. This simple recipe makes a nice luncheon dish. You can buy packets of instant aspic, but failing that use $\frac{1}{2}$ oz (15 g) gelatine as indicated on the packet.

Serves 4

2 lb (900 g) crab, cooked
$\frac{1}{4}$ pint (150 ml) mayonnaise

$\frac{1}{4}$ *pint (150 ml) melted aspic*
$\frac{1}{2}$ *pint (300 ml) whipped cream*

Remove the meat from the crab, setting a small amount of claw meat on one side to use as a garnish. Put the rest of the crab meat in a food processor and blend to a paste, or mash it well with a fork. Add the mayonnaise and melted aspic, and leave until almost set, then fold in the whipped cream. Pour the mixture into a soufflé dish, and sprinkle flaky bits of the claw meat, set aside as a garnish, lightly on the top. Chill in the refrigerator for 3 to 4 hours before serving.

Venison Pie 20th Century

Although there is no deer forest at Glamis, I am quite sure the Strathmores were sometimes given venison, or bought it, and in any case a collection of Scottish recipes without some using venison is unthinkable.

Serves 6

6 thin venison steaks from the haunch
venison fat or a piece of butcher's suet – enough
   to cover each steak with a thin layer
$1\frac{1}{2}$ tablespoons chopped fresh herbs: parsley, thyme,
   marjoram, chives, to taste
salt and freshly ground black pepper
1 oz (25 g) butter
1 tablespoon flour
$\frac{1}{2}$ pint (300 ml) good beef stock
1 tablespoon each of Harvey's Sauce and mushroom
   ketchup
2 tablespoons redcurrant jelly (optional)
1 small glass of port (optional)
12 oz (325 g) shortcrust pastry
1 egg, beaten

Pre-heat the oven to 180°C (350°F, Mark 4). Place a thin layer of the venison fat or butcher's suet over each venison steak. Then sprinkle the steaks with the chopped herbs, and salt and pepper to taste. Roll up each steak, and place the rolls in a pie dish.

Make a rich sauce by blending together the butter and flour to make a roux, then adding the stock, Harvey's Sauce, mushroom ketchup, and, if desired, the redcurrant jelly and port. Pour this sauce over the rolls of meat in the dish. Roll out the pastry on a floured board, and place over the meat, trimming away any excess pastry. Brush the top of the pastry with the beaten egg. Bake the pie in the pre-heated oven for 2 to $2\frac{1}{2}$ hours.

Mince Collops 20th century

This is another traditional Scots recipe from the Hon. Mountstuart Elphinstone, but quite different from the Scotch collops on page 71.

1 tablespoon lard or dripping
1 onion, finely chopped
1 lb (450 g) minced steak
$\frac{1}{4}$ pint (150 ml) stock or water
1 teaspoon salt
1 dessertspoon pinhead (coarse) oatmeal
freshly ground black pepper
1 tablespoon mushroom ketchup (optional)

Heat the lard or dripping in a large heavy pan, add the chopped onion, and fry gently for about a minute. Add the minced steak, and cook until browned, beating it well with a wooden spoon to keep it free from lumps. Pour in the stock or water, add the salt, and leave to simmer gently for 1 hour.

Stir in the oatmeal. Season with pepper to taste, and add the mushroom ketchup if desired. Cook for a further 5 minutes. Serve hot with fingers of toast on the side, or with mashed potatoes.

Grouse Soufflé 20th century

The strong taste of grouse suits this otherwise bland recipe, which makes a good luncheon dish.

> Serves 4
>
> 2 grouse
> 2 oz (50 g) unsalted butter
> 4 egg yolks
> cayenne pepper
> salt
> 4 egg whites

Pre-heat the oven to 200°C (400°F, Mark 6). Grease a soufflé dish well. Remove the breast meat from the grouse, and place in a food processor with the butter. Process to form a smooth paste (if you do not have a food processor, pound the meat with the butter in a mortar, then rub through a sieve). Blend in the egg yolks, and season to taste with cayenne pepper and salt. Beat the egg whites until stiff, then fold gently into the mixture.

Put the soufflé mixture into the prepared dish, and bake in the pre-heated oven for 20 minutes until well risen and golden brown. Serve immediately.

Cold Game Pie 20th century

This type of pie, very popular from Victorian times until the war, has no pastry, and is really a terrine. To make it properly is a long process, because one must first make a stock from venison or other game, and also pre-cook the tongues. The Hon.

Mountstuart Elphinstone says 'this pie is improved by the addition of a hare, grouse, or duck, and a glass of Port Wine'. If you follow this advice, cut up the additional meat into small cubes, and mix these with the minced venison and liver – it will give an interesting texture. Here is my version of his pie.

> Serves 8
>
> Stock
> bones from venison, hare, pheasant and/or duck
> 2 pig's trotters
> 2 carrots, sliced
> 2 sticks celery, chopped
> 2 onions, chopped
> fresh herbs: thyme, parsley, oregano, and a bay
>   leaf
> salt and freshly ground black pepper
>
> Pie
> 4 small deer tongues
> 1 carrot, sliced
> 1 onion, chopped
> 2 lbs (900 g) venison, skin and sinews removed
> 1 lb (450 g) deer liver
> 1 teaspoon finely chopped onion
> salt and freshly ground black pepper
> 8 oz (225 g) hare, grouse, or duck meat (optional)
> bacon fat, for frying
> 12 slices bacon, rind removed
> about 1 oz (25 g) parsley, chopped
> 1 small glass of port (optional)

Make the stock by roasting the bones and trotters until the meat on them is brown, then putting them with their juices into a large pan with the carrots, celery, onions, herbs, and salt and pepper to taste. Cover with water and simmer very gently for about

4 hours. Strain and leave to cool. Next day remove all the cold fat from the top, and use the clear jelly for stock.

Bring a large pan of water to the boil. Put in the tongues, carrot, and onion. Lower the heat and simmer for about 2 hours. Remove the tongues from the water, and when they are cool enough to handle, skin them, trim off the ends, and slice them thinly across the grain.

Pre-heat the oven to 170°C (325°F, Mark 3). Put the venison and liver through a mincing machine, or process in a food processor (do not, however, process them to a mush). Mix in the finely chopped onion, then salt and pepper to taste. (If adding the hare, grouse or duck, chop this meat into small cubes and mix these with the minced venison.) Melt the bacon fat in a frying pan, and fry the meat lightly, turning it over, then when it is pale brown leave it to cool.

Take a deep pie dish, put four slices of bacon in the bottom, and cover with a layer of the cooked venison and liver. Sprinkle with some of the chopped parsley, and grind on a little pepper. Then add a layer of sliced tongue. Begin again with the bacon, repeating the layers as before until the pie dish is full. Pour over about $\frac{1}{2}$ pint (300 ml) of the stock, and the port if desired. Cover the pie dish with closely-fitting foil or a lid, and stand it in a dish of water, so that the water comes about half-way up the sides of the pie dish.

Place this in the pre-heated oven for $2\frac{1}{2}$ to 3 hours. Remove the pie dish from the dish of water, and leave to cool.

While the pie is cooling, top it up with the remainder of the stock. When fairly cool, put in the refrigerator for at least 4 hours. Turn out and serve sliced with salads for a buffet lunch or a rather grand picnic.

WALES

Erddig Hall, Clwyd
C. Anne Wilson

Erddig Hall, Clwyd

In 1977 Erddig Hall became for a time the most famous house in Britain. In that year it was first opened to the public, having passed into the guardianship of the National Trust in 1973. It featured in television and radio programmes, and newspapers and journals carried stories about the stately home in north Wales where time had stood still for a hundred years or more. Not only the fine eighteenth-century furniture, but also many household objects of the eighteenth and nineteenth centuries had survived, while in outbuildings there remained an ancient family coach, two victorias, and several other outdated vehicles. Furthermore, a remarkable collection of letters, poems, memoranda, estate and household accounts, and cookery books dating from the seventeenth century onwards, and even earlier land-deeds, had accumulated in the house, and these too were transferred to the National Trust.

Erddig Hall, little more than a mile from Wrexham, was still without mains electricity or gas in 1973; and water was brought to it from the Black Brook in the valley below via a water-powered pump feeding tanks on the roof, and was regarded by Philip Yorke as a good deal purer than the chemically reinforced liquid from the waterworks. Philip Yorke III owned Erddig Hall and estate from 1966 to 1973. The house, built in the 1680s, had

been extended in the eighteenth century, and a dining-room was inserted in 1826. Thereafter there was little alteration to the fabric until the Coal Board began mining directly under the foundations after 1947, causing one end of the building to sink five feet and the other three and a half feet. As a result rainwater penetrated the roof above the centre, inflicting serious damage on the rooms below through damp and wet-rot.

Even before that time, while Philip's elder brother Simon was owner of Erddig from 1922 onwards, both house and grounds had entered upon a period of gradually increasing neglect and decay, exacerbated after 1939 by wartime difficulties. After 1966 Philip fought back with ingenious solutions to various small problems, but by the time he took over both the house and its furniture were badly in need of major conservation work. And when Philip spoke of his 'gardeners', he meant the sheep he had introduced to crop the lawns nearest to the Hall.

For Simon and Philip, the Hall and estate were a sacred trust handed down by generations of Yorkes, and it was because they were so deeply trapped in Erddig's past that they were unable to cope with the task of bringing it into the mid-twentieth century. Yet the house had been built by a man who had no connection with the Yorke family; and

John Meller, uncle of Simon Yorke I, who later purchased it, apparently had no connection with Wales prior to the chain of events that led him to make the purchase.

Erddig Hall is built on an escarpment formed by Wat's Dyke, some two miles east of Offa's Dyke. Celts of the ancient tribe of the Deceangli occupied the area in Roman times. Later their descendants struggled against the Saxons, and nearby Wrexham was a Saxon foundation. But the Saxons were driven eastwards again, and even after the Norman Conquest the region remained Welsh-speaking.

The English manorial system gradually penetrated the Welsh border counties. Some light is shed on local diet during the later Middle Ages by records of the food-rents paid in the commote of Merford, a few miles north-east of Erddig. In 1449–50 customary tenants paid a pig at Martinmas (11 November), in addition to a money-rent and certain days of boon-work on the lord's land. On 1 May some gave a lamb or kid, and others a fixed quantity of oats. In 1472–3, fifty-four hens valued at 1½ d. each were due to the lord at Christmas. Even in 1508 most tenants paid stated amounts of wheat and oats plus three hens as part of their total rent.

Oats provided oatcakes, gruel, and *llymru*, made from the finest part of the gruel or from water in which oats had been steeped (it was adapted as the 'flummery' of English gentry cookery books). Oats also supplied malt for ale. Barley, rye, and wheat were raised in the area as well, but only the well-to-do ate wheaten bread. Poorer families ate rye or barley bread or bread of 'mixed grains', sometimes called 'muncorn': the most usual combinations were wheat and rye or oats and barley. The hens contributed eggs, and the sheep, with perhaps one or two cows, yielded milk for cheese. Goats were plentiful; their flesh and that of the wethers was salted and dried, and through the lean months could be added in small amounts to the *cawl* (broth) of roots and herbs.

Glimpses of the diet of the Welsh nobility come from the poems of their personal bards, the *Beirdd yr Uchelwyr* (bards of the nobility). From about 1350 to 1650 a poet was retained on the staff of a great household to praise the lord's achievements and hospitality. By the fifteenth century the cooked dishes occasionally mentioned in the bards' poems had begun to reflect the kind of cuisine recorded in contemporary cookery books for the English nobility; and some of those books were probably translated into Welsh then (though the earliest surviving Welsh cookery manuscripts were written a century later). The sauces and meat stews enriched with spices and dried fruits, the *ffwrment* (frumenty) and *pasteiod* (pies), and the sweetmeats and *cwnfetts* (comfits) praised in the poems of the bards have their counterparts in English cookery of the time. One poem, at least, consists of a recipe. It describes the ingredients for the Welsh version of green sauce (*saws glas*), a familiar sauce in French and English cookery books of the period, made to accompany fish, especially sturgeon which then still reached the mouth of the River Dee.

The monasteries before the Dissolution (1539) also offered lavish hospitality, and the poets were welcomed at the abbot's board and wrote their poems of appreciation afterwards. Lewis Môn enjoyed brawn, beef, and a variety of birds at Valley Crucis Abbey in the early sixteenth century, and Tudor Aled wrote of guests there receiving brawn, bream, and an abundance of wine.

At that time, a few miles east of the Abbey, the Erddig estate was already in the making. David Gogh ap Howel ap Ieuan ap Llewelyn, named in a document of 1505, held lands in Erddig township, though his forebears may have settled there much earlier. His son John adopted a surname in the English style, taking the name 'Erthig' from his home ground. His descendants were the Erthigs of Erddig, and they built Erddig House, forerunner of Erddig Hall, on their land. But in 1598 the first John's grandsons sold part of their estate, including Erddig House, to Dr David Yale, Chancellor of Chester, and thereafter the Erthigs lived at Erddig Fechan (Little Erddig), a smaller house on their remaining land. (In all the documents consulted, Erddig was invariably spelled 'Erthig' until Lucy Hitchman's early twentieth-century cookery books produced the compromise 'Erdhig'. But throughout this account I have used the modern Welsh-based spelling 'Erddig' for the place.)

The outbuildings of Erddig Fechan terminated in a dairy, and below it in a cellar was a spring of exceptionally pure water, probably the 'Ffynnon Erthig ... a pure water much resorted to' mentioned by Edward Lluyd at the end of the seventeenth century. The water was in demand as far away as Chirk Castle, some ten miles off. Martha, daughter of the last male Erthig, owned Erddig Fechan at this period, and her husband Jonathan Moore received 7s. 0d. a week in 1702 'for sending the Erthig water to the Castle for 6 weeks'.

Dr Yale added more land to his Erddig estate, but in 1619 sold it all to Richard Davies 'citizen and vintner of London', who further enlarged the property. In 1653 he sold it to John Edisbury, steward of Chirk Castle. It then comprised Erddig House, together with '13 messuages, 6 gardens, 6 orchards, 2 water corn-mills', and several hundred acres of arable, pasture and woodland. The two corn-mills, 'two mills under one roof', originally called *Melin Coed y Glyn*, were later known as the French Mills. John Edisbury's father, a local landowner, had purchased the right to the 'toll and tollage' of the town of Wrexham at the King's Mill further down the River Clywedog, and the bronze bushel measure at Erddig Hall engraved 'A.D. 1663' may have been used by John to measure the corn ground at both watermills. He also enlarged Erddig House: hearth-tax returns of 1670 show that two of the six hearths (with their associated rooms) were newly installed. Seven years later the house passed, on John's death, to his elder son Josua.

In 1682 Josua was High Sheriff of Denbighshire, and at the peak of his influence and wealth. Among his contacts was Dr David Yale's great-grandson, Elihu Yale, then Governor of Fort St George, India. In April 1682 Elihu acknowledged a gift from Josua of '4 rundletts of Sandpatch (Sandbach) ale', which had arrived in good shape despite its long journey through 'ye torrid zone'. His response was to despatch 'one of yor vesselles fild with our best Mango Atcher' for Josua, and an oriental screen for his wife, Grace. Elihu, although born in American Boston, returned to north Wales after 1690 to live at Plas Grono, adjoining Erddig. Later still he sent gifts of books and money to the collegiate school in Connecticut which became Yale University.

Josua commissioned a new house, Erddig Hall, from the architect Thomas Webb of Middlewich in 1683. It was a fine rectangular brick building, 'eight roomes on a ffloor besides closetts' with additional outbuildings, constructed on the site of

Erddig House which was demolished. A walled garden was laid out on the east side, with a banqueting-house at either end of a walk running parallel to the Hall.

The contract for the carpentry work for the two banqueting-houses is dated 17 March 1685, when Josua still had fresh in his mind the success of the entertainment given in the previous July to the Duke of Beaufort, Lord President of Wales:

... att on admirable Walled Garden of Trees, Plants, Flowers, and Herbs of the greatest rarity ... where in a Banquetting-house a Collation of choice Fruit and Wines was lodged by ... Sir Richard Myddelton [of Chirk Castle], to entertain his Grace in this his flourishing Plantation.

So wrote Thomas Dineley. Months later Sir Richard settled his bills with Shrewsbury shopkeepers for the raspberry, redcurrant and apricot pastes, candied citron, orange and lemon peels, syllabub glasses, and other luxury items purchased for this occasion.

Grace Edisbury no doubt preserved the fruits and flowers of their new garden at Erddig Hall, as was the practice among gentlewomen, and some of her conserves may have been eaten by guests in the banqueting-houses. But the only surviving contemporary record of preserving at Erddig is in a letter of 1685 with a request on behalf of a cousin Mary to 'my cousin Bety Glegg [a relative of Grace then living at the Hall] to make her a bottel of Surrop of Clove giliflower and she will return her the Sugar with many thanks'.

The progress of the garden is mentioned in letters to Josua when he was away from Erddig in the 1690s: the building of new hotbeds for melons, and the setting of gilliflower seeds in one letter; a gift of cabbage-lettuce in another; and the 'wall-fruit', apples, pears, and cherry-standards, that 'hitt very well' in a third. But by then he had heavier concerns on his mind, for it was clear that the yield of the estate, even including tenants' rents, tolls from the corn-mills, sale of timber, and income from the coal mines on Erddig land, could not pay off the large debt incurred in building and furnishing the Hall; and Josua's own speculations in copper and lead mines merely increased his losses.

Josua and Grace spent more time in London, where he tried to raise money in other ways. But he was an incompetent man of business, and perhaps overgenerous to relatives. His cousins Francis and Kenrick came to live at Erddig Hall, and Elizabeth Lea, a connection of Grace, also moved in and acted as housekeeper. 'I do not know how Mr Edisbury likes his diet,' she wrote to Josua, 'I get him one dish every dinner, butter and the good ould cheese.'

Elizabeth Lea also sent Erddig produce to Josua and Grace: plump hens, occasionally a turkey or goose, butter, and cheese. The steward, John Williams, sent woodcocks and hares. The journey from Erddig to London took three days, yet it was common for presents of meat or fish to be despatched over comparable or greater distances in the seventeenth and eighteenth centuries. If freshly killed or caught, they could survive such journeys in an edible condition provided the weather was not too warm, and well spiced sauces and stews could mask the flavour of meat or fish already past its prime.

Josua's absences kept him from supervising

improvements made on the estate. His cousin wrote about the French burr millstones installed in the double watermill: 'French mills in very good repute for quick grinding, but the one that *does* go drowned in water & only one of them can go at a time, the arch through which the water goes being too narrow.'

We do not know how that problem was solved. But Josua's liabilities increased, and he had to let Erddig Hall to tenants. One of his creditors was Elihu Yale who lent him £2,000 in 1705. His brother Dr John Edisbury, a Master in Chancery, also made loans and gifts to Josua in the mistaken belief that Erddig was basically solvent. To do this John used monies deposited in Chancery, and when discovered he was disgraced and imprisoned; and the whole estate was put up for sale to satisfy its creditors.

John Meller, another Master in Chancery, offered the best price, and was accepted. In 1716 he began to spend time at Erddig Hall, at first sharing it with the latest tenant. Nevertheless he held a feast for the estate's other tenants in 1717, and the following year the creditors were finally paid off (including Elihu Yale who received £3,511). By then John Edisbury was dead, and so, probably, were Josua and Grace, though the dates of their deaths are unknown.

John Meller was a bachelor, and his sister Aliza lived at Erddig with him until her marriage in 1723, and for long periods thereafter. Another sister, Anne, was married to Simon Yorke, and their son, Simon, gave John much help over the furnishing of Erddig Hall, acting as his agent in dealings with tradespeople in London. A third sister, Elizabeth, was already married in 1681 when the sixteen-year-

old John sent his 'duty to my brother and sister Mynne' in a letter to his father. Nothing more is known about her, though her granddaughter, Frances Watts, was named in John's will of 1732.

But Elizabeth has a special interest for us, because she must have owned the earliest cookery book in the Erddig archive (D/E/1203). It is a smallish notebook, and the two final leaves record weekly rent payments from Christmas 1684 to Lady Day (25 March) 1686. On the first leaf is written: 'To be left at an ironmonger at the ffalcon on St Margaret's Hill in Southwark / for Mr Thomas Mynne at his house in Red Lion Court, in Wattling Street.' The following leaves contain culinary, cosmetic, and medical recipes; and after them come several blank leaves and places where others have been torn out.

The cookery recipes are comparable to others in later seventeenth-century collections. Four simple sauces for pigeons, green geese (see page 106 for recipe), stubble geese, and a turkey respectively, are followed by instructions for roasting venison, boiling small fish, frying chickens, and drying neats' tongues. 'To make spiced cacke' is next, followed by 'a sauce for a capon', rice pudding, 'puff paste', 'ipocras' (spiced wine – see page 106 for recipe) and 'to boyle creme'.

Preserved 'soletes' (salads) follow: cucumbers, samphire, broom buds (see recipe on page 107), and herbs pickled with salt and vinegar, and 'Vialets, primroses, coueslepes, gilliflouers or any kind of wholsom flouers' with sugar and vinegar. Then come conserves: pippins red and white, cherries, gooseberries, apricots, quinces, and rosemary flowers either preserved in sugar syrups or candied. Cosmetic recipes are intermingled, and medical ones follow, with a lone cookery item 'To bake a leg of beef on claret' in a different hand inserted in the middle. Although the culinary recipes at the front could well have been copied in before the book was put to temporary use as a rent book, at least some of the remedies were added later; the formula for 'Dr Blackborne Dyet Drink' is written all round one section of rent entries.

John Meller kept a notebook (D/E/2547) titled 'My own physical observations', in which he collected medical recipes with comments on their efficacy. When his eyes troubled him late in life, his sister Anne wrote to recommend the herb eyebright, taken in distilled form with sugar or as a tea; 'if it be not to be had in Wales', she offered to 'have it from our market and either still or dry it and send to you'. John may have retained Elizabeth's book for the sake of its remedies and diet-drinks rather than for its old-fashioned cookery recipes.

John was a successful lawyer, and he had inherited family property in Derbyshire. He brought to Erddig Hall the thing it most needed: money. He added new wings to the house, enlarged the garden, and purchased more land adjoining the estate. He bought magnificent furniture for the main rooms, including the outstanding state bed and the chairs with silvered frames still to be seen at the Hall. He also valued good food and fine wines.

Much of the former was supplied by the estate. Among John's earliest purchases for Erddig were fruit trees, and in 1718 he drew up a lengthy list of the many named varieties of peach, plum, pear, nectarine, apricot, and cherry trees growing against the walls of the kitchen garden, the 'hartychoak' garden, and the hall court. The orchard contained

freestanding apple trees, and also vines, nectarines, and peaches.

The 'best garden' was extended eastwards, with a long ornamental canal at its east end. Nearby was the fishpond, a valuable resource. Thomas Parry wrote from Chester in August 1729 (D/E/1542, 100), 'Knowing how careful you have been to stock your ponds with all manner of fish' to request John to spare some perch fry 'for a Noble Person of my Aquaintance'. They were to be conveyed live, 'the Noble Person knowing of a particular Method to carry them in Bladders, etc.'

Meat was killed on the estate, and eaten fresh during most of the year. Bacon and hams were salted in the 'wett larder', recorded in an inventory of 1726, and beef and mutton too may have been lightly salted there for better keeping in hot weather. With a staff of twenty-five or thirty to feed (Waterson's estimate for the 1720s), plus the Meller family and guests, even the oxbeef would not have needed very long keeping. For the family table, variety was provided by poultry, doves from the dovecot, and game-birds shot on the estate.

The servants may have known traditional Welsh salted mutton and goatmeat in childhood, but at Erddig Hall they would have received the conventional English servants' diet: beef, mutton, and bacon. The servants' dinners ('for ye Hall') are recorded, in addition to the fare for the family table, in two of three menus surviving from the 1730s:

Tuesday Octo.r 13th 1730 Dinner
A Fry'd Soal
Stewed Apples}   Sallet   {Goose Roasted
Ribs of Beef Roasted

—————————

Boiled Beef for ye Hall

20 Sept. 1732 Wednesday Dinner
Knuckle of Veal & Bacon
Chine of Mutton roasted}   *{Pudding*

—————————

Leg of Mutton boiled for ye Hall

31st Octob.r 1733 Menu for Wednesday Dinner
Leg of Pork boiled
Couple of Chickens roasted}   *{Apple Pyes*
Fillet of Veal roasted
            (D/E/1542, 63 and 62; D/E/2551)

At the time there were two servants' halls (though the menus make no distinction). The 'New Hall' containing three long tables and nine forms was probably used by the lower servants, and the 'Old Hall' with its two long tables, '2 arm Kane Chares and 8 old Kane Chares' by the upper ones. Junior servants would have acted as waiters for both, eating later themselves.

The menus were reminders for the cook. They show that dinner at a gentleman's table in a smaller country house still comprised a single main course (though more substantial than the solitary cooked dish with bread and cheese on which Josua Edisbury's cousin dined), except when important guests were present. The layout of each menu shows which position the dishes would have occupied on the dinner table. Boiled meat was cooked with roots and herbs. Roast meat was accompanied by sauces (not mentioned here). The starch element was supplied by a pudding or by bread. The meal was rounded off with a dessert of fresh or preserved fruits, and perhaps a light creamy dish prepared by the housekeeper. John Meller expected well

cooked main courses, for he paid his cook £21 a year in 1725, when his housekeeper and butler each received £10.

Cheese and butter were prepared in the 'Cheese Roome' and 'Darry' mentioned in the 1726 inventory; and bread was baked in the bakehouse from flour ground at the mills. The right to the corn-toll had been transferred, and John Meller's bronze bushel corn-measure, now in the dining-room at Erddig, is inscribed: 'FROM HIS MAIESTYES EXCHEQVER FOR THE USE OF IOHN MELLOR ESQ[R] FEE FARMER OF THE TOLL WITHIN THE TOWN OF WREXHAM IN THE COUNTY OF DENBIGH ANNO DOMINI 1716'. The 'Account of the Toll taken up at both the Mills', July 1721 to October 1722 (D/E/366), shows payment made in kind and part sent to Erddig Hall, comprising 'mault' (barley-malt for brewing), 'wheat' (flour for bread, pies and puddings for the family's table) and 'mixed corn' (flour for the servants' bread). 'Muncorn' was now usually a blend of wheat and rye (still sold in markets along the north Wales border as late as the 1880s). It could be further mixed after purchase. At Chirk Castle on 2 March 1723, two and a half measures of rye were bought 'to make household bread', plus '3 Measures of White Muncorn to Mix with the Rie'.

The brewhouse at Erddig Hall supplied small beer for the servants, who drank it at every meal including breakfast, and strong beer, given to them on special occasions but always available for John Meller and his guests. But John was more interested in fine wines. He had large vaults, with lead ceilings to exclude damp, constructed under the carriage-sweep before the front entrance at Erddig.

Thomas Beech, a Wrexham wine-merchant, was

eager to please him. 'I have with some difficulty,' he wrote, 'procured for you 5 dozen Excellent French Claret, $\frac{1}{2}$ Haut Bryan and $\frac{1}{2}$ Margauz. I was concerned for your disappointment in the hogshead of claret, and resolved if possible to procure you some worth yours and freinds' drinking.' In the same letter he offered a hogshead of red Port 'as good as I ever drank'. Wines despatched to Erddig in the hogshead were rested awhile in the vaults, and then bottled by the butler. Wrexham was conveniently near the port of Chester, and could supply Erddig Hall with many luxury imports, such as wines, oranges, lemons, dried vine-fruits, and salad oil; and also with shellfish and seafish.

John Meller died in November 1733. Sixteen months earlier he had made a will bequeathing Erddig to his nephew Simon Yorke.

From 1733 to 1922 Erddig Hall had just five owners: Simon Yorke I, his son Philip I, grandson Simon II, great-grandson Simon III, and great-great-grandson Philip II. Surviving letters and documents tell of the marriage of Simon I to Dorothy Hutton in 1739; of the birth of their only son Philip four years later; and of how Philip, aged only five, was sent away to Wanstead, Surrey, for his schooling, and thereafter to Hackney and then Eton. The same sources also yield much information about the day-to-day running of the estate.

Each owner of Erddig increased the property by purchases of adjacent land, but this did not automatically yield rich profits. In good seasons prices fell, but expenses still had to be met. John Caesar, the steward, wrote to inform Simon, staying at Chester during the winter of 1750, that 'Barley takes but a low rate, am bid for yours but 18s.0d. a measure'; and that a recent gale had stripped

tiles from the roof of Erddig Hall and 'whirled rotten sticks from the big Elm trees' to shatter the windows in several rooms. Tenants' rents came in slowly, because they had lost cattle through distemper, or had to wait until crops were harvested or cheeses had ripened and could be sold.

Caesar wrote too about the buying and selling of cattle at local markets. In a letter about the sale of an Erddig heiffer and a cow, he added, '. . . and one heiffer we had killt today, and as many choice pieces as William can carry besides the Linen we shall send by him for your use tomorrow.' The rest would have fed the Erddig servants. He reported progress in the garden: 'wall-fruit' (cherries, plums and pears) nailed to their walls; gooseberries, currants and strawberries planted on newly-dug ground in the 'nursery'; apple-trees set to border a gravelled walk in the 'new garden'.

The butler's wine day-book from the early 1740s (D/E/372) sheds some light on the Yorkes' meal arrangements. The entries show that red wine was served daily at both dinner and supper, white less frequently and usually at supper. The quantities vary, reflecting the number of guests present. Madeira appears occasionally, probably drunk by the men after the meal.

Wine issued for cooking also appears, for instance red wine 'to ye cook for carp' on Monday, 15 September 1740, and again on the two following Fridays (Hannah Glasse in *The Art of Cookery*, 1747, gives a recipe for a rich, red wine-based sauce for carp, and another for baking the fish in red wine). On Friday, 26 September, white wine went 'to Mrs Barbara for solububs'. The cook received red wine 'for sago' on Thursday, 23 October. Sago boiled in water, and mixed with a little wine and sugar made a light gruel for invalids (also recorded by Glasse). 'White wine for whey' recurs at intervals, and wine whey (milk, wine and boiling water combined, the curd removed, and the liquid slightly sweetened and flavoured with lemon or balm) was another invalid drink of the period.

In January 1741 the cook received red wine for sauce for a tongue on one day, and for 'tongue and udder' on another; and white wine for waffles (an early mention of this American-Dutch name for wafers) on a third. On 25 August there was red wine for collared beef (big pieces of beef flank, pickled for several days, then rolled and baked with wine in a deep pot). The red wine record on 27 May 1742 includes 'part for stewed duck'; and two days later white wine was issued for jellies.

Simon's personal account-book (D/E/365) shows payments for 'wine' and 'Madeira wine'. Tea and chocolate cost him £4.5s.0d. on 26 May 1743, and chocolate a further £1.16s.0d. on 12 October. Chocolate was a breakfast beverage, to accompany plain cakes or diet-breads. Simon and Dorothy drank it in the later 1750s from the Chelsea porcelain chocolate-cups still displayed in the saloon at Erddig. Tea could be a breakfast beverage too, but was often taken after dinner, when the gentlemen had finished their wine and rejoined the ladies.

After Eton, Philip's education was continued at Cambridge, and then at Lincoln's Inn. Dorothy wrote to him there in 1765 about the servants' board wages while she and Simon were absent from Erddig: 'They are to find nothing for themselves but ale, sugar and bread, and they have some small stock to begin with. This will prevent strangers soaking them whilst we are gone, as too

many have got on that footing at Erthig ... Liberality of Living causes Straitness of Money.' The Yorkes at this period could not afford to uphold the Welsh tradition whereby the great house offered hospitality to all comers (a custom that had earlier contributed to Josua Edisbury's downfall). Yet Dorothy tried to maintain a just balance, adding in the same letter '... whilst I keep house I shall never pinch my Servants. A large house in Wales is the worst thing in the world to manage.'

Her responsibilities increased when Simon died in 1767, for Philip remained in London while she supervised affairs at Erddig. On visits home Philip organized improvements, having the water-meadows drained and the corn-mills rebuilt to increase their output. For he was courting Elizabeth, sister of his college friend Brownlow, and her father, Sir John Cust, considered Philip's income far too low to support them both.

Even in London Philip still enjoyed Erddig fare. Dorothy, off to stay at Bath in November 1768, wrote: 'I imagine you will like your servants ... to be on board wages; if so, I should think you might have your mutton from home, which is now very fine.' Later, in May 1769, Dorothy reported on Erddig's garden produce: 'I have had many good things out of your garden, and several pigions'; and less happily in September: 'You need not lament [missing] your fruit this summer ... few peaches, bad nectarines, swarms of wasps on everything. We have a great plenty of greengages, which they eat fast.' But the same letter stated: 'Your wheat is very fine and got in.' And work on the mills was nearing completion. On the day the tiles arrived to re-roof the King's Mill, '23 carters dined in your Servants hall, near 50 men with Carters,' Dorothy informed Philip, 'and I endeavoured to please them with plum pudden and beef sufficient, with your strong beer and ale ...'.

In January 1770 Sir John Cust died, and a month later Elizabeth came of age. Plans for the wedding went ahead, despite the sad death of Philip's young sister, aged only sixteen, in April. Elizabeth and Philip began their married life in July 1770, but not at Erddig; for Philip rented a house at Northaw, Hertfordshire, within reach of London, as their first home.

The second oldest Erddig cookery book has the title-page inscription: 'A Receipt Book 1765', so one might expect this to be Elizabeth's book, begun when she was sixteen in anticipation of her marriage. But internal evidence tells another story.

The book (D/E/2551(a)) contains cookery recipes written in a neat sloping eighteenth-century hand on pages numbered to 117, followed by several unnumbered pages with recipes in a different hand. There are many cakes and puddings, but among them some savoury dishes, pickles and fruit preserves, possets, and wines. At the back a collection of medical and household recipes occupies pages 9 to 18, followed by ten unnumbered leaves containing similar material. Pages 1 to 8 there have been removed, as have a few leaves at the front of the book.

On page 70 the 'Marble of calves head' ascribed to Mrs Watts, Dereham, is dated 1782. But by then Elizabeth was dead. Furthermore the top right-hand corner of the title-page carries the initials 'K.S.'.

On page 65 of the cookery recipes is written: 'Here ends the Receipts taken from Mrs Turner's book.' Mrs Turner's name also heads a mincemeat recipe on page 10. Another recurring name, attached to

three recipes, is Mrs Scott; and in the household section there is a recipe for blacking attributed to the Revd C.L. Scott. For several cookery recipes the name of the donor is followed by her place of residence, and the places, including Dereham, Fransham, Horsford, and Wymondam, are in Norfolk. In a few recipes the command to 'braid' the mixture through a sieve or colander occurs, and this dialect word also belongs to East Anglia.

Philip Yorke II of Erddig married in 1902 Louisa Matilda, daughter of the Rev T.J. Scott and granddaughter, through her mother, of John Barnard Turner. The Scotts were a many-branched family with estates in Norfolk, and had intermarried with the Turners before: Sarah Anne Turner, daughter of Captain Sackville Turner, married the Revd Thomas Scott in 1795. Louisa brought her own family records and heirlooms to Erddig, among them an account of the death by shipwreck of Captain Sackville Turner and his wife, and the silver sword presented to Lieut. Barnard Turner in 1761. She may also have brought the 1765 cookery book to Erddig, and 'K.S.' could have been a 'K. Scott' from whom it had passed to Louisa's Scott or Turner forebears.

Elizabeth Cust grew up at Belton, near Grantham. There she would have begun her own cookery book, perhaps no more than fifty miles from where 'K.S.' was compiling hers, and it would have contained very similar recipes. Gentry cookery followed a fairly universal pattern in most parts of the British Isles in the eighteenth century; the places where it remained furthest from the norm were those most remote from towns and main roads, and thus least accessible to new culinary ideas and foodstuffs. Neither Belton nor Erddig was at all inaccessible. Erddig could draw on Chester,

Shrewsbury and Wrexham for luxury foods, as could other gentlemen's homes in Denbighshire and Flintshire. Since the days of Henry Tudor most Welsh gentry families had kept contacts with friends and relatives in London, and absorbed English culture in a variety of ways, including ways with food. The cuisine of the Yorkes and their neighbours in the mid-eighteenth century would have differed little from that demonstrated in the 1765 cookery book.

When Sir Watkin Williams-Wynn of the famous Welsh family came of age in April 1770, a great party for perhaps as many as 15,000 people was held in the Park at Wynnstay, not far from Erddig, where a huge ox was roasted. The list of provisions (D/E/1542, 203) records prodigious amounts of meat, poultry, game, and fish – plus 60 barrels of pickled oysters, a hogshead of rock oysters, and 20 quarts of oysters for sauce. This was Welsh hospitality at its most generous and ostentatious. But the sweet dishes, including 34 rice puddings, 24 pound cakes, 60 Savoy cakes, 30 sweetmeat cakes, 144 ice creams, and 'rockwork shapes, landscapes in jellies, blancmange, etc.' are all typical of the confections in contemporary English cookery books, both printed and handwritten.

For 'real' Welsh food it was necessary to go much further west. Thomas Pennant, a friend of Philip Yorke and author of *A Tour In Wales*, described there (Volume 2, 1781) his visit in the early 1770s to Cwm Bychan, near Harlech, the home of Evan Lloyd, a Welsh gentleman who gave him: '. . . a most hospitable reception and in the style of an ancient Briton. He welcomed us with ale and potent beer to wash down the Coch yr Wden, or hung [i.e. salted and smoked] goat, and the cheese compounded of the milk of cow and sheep.' The

cheese was made in summertime when Evan Lloyd's men took his flocks and herds to the high pastures 'among the Hafodtys, or summer dairy-houses'. Nearer home was a little wood, a meadow often grazed by deer, and 'a pretty lake swarming with trout'. Pennant commented on the great wooden oatmeal chests in the Lloyds' home, adding: 'The family lay in their whole store of winter provisions, being inaccessible a great part of the season by reason of snow. Here they lived for many generations without bettering or lessening their income.' Pennant's own family had lived in Flintshire for several generations, but he clearly regarded the Lloyds' arrangements as belonging to another world.

There is a marked contrast too with Erddig's dependence upon markets and merchants. Moreover Erddig's income was bettered twice in the eighteenth century, first by John Meller and secondly through Dorothy and Philip Yorke's inheritance of 1770. This inheritance, from Dorothy's bachelor brother, James Hutton, was a valuable house and estate at Newnham in Hertfordshire, acquired after some anxious years of waiting on the Yorkes' part. James had strongly opposed Philip's marriage, and already had an illegitimate son as an alternative heir. Moreover he had frequently been on his deathbed before, but each time had recovered. Philip's wedding in July 1770 apparently deprived him of his *raison d'être*, and the Yorkes after all inherited Newnham.

Philip and Elizabeth's home at Northaw was a convenient base from which to organize affairs at Newnham. Soon Philip wrote to the Erddig steward, John Caesar, 'your mistress desires by the return of the post that you will on consulting Mary Rice [the cook] let her know what kitchen utensils are most wanted at Erddig', with a view to supplying them from Newnham. In due course valuable furniture and silver were also sent from Newnham to embellish Erddig Hall.

Newnham was later let to tenants, but in summer 1771 Philip himself made arrangements for bringing in the harvest, and he sent to Caesar for five horses from Erddig, accompanied by a man and a boy 'both talking English' – a reminder that although the regular servants at Erddig were bilingual, some occasional workers were solely Welsh-speaking. This situation increased Philip's dependence on his steward, who was often left in charge for long periods during his master's absences in London (Philip sat as MP for Helston, Cornwall, from 1774 to 1784), or at Newnham, or Belton, or on duty with the militia.

The income from Newnham allowed Philip to make alterations at Erddig. The saloon was enlarged, the state bedroom relocated on the floor above, and some domestic offices were rebuilt. A large new kitchen was constructed, with a handsome Venetian window. It was freestanding because of Philip's great fears about fire-risks (it was joined to the house by a corridor only in 1834). Three wide arched recesses occupy the south side. The cooking-range is under the central one, and over the south arch are inscribed the words 'WASTE NOT', and over the north one 'WANT NOT'. The fine window and careful motto show that Philip had absorbed from Dorothy the particular Yorke blend of generosity and frugality.

The servants' earnings at Erddig were often well below the contemporary 'going rate', but Philip liked to reward special service, though he was quick to show displeasure when required tasks were not

accomplished. In November 1770 he wrote to Caesar:

During the frosts Worral should see the Ice house properly filled and if necessary an outer door made to it. I shall not forgive him ... if the Ice is suffered to be lost as it was last Year. Some one labourer should be appointed to the care of it ... If he did his duty well in it, I should give him a present on that Account.

The ice would later be broken up in small amounts and brought indoors to be packed around containers in which various iced creams were made.

The following summer Philip instructed that the dairymaid who had brewed the household beer during his last visit to Erddig 'with diligence and readiness of spirit' be rewarded with 2s.6d. 'as a mark of my approbation'; and also that the tenants' servants who drove teams to cart stone for some of his building work 'be treated with bread and cheese and small beer. Let them have such refreshment with due economy and moderation ... You know when the whole is finished I mean them a more generous treat.'

Similar caution prevailed when, shortly afterwards, Philip announced the birth of his eldest son, Simon:

I would dedicate to this joyful occasion a Hogshead of my Strong Beer ... You will not give out that I mean any such benefaction, but only call in the workmen some day after they have finish'd their work and give them a quart of beer to drink their Mistress' Health.

Tenants or neighbours' servants who called 'to enquire after us' were also to be given 'a draught' with bread and cheese – but without ostentation.

The household beer was a constant concern for Philip. Worried in January 1775 lest the cellar door be left open, allowing outside workers to slip in unnoticed, he had a new complaint in June: the small beer recently served at his table had been 'particularly noted for strength', and he urged Caesar to 'minutely attend the Brewer' to ensure that 'the Small Beer be of no increased strength whatever to what it was in my Father's time'.

The beer was brewed in the brewhouse, and piped through to the appropriate cellars in the vault via lead pipes, which had been repaired and re-laid in 1768. Ale, also called 'strong beer', required 7lb of hops according to the butler's book for 1774 (D/E/418); for small beer, 4lb sufficed. More malt was used for ale, too, and it took longer to mature. In 1774 it was brewed three times in July, twice in October and three times in December; small beer was brewed every few days in August and September, twice in October, twice in November and three times in December. Barm to set the liquor working was occasionally purchased, but was usually saved from one brewing to the next.

Brewing was Philip's domain, but the dairy was Elizabeth's. Her letters to Caesar in spring 1773 (D/E/569) show, in mid-April, her desire for the dairy 'to produce more plentifully, the quantity of butter does not sound much for eight cows', and also for accounts to be kept of 'the price of the butter when it is potted in the same manner as when it is sold'. By mid-May she was well pleased by increased butter output, and was already looking forward to cheese-making which would replace butter production later in the summer: 'I would have you send the number [of cheeses] we make in

a week, and also the weight they weigh then, though the weight is not to be entered in the dairy book until the year following.'

The best Cheshire cheeses were ripened for a year, and north Wales cheeses, by then nearly as well-known in south-eastern England as the Cheshire ones, were made in similar style. Erddig's neighbour, Sontley Farm, sent its cheese by wagon to London, and a Sontley cheese-wagon on a return trip is said to have carried back the Coadstone statue that adorned one of Erddig's woodland walks. Erddig's own cheese-making seems to have been small-scale, no doubt intended primarily to provide the servants' suppers through the year, with any surplus sold locally. Elizabeth was careful about the by-products, however, and required part of the whey to be made into whey-butter for the family, and the rest to be used to fatten pigs bought in by Caesar for that purpose.

The Yorkes were not always self-sufficient in butter. Household accounts show that in December 1778 they bought in several pounds at 6d. a pound. Their nearness to Wrexham market (where Erddig butter was still being sold in 1856), and to other local fairs and markets allowed them both to sell butter, eggs, cheeses, and livestock when supplies exceeded household needs, and to buy them in as required at other times.

That Dorothy Yorke missed Welsh butter when she went to live in the London house she inherited from her brother is clear from her companion's letter of October 1771 to Mrs Caesar at Erddig:

My Mistress desires one favour of you which is to buy her some salt Butter, that you sent last year was very good ... My Mistress would be glad to have at least a Hundred and a half . . . I dare say it will be dear, but it is not near so good here. (D/E/565)

The domestic fowls were cared for by the kitchen- and dairy-maids under Elizabeth's general supervision (one letter, D/E/569, records her distress at the loss of turkeys allowed to escape in her absence). The rabbit warren was another source of meat for the family table. Philip sent a request to Caesar in July 1771 for John Jones, the gardener, to 'raise a stock of young rabbits in the warren against we come down'. But both poultry and rabbits were bought in occasionally.

A necessary purchase was preserving salt, for hams and bacon, for short-term preservation of other meat, and also for pickling liquids such as were made when preparing collared beef. '1 bushel salt' cost 4s.6d. on 10 December 1778, and a week later 'another bushel of salt' was bought for the same sum. Although a large meat animal was slaughtered every few days in the 'fleshyard' at Erddig, meat was also purchased in Wrexham, again to supply variety for the Yorkes' meals. The 1778–9 housekeeper's accounts (D/E/421) include legs of veal, a calf's head, and other meats not specified and possibly obtained over a long period, which added up to a butcher's bill for £3.13s.10d. Even sausages and black pudding were bought on 1 January, which suggests that the servants were spared the task of slaughtering a pig and coping with its blood and entrails during the Twelve Days of Christmas. Sea-fish, cockles, mussels, shrimps and oysters, and lemons and 'Chiney' oranges were bought quite often.

Erddig's working dairy was among outbuildings close to the Hall, but Philip also built for Elizabeth an ornamental dairyhouse deep in the parkland to the north-east. It was evidently a dairy of the Marie Antoinette variety (later described by the Hon. John Byng in *The Torrington Diaries* as 'out of all character, having never held one bowl of milk'); and when Elizabeth's sister Anne married Jacob Reynardson in the Yorkes' own chapel in September 1775, a small family wedding breakfast was held in Elizabeth's dairyhouse. By then the two banqueting-houses were no longer in fashion for private entertainments, and had perhaps already been taken down when Philip had some internal garden walls demolished.

Sadly, Elizabeth did not enjoy her new dairyhouse for many summers. On 31 January 1779 she died of fever following the premature birth of her seventh child. She was not quite thirty. Her portrait by Francis Cotes shows her, sweet-faced and elegant, in shepherdess dress; and her letters make her a very real person to today's reader, gently teasing Philip while they were betrothed, and taking her household responsibilities very seriously after their marriage. The baby, Dorothy, nourished by a wet-nurse, thrived, and eventually became the longest-lived of Elizabeth's children.

For a while the Yorke children were cared for by the servants under Philip's supervision, and they also spent time with their aunt, Anne Reynardson. During 1782 Philip's friendship deepened with a beautiful Welsh widow, Diana Meyrick, daughter of Robert Wynne from whom she had inherited Dyffryn Aled, her house at Abergele. Philip, absent again from Erddig, wrote instructing his gardener, John Jones, to send weekly, by a careful messenger, 'the best basket of fruit he can from time to time collect to Mrs Meyrick at Abergeley'; at the same time he was to send 'pigeons from the Dovehouse . . . and . . . the finest vegetables'. Soon the children had a kindly stepmother, and in due course six stepbrothers and sisters. The family lived partly at Erddig and partly at Dyffryn Aled, and the Erddig housekeeper's accounts of the late 1790s record several payments of 2s.0d. to messengers who carried urgently needed items, such as medicines, between the two houses.

Occasional food-related entries in Philip's pocket-books during the 1780s suggest little change in the way the Erddig estate was run. He still stocked the fishpond: on 10 October 1782 he deposited there seven carps, thirty-two perch, and ten tench (D/E/385). Food-gifts were still sent to London, now from son to mother: 'Nov 24th 1785, Sent box of six woodcock to my mother through Mr Hughes of Abergelog.' Wages were still carefully recorded: in September 1784 Caesar was directed to agree with the outdoor labourers at Erddig for 10d. a day in winter and 1s.0d. a day in summer, 'being the same I give at Dyffryn'. But in January 1787 John Caesar the younger, who had succeeded his father as steward, vanished from the scene after it was discovered that the two Caesars had between them mulcted the estate of £785 over several years.

Philip's relations with other servants were happier. Mary Rice, the cook, was a recipient of the earliest of his verse tributes. He composed a special prologue for his son Brownlow to recite at a family performance of Shakespeare's *Henry V* in New Year 1786:

You cook for me and shall not I again
Give Mary Rice some pleasure for her pain;
Her pies indeed are excellent and good,
And I will pay her in dramatic food.
To Gard'ner John I owe but little less,
I prog his peaches and his apples dress,

His fairest apricots I pull and plunder . . .

In the 1790s Philip had portraits painted of some Erddig servants with his biographical verses introduced into the composition. Those for Jack Nicholas, the kitchen man, identify him as:

. . . him that waited on the Cook
And many a walk to Wrexham took,
Whether the season cold or hot,
A constant Porter to the pot:
Then in the Kitchen corner stuck,
He pluck'd the fowl, and drew the duck,
Or with the basket on his knees,
Was sheller-general to the peas . . .

Purchases recorded in the housekeeper's accounts, 1798–1806 (D/E/429) include citrus fruits, 'coffy', salmon, and seafood; and occasionally 'a quarter of lamb and head', 'a loin of veal and head', ducks, fowls, and sides of venison. Early peas were bought on 5 April 1798, and late damsons on 17 October 1803. On 18 June 1798 'cakes and piklets' cost 6s.0d. Quite often, both in these accounts and the later ones of 1810–15, a dozen or less muffins and 'lite cakes' were bought, the former at 1d. each, the latter at $\frac{1}{2}$d. Pikelets, muffins and light cakes (see recipe on page 114) were Welsh specialities, often made at home on the bakestone, but it is easy to believe that Philip, with his fear of conflagrations, would forbid the use of a bakestone in the kitchen. Also, the muffins and light cakes may have been bought for the tea-table in the housekeeper's room, rather than the breakfast-table of the Yorkes.

When Philip died in 1804, Simon II inherited Erddig, and Diana and her children returned to Dyffryn

Aled. Simon had been MP for Grantham from 1793–1802, but his interests were now centred in Wales. He sold Newnham, and purchased more land adjoining his Erddig property and also Erddig Fechan, which the last direct descendant of the Erthigs, Martha Moore, the unmarried granddaughter of Martha Erthig Moore, had bequeathed to a distant Moore relative. The house was let to tenants until 1886, when Simon's son had it taken down.

In 1807 Simon married Margaret Holland of Teyrdan, a Denbighshire neighbour. Brownlow and Dorothy (the only other survivors of Elizabeth's children) joined with their eldest stepbrother, Piers Wynn York, to buy a magnificent Spode china dinner-service in Indian-tree pattern as a wedding gift. Its size was complemented by the extensive *batterie de cuisine* in the kitchen. By 1834, when an inventory was made, this comprised a vast array of objects, some present in large numbers, e.g. twelve copper moulds, four tin moulds, three copper frying pans, twenty-four copper cups, seventeen tin pots, twenty-five copper stewpans, twelve tin dishcovers, six pewter water-plates, three mills.

Until 1826 main meals were taken in the saloon, with the table removed betweentimes and stored elsewhere. Simon then commissioned a new dining-room, designed in classical style by Thomas Hopper, to fill the area once occupied by the state bedroom and dressing-room. A gift of mahogany dining-table and chairs from Margaret's brother allowed them to entertain in fashionable mode.

The housekeeper's accounts for 1810–15 (D/E/421) tell a similar story to earlier accounts, with barm, eggs, oranges, lemons, and fish of various kinds, especially salmon in summer, among the more frequent entries; and less often, ducks, fowls, sides of venison at 10s.6d., and 'biskets'. The six dozen oranges purchased for 15s.0d. on 24 March 1813 were doubtless for orange marmalade, prepared in those days in March or April. Early potatoes were bought three times in June 1810 – a single pound for 1s.0d. or 1s.6d. as a once-a-week treat. Mushrooms were purchased several times each year in late summer; and on 19 July 1813, 3s.0d. was paid for samphire. Twenty years on, Simon's account with K. Briscoe of Wrexham (D/E/442) has a more modern aspect with Italian paste (pasta), Burgess's essence of anchovies, and a packet of curry powder, but includes also verjuice, isinglass (for jelly-making), salad oil, lemon pickle, ginger, saffron, and cochineal, all interspersed with household materials such as lamp oil, red-lead, and drab-coloured paint.

In 1830 Simon had portraits painted of servants for which he too composed verses. His woodman, Edward Barnes, acted as Erddig's brewer, and was a fine fisherman, though overfond of *cwrw da* (good Welsh ale). His gardener, Thomas Pritchard, had formerly helped the gamekeeper ('Of Cock and Partridge rung the knell / And loudly call'd as dead as Hell'), and cared well for the fruit-trees, and the melons and cucumbers grown 'by glass and frame'.

Simon III, elder son of Simon II and Margaret, inherited Erddig in December 1834. He thereupon made an inventory of the contents of the Hall. From the 1850s onwards he commissioned several portraits of the servants, both singly and collectively, first by daguerrotype, and then by photography. To accompany these he, and later his son Philip, wrote the now traditional verses.

Changes to the domestic economy came slowly. For many years meat was still home-killed. The 'Account of Sheep slaughtered at Erddig Hall' for 1837 (D/E/426) records one every few days, of weights varying from 37 to 77 lb, plus a Welsh 'llamb' of 20 lb on 26 May. Also listed are sheepskins sent to a Mr Jenkins to earn some extra income. Pork pigs were killed at the rate of four a month in winter, fewer in spring and September, and none in the summer months without an 'r'. In February two enormous bacon-pigs of 285 lb and 375 lb were slaughtered, a fortnight apart to allow time for the first stages of salting, and for coping with the by-products.

In 1846 Simon married his cousin Victoria Mary Louisa Cust. The arrival of the newly-wed couple at Wrexham on 28 August was celebrated by a procession through the streets. A very long poster (D/E/1216) details the participants: a band, followed by three wagons each containing an ox and four sheep, and a fourth with just four sheep, all drawn by horses decorated with crimson and white favours; members of the Prince of Wales' Ancient Foresters 'with their splendid regalia ... the Committee, tenantry and friends of the house of Erthig with crimson and white favours'; plus various others. Eight hundred children were regaled with tea and plum cake at their respective schools, and then lined the route. The procession met and escorted the young Yorkes through Wrexham, and on to the Erddig lodge gate, where they were greeted with 'a salute of canon'. It was all funded by subscription, and the animals were later slaughtered and their meat distributed to 'the Poor, on production of a ticket from a subscriber'. The subscribers themselves shared a special dinner at the Wynnstay Arms Hotel the following week.

Victoria brought with her a cookery book begun in 1839 when she was fifteen (D/E/2794). The thick notebook with its mottled brown cover includes recipes collected while she was lady-in-waiting to Queen Victoria, such as 'Melt Bur. – H.R.H. D[uchess] of Kent' (a white sauce of milk thickened with a flour and butter liaison, so novel to Victoria that she named it from the ubiquitous earlier sauce of melted butter beaten with a very little flour), and perhaps 'Lord Sandys sauce called Worcester Sauce'. Among her foreign recipes are American puddings of cornmeal, a Swiss pudding, Italian *pasticiotti*, and *boudin de lapereaux*.

To her Erddig life must belong the cream cheese recipe from Nerquis (a few miles away), and probably 'to make toasting cheese with 3 cows milk [i.e. 3 milkings]', annotated: 'ready in 6 weeks for toasting' – a reminder that toasted cheese had been a Welsh favourite since medieval times. Among several drinks is an 'ale posset very good for nursing mothers'. A recipe for 'watercakes', thin flour and butter biscuits, with the note, 'ammonia powder makes them crisper', must have been acquired by Victoria early on, for during the 1840s this ill-tasting raising-agent was well on the way to being superseded by baking powder.

Victoria's second, later cookery book, a slightly smaller brown-covered notebook, gives no fewer than three recipes for home-made baking powder. This book has many cake recipes, plus a few savoury dishes, e.g. cockscombs fried in butter, a chaudfroid of quails and another of lamb cutlets 'from the cook of The Blues'. Coconut is used in a pudding, a soup, and a coconut pound cake. And tomatoes also appear, always cooked in a sauce or soup.

Victoria's books reflect her real interest in cookery, corroborated by Simon's account of groceries consumed at Erddig during 1850 (D/E/451). Black and white pepper, Carolina rice and Patna rice, rice-flour, pearl sago, and several spices appear there. Tea was now a drink for the servants: an 1848 list has '54 lb. servants tea at 3s.4d. lb.'. Nevertheless, beer was still important, especially for the men-servants, though it ceased to be home-brewed. The beer-book for 1881 (D/E/2790) records two barrels of beer delivered twice monthly by a brewer, adding up to the consumption of 864 gallons over six months.

The 'Account of the servants' allowed meals', 1850–51 (D/E/2362) states, usually, nine males and nine females, plus the occasional caller, such as the post-boy, who also ate in the servants' hall. Larger groups ('4 ladies maids, 8 strange menservants' on 14 March) appear when the Yorkes had visitors. By 1866 the number of servants fed regularly had dropped to three or four males and seven or eight females (D/E/461).

The small-scale sale of produce continued. Erddig butter, sent to Wrexham market every few days in quantities from 5 to 16 lb, raised £5.14s.0d. during April and May 1856, less a market toll of 4d. (D/E/453). It was sold until late September in 1856, but over a shorter season in succeeding years, and only in May in 1860.

Care was taken, too, in recording the game shot by Simon Yorke and his friends, and the beneficiaries – other friends and tenants – who received the carcases. In 1875 the bag was listed according to its destination (D/E/2707): 20 hares given away, 30 consumed; 40 partridges sold at 1s.3d. each, 85 given, 270 consumed; 30 pheasants sold at 3s.3d.

each, 36 given, 54 consumed; two woodcocks sold at 2s.0d. each, two given, and one consumed. This careful accounting underlines the fact that no further large acquisitions came to Erddig after Simon II sold Newnham, and the Yorkes were having to live carefully again (in 1897 a housekeeper was dismissed for disposing of pheasants without Philip II's knowledge).

Simon III died in 1894, and Victoria the following year. Their elder son Philip inherited Erddig Hall. He had spent much of his time abroad and in London following a failed marriage, but his wife's death eventually released him, and in 1902 he married Louisa Scott (mentioned earlier in connection with the 1765 cookery book).

Louisa herself seems to have arranged the local celebration of their marriage in the form of tea parties, and the 'account of expenditure for 6 School Treats and two large parties of tenants and Mayor and Corporation (200 at each party)' in her personal account-book (D/E/464) shows considerable dependence on Wrexham shops for the supply of cakes, buns, and bread. In her early married life at Erddig she had to cope with a series of unsatisfactory housekeepers before Miss Brown held the post from 1907–14. Thereafter Lucy Hitchman, formerly nurse to Louisa's sons, Simon and Philip, acted as housekeeper in the war years.

Among the men-servants was John Jones, the coachman, a good shot in his spare time. His photograph of 1911 (on horseback, with Simon on a pony with a leading-rein) is accompanied by Philip II's verses, including the couplet: 'And sometimes will supply the Cook/ With hare and rabbit, or a rook.'

Louisa compiled two of the four latest cookery

books in the Erddig archive (D/E/2794): a small black-covered book with the title 'Special Recipes 1911', and a taller, thin black-covered book in the same hand bearing her signature, with an index of soups, sweet, and vegetarian dishes, dated 6 January 1915 at the end. The two remaining books are in a fluent but different hand. One is signed 'L.A. Hitchman' inside its blue mottled cover. The other, a thick book with a shiny black cover, contains many economical recipes for wartime cookery (e.g. bone soup, 'very nourishing', and 'a delicious sauce for boiled sheep's head'), and was perhaps begun when Lucy became housekeeper, though several of its recipes are attributed to her predecessor, Miss Brown. The mottled-cover book also has some recipes from the wartime period, e.g. 'Guards pudding, Erdhig, 1915', and a heading on the following page, 'Wartime Recipes 1914–17'. But the 'plumcake, Erdhig 1890' (see recipe on page 119) in the same book comes from an earlier source. That there was close co-operation between Louisa and Lucy is clear from the occasional recipes copied by Louisa herself into Lucy's books.

Several non-alcoholic fruit and cereal drinks recorded by Lucy in her mottled-cover book are a reminder that the Yorke family had become largely teetotal. They were also now largely vegetarian, and an entry in 1917 in Louisa's account book reads: 'Vegetarian suet, 10s. 6d. (this was returned)'.

As might be expected, the wartime entries in Louisa's account book show a decline in Erddig's living standards: 'tinned salmon, 2s.3d., condensed milk, 1s.3d., margarine, 1s.0d.', interspersed with canary-seed, dog-biscuits, and wool for socks. Nor did they ever really recover.

The food and recipes in Louisa's and Lucy's cookery books tend to be ordinary and plain: 'rabbit mould', 'sham potatoes', 'how to bottle peas', and 'Mrs Crump's sponge-cake' are typical examples. One of the more exotic is 'nun's puffs' – unadorned profiteroles – supplying an inexpensive sweet. A menu for a special dinner about 1920, 'Sago soup, 6d., Lobster cutlets, 1s.0d., Compote pigeons, 2s.6d., Pineapple pudding, 10d., Sardine rolls, 6d.' showed more imagination, but was hardly extravagant. Louisa's tastes were not sophisticated: the salads she thought noteworthy were tomatoes, cucumber, and spring onion; and mustard and cress, beetroots, cold sliced potatoes, and hard-boiled eggs.

Lucy married the groom, Ernest Jones, and they both left Erddig. But she returned again to help out as housekeeper during and after the Second World War, and household accounts for 1946–51 (D/E/2714) in her handwriting again record dull and restricted food: rations, sausages, carrots, tinned peas, tinned meatloaf. Black pudding was still a favourite, as it had been at Erddig in the eighteenth century, but it probably fed Lucy and John Jones, former coachman, then acting as gardener and odd-job man, since the Yorkes continued to be vegetarian.

In 1910 Albinia Cust wrote: 'At Erthig Hall in the twentieth, the nineteenth century still reigns supreme.' Even after 1922, when Simon IV, Louisa and Philip II's elder son, succeeded his father as owner of Erddig, this judgement was not inaccurate. Louisa lived on until 1951. But Simon became increasingly reclusive, despite a short period in the Army during the Second World War. He failed to repair or modernize the house, and seems to have had little personal interest in food, or the exchange of hospitality. But he continued to buy further pieces of land on the edges of the estate.

His brother, Philip III, who acquired Erddig on Simon's death in 1966, was more sociable. But because of his vegetarianism and the neglected or damaged state of many rooms at Erddig Hall, Philip's hospitality usually took the form of a tea of bread and butter, jam, and cakes, shared with his visitors in the servants' hall.

While Philip dragged on his negotiations with the National Trust through more than six years, land prices were rising. And it was the sale of building land on the Wrexham side of the estate, together with compensation from the Coal Board (a fault had been reached in the coal seam under the Hall, and mining operations there had ceased) that allowed the Trust to take on the costly task of restoring Erddig Hall and its furniture. On the evening Philip signed the deed of gift, the solicitors and Trust representatives took him out to celebrate with the best teetotal vegetarian meal the local Chinese restaurant could produce.

Recipes
by Jennifer Stead

Hippocras 17th century

In the late Middle Ages, Hippocras, a sweet spiced wine, was served with great ceremony, along with spices and comfits, as a pleasing digestif at the end of a grand feast. This custom developed into the elaborate Tudor and Stuart banquet, served separately from the meal, often in a specially built room or banqueting-house on the roof or in the garden.

On 17 March 1685, Josua Edisbury of Erthig drew up a contract with Philip Rogers, who was to undertake the carpentry work for two banqueting-houses 'att [each] end of ye long walk att Erthigg'; this arrangement of twin banqueting-houses was quite common. Thomas Badeslade's aerial view of 1739 shows them still *in situ*, but they disappeared some time after this.

Hippocras can still be enjoyed today as an unusual cordial at the end of a meal. The Erddig recipe called for $\frac{1}{2}$ lb sugar to a pint of wine, but other contemporary recipes use only 1 oz to a pint, so the sweetening was very much a matter of taste.

Makes 6 glasses

$1\frac{3}{4}$ pints (1 litre) white or red wine
2–4 oz (50–100 g) caster sugar
2 level tablespoons ground ginger

2 teaspoons ground nutmeg
$\frac{1}{2}$ teaspoon ground cloves

Stir all the ingredients together until the sugar is dissolved, and leave in a non-metal jug, covered, in a cool place to infuse for 24 hours. Then strain through coffee filter paper, and re-bottle.

Sauce for Green Goose 17th century

'Tacke the iuyce of sorill and sugear Mixed togeather with a feue scalded guesberys' – this produces a bright green sauce with a bright green taste. Field sorrel (*Rumex acetosa*) or wood sorrel (*Oxalis acetosella*) may be used. This sharp sweet-sour sauce was eaten as a welcome relish (rich in Vitamin C) in early summer with young goose or veal: a green goose means a young one. The only comparable green sauce surviving today is mint sauce, which accompanies lamb. This sorrel and gooseberry sauce is also good with fish, especially oily fish such as mackerel

Serves 4

2 oz (50 g) sorrel
1 oz (25 g) caster sugar
4 oz (100 g) tart young gooseberries (optional)

Wash the sorrel, and pat dry in kitchen paper, then mince it finely (a Mouli Parsmint does the job very well); each 1 oz (25g) of leaves should produce 1 tablespoon of juicy pulp. Mix in the caster sugar. You may use the sauce at this stage, if you wish. If adding gooseberries, cook them till just soft in the minimum of water, cool and add.

Pickled Broom Buds 17th century

Broom buds were used as a native substitute for expensive capers from the Mediterranean. Both broom buds and nasturtium seeds possess the essential goaty flavour of the capric acid in capers. Pickled from late April to May, 'which afterwards being washed or boiled,' wrote Gerard in his *Herball* (1597), they 'are used for sallads as capers be and be eaten with no less delight.' (Salad here means a relish.) They featured at the coronation feast of King James II.

> 1 pint (600 ml) white wine or cider vinegar
> 1 heaped teaspoon salt
> broom buds (immature flower buds picked on a
>   dry day), enough to fill a 1½-pint (900-ml)
>   glass preserving jar

Boil the vinegar with the salt, and allow to go cold. Pack the buds into a 1½-pint (900-ml) glass preserving jar (or several smaller jars), pour the cold vinegar over, and screw on the lid tightly.

Nasturtium flower-buds and pods may be pickled the same way.

Orange Custard 18th century

The sharp flavour and cool smooth texture of this dessert is just right after a rich main course. Substitute lemons when Seville oranges are not in season.

Serves 4

> 3 whole eggs
> 2 egg yolks
> juice of 4 Seville oranges (or lemons), plus 1
>   teaspoon finely grated rind (optional)
> 3 oz (75 g) sugar
> 8 fl oz (250 ml) boiling water
> 1 tablespoon orange flowerwater (or rum or
>   brandy)

Beat the eggs well, then put them with the orange juice, and finely grated rind if using, and the sugar in a pan, and add the boiling water. Stir patiently over a very low heat until the custard thickens, but do not boil or the custard will scramble.

Add the orange flowerwater and stir until the custard cools. Pour into a 1-pint (600-ml) dish or into four individual glasses. Serve chilled.

Orange Shrub 18th century

Shrubs became popular in the early eighteenth century. This is similar to lemon brandy (see recipe used at Glamis on page 74), but without the water, and makes a good after-dinner drink. The Seville orange season was longer in the eighteenth century than it is today, but shrub can also be based on lemons. The Vitamin C, preserved by the rum, could have helped to stave off scurvy in winter – 10 mg daily are enough – when few fresh fruits or vegetables were eaten.

Use either oranges or lemons, but do not mix the two.

Makes 1 pint (600 ml)

> 1 large or 2 small Seville oranges (or lemons)
> 2 or 3 sugar lumps

4 oz (100 g) caster sugar
16 fl oz (500 ml) rum

Wash and dry the fruit. Rub the sugar lumps over the skin to absorb the oil, then peel the oranges very thinly. Squeeze out the fruit; there should be about 2½ fl oz (75 ml) of juice.

Add the sugar lumps, the juice, the peel (if using lemons don't add the peel) and the caster sugar to the rum in a clean well-stoppered glass jar, and leave for 24 hours. Strain through a coffee filter, and bottle.

Sweet Puddings 18th century

This is a typical eighteenth-century dessert: the mixture is similar to Prince Albert Pudding (see page 78), but it is baked in cocotte dishes rather than steamed whole. The little puddings look pretty turned out on a handsome platter.

Makes 8 (2 per serving)

1½ oz (40 g) candied orange peel, finely sliced
2 oz (50 g) fresh white breadcrumbs
1 oz (25 g) ground almonds
2 oz (50 g) sugar
juice and finely grated peel of ½ lemon
4 oz (100 g) soft butter
11 fl oz (340 ml) boiling milk
3 whole eggs
2 egg yolks

Sauce

¼ pint (150 ml) sweet white wine
2 oz (50 g) unsalted butter
1 oz (25 g) sugar, or more to taste

Pre-heat the oven to 180°C (350°F, Mark 4). Grease

8 cocotte dishes (or other individual-portion ovenproof dishes) and place two or three slices of the candied peel in the bottom of each. Place the breadcrumbs, ground almonds, sugar, lemon juice and rind, and butter in a bowl, pour on the boiling milk, and mix very well. Beat the whole eggs and yolks well together, and add to the mixture.

Place the cocotte dishes on a baking tray, and divide the mixture equally between them. Bake in the middle of the pre-heated oven for 40 to 45 minutes or till golden. If turning out, allow them to stand in a warm place for 10 minutes, then carefully loosen the edges and turn out onto a hot platter. Serve with the sauce, made by gently heating all the ingredients together until well incorporated. Any leftovers are good eaten cold.

Cambridge or Milk Punch 18th century

This makes a welcoming drink for winter guests, or a comforting nightcap. It is attributed to a Mrs Beckwith, and if you followed the original recipe would be exceedingly sweet; I have reduced the sugar.

Makes 4 glasses

1½-2 oz (40–50 g) caster sugar
1 piece of cinnamon stick or ¼ teaspoon ground cinnamon
16 fl oz (500 ml) milk, plus 1 tablespoonful
1 egg
1 wine glass of mixed brandy and rum

Put the sugar, cinnamon, and 16 fl oz (500 ml) milk in a pan, and heat very gently until boiling. Simmer for 1 to 2 minutes stirring, then remove the cinnamon stick. Beat the egg with the tablespoon of milk, pour the warm milk over this, and stir to mix well. Return the mixture to the pan, and heat very gently without boiling, stirring all the time, until it thickens very slightly (it should appear slightly opaque on the back of a wooden spoon). If it is in danger of curdling, dunk the pan in a bowl of cold water (have this ready, just in case). Pour in the rum and brandy, and stir well. Drink warm or cold.

Rice Apples 18th century

These are baked apples, stuffed with a ground rice and almond filling. Beef-red 'beefins' (biffins), a Norfolk speciality, are stipulated in the recipe. The apples were to be hollowed rather than merely cored, but for simplicity core them only. I have invented marzipan plugs for the bottoms, as the filling tends to run out.

Serves 6

12 fl oz (375 ml) milk
2 oz (50 g) ground rice
2 oz (50 g) butter
1 oz (25 g) ground almonds
1 tablespoon orange flowerwater
1 oz (25 g) sugar (or to taste)
2 eggs, beaten
marzipan for plugging
6–10 good flavoured apples (Cox's orange pippins work well)

Pour the milk into a thick-bottomed pan, and when it is getting hot, gradually sprinkle the ground rice into it, stirring continuously, and cook, stirring all the time, until the mixture thickens. Turn down the heat, and continue stirring for about 5 minutes longer, making sure it doesn't burn. Remove from

the heat, and add the butter, almonds, orange flowerwater, and sugar, then last of all the eggs. Stir well, and set aside.

Pre-heat the oven to 180°C (350°F, Mark 4). Core the apples, and plug the bottom of each with a little marzipan. Then score the skin around the middles to prevent bursting. Arrange the apples in a buttered dish which just fits them so they support each other, and pour any unused filling around them. Bake in the pre-heated oven for 30 minutes to an hour, or until cooked but not mushy. 'When sent to Table prick what Sweetmeats you please on the Top' – pieces of angelica look pretty.

Tops and Bottoms 18th century

The manuscript cookery book of 1765 marked 'K.S'. has two recipes for tops and bottoms, which says something about their popularity. They are rusks, a speciality of Norfolk and Suffolk, which were particularly enjoyed at breakfast.

Makes 16

1 lb (450 g) plain flour
1½ teaspoons easy-blend yeast
3 oz (75 g) salted butter
2 small eggs, lightly beaten
7 fl oz (200 ml) warm creamy milk

Sift the flour and yeast, and rub in the butter roughly. Add the eggs to the warm milk (the mixture should be tepid), and mix into the flour and yeast to make a nice slack dough. Knead this lightly for a moment, then place in a warm floured bowl, cover with cling film, and leave in a warm place until doubled in size (1 to 2 hours).

Pre-heat the oven to 220°C (425°F, Mark 7). Divide

the dough into 16 2-oz (60-g) pieces, and gently form these into balls. Arrange on buttered baking sheets, and bake in the top half of the pre-heated oven for 10 minutes. Take them out, and with a sharp knife cut carefully in half round the middles, returning them cut sides up to the oven, now set at 150°C (300°F, Mark 2) for a further 10 minutes. At this stage, they can be eaten hot straight from the oven, and are quite delicious plain, but are especially good with thick cream and jam, rather like superior scones.

They can also be dried to make rusks. Leave in the oven, turned down to 135°C (275°F, Mark 1), and continue to cook for a further 45 minutes. Store in tins.

Yeast Puddings 18th century

The recipe for these little puddings, found in the manuscript cookery book of 1765, marked 'K.S.', is attributed to a Mrs Stoughton of Wymondham. Three puddings make one average serving.

Serves 4

4 oz (100 g) plain flour
1 teaspoon easy-blend yeast
a grating of nutmeg
finely grated zest of 1 lemon
2 oz (50 g) sugar
4 eggs, well beaten
8 fl oz (250 ml) warm milk

In a bowl mix together the flour, yeast, nutmeg, lemon zest, and sugar, and make a well in the centre. Add the beaten eggs to the warm milk (the mixture should be tepid), and pour into the well. Whisk to form a smooth thin batter, then cover

this with cling film, and leave to stand in a warm place until well risen (1 to 2 hours).

Pre-heat the oven to 200°C (400°F, Mark 6). Butter 12 cocotte dishes, cups, or patty pans well, and heat them in the oven for 1 minute. Stir the batter, and pour it into the containers to fill them three-quarters full (3 fl oz, 90 ml in each). Bake in the top half of the pre-heated oven for 15 minutes. Serve hot, either in the containers or turned out, with the same melted butter, sugar and white wine sauce as served with the sweet puddings (see page 108).

I have also used one buttered $1\frac{1}{2}$-pint (900-ml) dish, and baked the pudding in this for 25 to 30 minutes, adding cooked cherries to the batter.

Liver Sauce for Chicken 18th century

This makes a pleasant sauce; if thickened a little more it make a good filling for 20 small vol-au-vents. The recipe, attributed to a Miss Josscelyn, begins 'Take the liver & Boil it. Braid it up quite fine'; the word 'braid' comfirms this writer's origin as East Anglian – it means to press through a colander or sieve.

Serves 4

8 oz (225 g) chicken livers
8 fl oz (250 ml) water
1 good chicken stock cube
5 fl oz (150 ml) double cream
beurre manié, made by blending together 1 oz
    (25 g) plain flour and
    $\frac{2}{3}$ oz (20 g) butter
(a grating of nutmeg)
1 dessertspoon lemon juice

Cut any greenish parts from the livers. Boil the water and dissolve the stock cube in it. Simmer the livers in the stock very gently for 10 minutes, then take them out, and mince finely or blend.

Replace the liver in the stock, and over the heat add the cream and little bits of beurre manié, stirring vigorously until thick. Strain (optional), and then add the nutmeg. The sauce may be prepared in advance to this point. Stir in the lemon juice just before serving.

Lemon Mince Pies 18th century

Lemon mincemeat makes an interesting change from the usual apple mincemeat. The manuscript says 'you may add at leisure what spice you please'; I have added only nutmeg and cinnamon. Make open tarts in the traditional oblong shape of a manger.

Makes 24

1 medium lemon
3 oz (75 g) currants
2 oz (50 g) raisins
4 oz (100 g) brown sugar
3 oz (75 g) suet, grated
1 oz (25 g) candied peel, chopped
$\frac{1}{2}$ nutmeg, grated
1 teaspoon ground cinnamon
12 oz (325 g) puff pastry

Wash the lemon and boil for 30 minutes, then change the water and boil for another 30 minutes. Cool, then halve it, and using your fingers, scoop out all the flesh into a sieve set over a mixing bowl. Rub the flesh with a wooden spoon through the sieve to remove any pips and tough integuments. Add the sugar, suet, candied peel, nutmeg and cinnamon. In a food processor chop the boiled lemon peel, raisins and currants, and add these to the mixing bowl. Pack into a jar or basin, cover, and keep in a cold place. It is ready to use in 7 to 10 days. This is stiffer than apple mincemeat, and won't run. If you want to moisten it, add brandy.

Pre-heat the oven to 220°C (425°F, Mark 7). Roll out the pastry on a floured board until about $\frac{1}{16}$ inch (1.5 mm) thick, and with a sharp knife cut oblongs 2 x 4 inches (5 x 10 cm). Lay these on an ungreased baking sheet, and put a line of mincemeat down the middle of each (for round tarts use shortcrust or flaky pastry, as puff paste may balloon and throw the filling off). Bake in the pre-heated oven for 10 to 12 minutes. Serve crisp and hot.

Bread Dumplings 18th century

These dumplings, attributed to a Mrs Watts, have a Norfolk origin, but dumplings were certainly made at Erddig. An entry in the housekeeper's accounts on 11 June 1799 reads: 'Nets for dumplins 1s.10d.' The nets were an extra convenience to ease the removal of the dumplings from the cooking pot when done. The dumplings in this recipe can be prepared an hour or so ahead, and cooked at the last minute. The sauce may be made in advance, and reheated just before serving.

Makes 14 to serve 3 to 4

6 oz (150 g) fine white breadcrumbs
4 oz (100 g) suet, finely grated
4 oz (100 g) currants
1 oz (25 g) ground almonds
1 rounded tablespoon sugar
$\frac{1}{2}$ nutmeg, grated
pinch salt

111

2 oz (50 g) chopped candied peel or the finely
grated zest of 2 oranges
2 eggs, size 3

Boil at least 6 pints of water in a very large saucepan
or preserving pan. Mix all the ingredients to a *very*
stiff paste – add more breadcrumbs or ground
almonds if it's not stiff enough. Roll into 14 balls,
drop these into the pan of boiling water, and boil
rapidly for 15 minutes. After five minutes they rise
to the surface and expand. At this stage gently
loosen with a fish slice any that stick to the bottom
of the saucepan.

When they are done, transfer the dumplings with a
slotted spoon to a hot dish and serve at once with
the same butter, sugar and wine sauce as served
with the sweet puddings (see page 108).

Sweet Pretty Cakes 18th century

This recipe comes from a Mrs Grigson. The little
rock cakes are indeed sweet – you may reduce the
sugar and add more butter if you wish. The almonds
should not be chopped too small.

Makes 20

8 oz (225 g) plain flour
8 oz (225 g) caster sugar
$\frac{1}{2}$ teaspoon ground mace
2 oz (50 g) butter
2 oz (50 g) currants
2 oz (50 g) candied peel, chopped
2 oz (50 g) blanched almonds, roughly chopped
2 eggs, size 3, well beaten

Butter two large baking trays. Pre-heat the oven to
200°C (400°F, Mark 6). Sift together the flour,

sugar, and mace, and rub in the butter. Add the
currants, candied peel, and almonds, and mix well.
Add the eggs, and mix well together.

With two forks make rough heaps of the mixture,
10 to each baking tray, and bake in the centre of
the pre-heated oven for 12 minutes or till done.

Sack George's Cakes 18th century

The only raising agent in these cakes is the air you
beat into the eggs; chemical baking powders did
not start to appear until the end of the eighteenth
century. The cakes are delicately scented with
sherry or rosewater. Eat them fresh, crisp, and hot
with China tea.

Makes 24

10 oz (275 g) plain flour
8 oz (225 g) caster sugar
1 teaspoon ground mace
$\frac{1}{2}$ nutmeg, grated
8 oz (225 g) butter
8 oz (225 g) currants
3 eggs
2 tablespoons sherry or rosewater

Pre-heat the oven to 190°C (375°F, Mark 5). Have
ready two trays of 12 bun tins lined with paper
cases. Sift the flour, sugar, mace, and nutmeg
together. Rub in the butter, and add the currants.
Beat the eggs well till very light and frothy, then
beat in the sherry or rosewater. Mix with the dry
ingredients. Spoon the mixture into the paper cases
in the bun tins, and bake in the pre-heated oven
for 25 to 30 minutes.

Ramekins 18th century

The word ramekin we now take to mean a little
china dish, similar to a cocotte. But originally
ramekin meant toasted bread, or toast covered with
a cheese mixture and baked, or a cheese mixture
baked in little paper cases, or in a special mould.
The French version – ramequin – of this Flemish
word appeared in England in the late seventeenth
century to describe a dish that could include,
besides cheese, anchovies, wine, eggs, mustard, etc.,
and was just a more fashionable elaborate baked
version of the native toasted cheese called 'rabbit'.
In England the cheese called for was usually
Cheshire, being high in fat and a good melting
cheese. Ramekins were very popular – the K.S.
1765 manuscript cookery book (D/E/2251(a))
contains several versions. This one, from a Lady
Martin, is simple, creamy, and mild; it makes a
good lunch dish.

Serves 2 to 4

4 oz (100 g) Cheshire cheese, grated
2 oz (50 g) butter
2 eggs, beaten
3–4 slices of good white bread, toasted
milk for dipping

Pre-heat the oven to 190°C (375°F, Mark 5). Mash
the cheese, butter, and eggs together with a fork.
Take the slices of toasted bread, dip them in the
milk, and lay them on the bottom of three or four
small ovenproof dishes. Spoon the cheese mixture
over the toast, leaving some toast uncovered around
the edge. Bake in the middle of the pre-heated oven
for 15 minutes. Serve while still warm and the
toast edges crisp, with a green salad.

This recipe also works well, when baked in one
large (2-pint, 1.2 litre) pyrex dish. Bake in the pre-
heated oven for 25 minutes.

Pea Soup 18th century

This is a hearty winter soup. Use newly-bought
green split peas with the specification: no need to
soak. Do not use peas you have had for some time,
as old peas will not soften.

Serves 4

8 oz (225 g) green split peas
1¾ pints (1 litre) water
3 or 4 sticks of celery
1 medium onion
white part of 1 leek
4 anchovy fillets, chopped
2 teaspoons soy sauce
2 teaspoons mushroom ketchup
parsley, finely chopped, to garnish

Pick over and wash the peas, put them into a pan
with the water, and bring to a boil, then skim.
Simmer, covered, for 20 minutes. Clean or peel,
then chop the vegetables very small, add to the
pan, and cook for a further 40 to 60 minutes or
until tender. It is important not to add any salty
seasoning up to this point, as salt hinders the
softening of the peas.

Put the soup through a food mill or blender, if you
wish, then return it to the pan, and add the
anchovies, soy sauce, and mushroom ketchup. If it
is too thick, add some water or single cream.
Adjust the seasoning, and serve with a sprinkling
of fresh chopped parsley.

Oyster loaves 18th century

These make a pretty side dish for a first course at dinner. The recipe, from the manuscript cookery book marked 'K.S.' of 1765, is attributed to a Mrs Hazel.

Serves 4

> 4 soft white bread rolls, weighing about 2 oz (50 g) each
> 4 oz (100 g) butter, melted
> 12 small oysters
> 1 tablespoon thick cream

Preheat the oven to 220°C (425°F, Mark 7). Scoop a large hole in the top of each roll (to fit 3 small oysters plus sauce). Crumble the bread that has been removed to form crumbs, and set these on one side. Brush the rolls with half the melted butter. Toast them in the oven until lightly golden. Sauté the oysters gently in the remaining butter until the edges curl, and add the reserved crumbs; this takes 2 minutes. Stir in the cream, fill the rolls with this mixture, and serve at once.

Welsh Light Cakes Traditional

Light cakes made with buttermilk are little pancakes or drop scones, that were served to visitors for afternoon tea in many butter-making districts of Wales. In the Erddig housekeeper's account book of the early years of the nineteenth century, appearing in the weekly lists of expenditure, for example 'washing 1s.6d., soles 9s., turkey 9s., eggs 3s. 6d., 3 lemons 6d., barm 1s. 6d., charity 1s.', are regular entries for 'muffings' at 1d. each and 'lite cakes' at ½d. each, bought only 12 or 6 at a time, but sometimes only 2. These were probably purchased by the servants when they went on errands to Wrexham.

The following is based on a traditional Welsh recipe (there is no recipe in the Erddig books). The buttermilk makes these little pancakes especially light, and gives a subtle flavour. Baking soda began to be used in Britain in the early nineteenth century.

Makes 16

> 4 oz (100 g) plain flour
> 1–2 oz (25–50 g) sugar (optional — they are much nicer without)
> 1 large egg
> ¼ teaspoon baking soda
> 3 fl oz (90 ml) buttermilk or plain yoghurt

Have ready an iron griddle or bakestone heated and greased with butter. Sift the flour, and add the sugar (if using). Beat the egg till very light and frothy. Dissolve the baking soda in the buttermilk or yoghurt; it will foam. Make a well in the dry ingredients, and pour in the egg, and the buttermilk or yoghurt and baking soda mixture. Stir at the edge of the liquid, so that the flour is gradually incorporated from the sides, to form a smooth thick batter.

Drop the batter by the dessertspoonful onto the griddle, to make little pancakes about 3 inches (7.5 cm) in diameter. When bubbles on the tops begin to burst, and the pancakes are lightly brown underneath, turn and finish cooking (about 3 minutes on each side). Your griddle should not be too hot. The pancakes will have crisp edges, and a lovely light texture. Eat as soon as possible with chilled butter. They are also good with cream cheese.

George the 4th Pudding 19th century

This is a very rich and irresistible cold pudding. The recipe is from Victoria Cust's manuscript cookery book, begun in 1839. It needs no accompaniment, even though Victoria has written 'pour sauce over it to fancy'. She begins 'Take a pint of thick cream'. This was the old wine pint of 16 fl oz, which was changed to the imperial 20 fl oz pint in 1878.

Serves 6

16 fl oz (500 ml) thick double cream
peeled or grated zest of 1 lemon
1 oz (25 g) sugar
1 piece blade mace or $\frac{1}{4}$ teaspoon ground mace
6 egg yolks, mixed with a fork

In a thick-bottomed pan very gently heat the cream, lemon zest, sugar, and mace, and simmer on the lowest possible heat for about 30 minutes, stirring frequently to make sure it does not burn. Cool it until it is just warm, then sieve, taking out the mace, and forcing the lemon zest through the sieve. (Don't worry if it will not go through, discard it, the flavour will be in the cream.) Mix in the egg yolks, and pour into an oiled 1-pint (600-ml) earthenware mould or pudding basin, tie aluminium foil over the top, and place in a deep pan of boiling water, the water coming half-way up the mould or basin. Cover the pan, and simmer very gently for 45 minutes.

Allow the pan to cool to a safe temperature before lifting out the pudding. Test the centre of the pudding with a skewer – it should be softish in the middle, but not sloppy. If it is insufficiently cooked, return to the pan, and simmer until cooked. Before it goes completely cold, turn out of the mould or basin onto the serving dish, and chill for several hours before serving.

Cheese Balls 19th century

These are intensely cheesey. Serve them hot or cold as canapés. If a less intense flavour is required, substitute breadcrumbs for some of the Parmesan.

Makes 20

1 egg, size 2
$2\frac{1}{2}$ oz (60 g) unsalted butter, melted
5 oz (125 g) Parmesan cheese, grated
4 heaped tablespoons fresh white breadcrumbs
lard for deep-frying

Batter

1 egg
1 tablespoon milk
1 well-rounded tablespoon plain flour

Beat the egg, add the butter, the Parmesan, and 1 heaped tablespoon of the breadcrumbs, and mix it well. With two teaspoons, make 1-inch (2.5-cm) balls from the mixture, and refrigerate them for at least 30 minutes.

To make the batter, whisk the egg with the milk and flour until smooth. When ready to cook the balls, dip them in the batter, then in the remaining breadcrumbs (they can be prepared ahead up to this point), and fry in deep lard for 1 minute, or till golden and cooked through. Drain them on kitchen paper. Eat hot or cold.

Yorkshire Parkin 19th century

It is delightful to find this recipe in Victoria Cust's manuscript cookery book dated 1839. It is an example of a regional recipe migrating, as so many did in the late eighteenth and early nineteenth century, when the educated classes increasingly took a cultural interest in regional foods, so one should not really be surprised that this vulgar cake turns up in a gentry house. Oatmeal parkin, under other names and in various forms – biscuit, griddle-cake or oven-cake – at first sweetened with honey, then from the late seventeenth century with treacle, had for centuries been the poor man's gingerbread in northern England and parts of Scotland. This luscious soft type of parkin spread from Yorkshire. Victoria's is the earliest documented 'primitive' parkin recipe (before it became sophisticated with baking powder or soda, eggs, and flour) that I've seen. When this recipe was written down, treacle was sweeter and less pungent than our black treacle, so I've tempered the latter with golden syrup, and I've increased the butter slightly. I've also reduced Victoria's massive quantities. Victoria's is a rubbed-in mixture, but the following is also authentic.

Makes a 7-inch (18-cm) cake

4 oz (100 g) butter
4 oz (100 g) black treacle
8 oz (225 g) golden syrup
12 oz (325 g) medium oatmeal
1 rounded teaspoon ground ginger

Pre-heat the oven to 150°C (300°F, Mark 2). Warm the butter, treacle, and syrup till only just melted. Mix in the dry ingredients. Butter a 7-inch (18-cm) diameter cake tin or ovenproof dish, and pour the mixture in. Bake it in the middle of the pre-heated oven for 1 hour. It's best if taken out of the oven when still moving a little in the centre, but dry to the touch.

This parkin is crunchy at the edges and gooey in the middle. It is lovely if eaten hot (beware burning the mouth) with buttered apples, or (and this is unorthodox) with thick yogurt mixed with sliced stem ginger and grated orange zest. If you can leave it unmolested in its dish open to the air for a week, you'll find it has softened to a delicious sticky mass.

Biscuits (Grandmama) 19th century

These plain biscuits are nice eaten fresh from the oven with butter or cream cheese, and an intensely flavoured jam, such as damson. Or eat them cold with cheese.

Makes 48

8 oz (225 g) plain flour
pinch of salt
8 oz (225 g) thick double cream
$\frac{1}{2}$ egg, beaten

Pre-heat the oven to 190°C (375°F, Mark 5). Butter two baking trays. Sift the flour and salt together, and make a well in the centre. Mix the cream and egg, pour into the well, and stir with a fork until the ingredients are smoothly incorporated. Chill the dough for 30 minutes.

Roll out the dough until about $\frac{1}{16}$ inch (1.5mm) thick, cut into rounds $2\frac{1}{2}$ inches (6 cm) in diameter, or into squares, and use a palette knife to lift them onto the prepared baking trays. Bake in the top half of the pre-heated oven for about 10 to 12 minutes, or until puffy and lightly golden. Do not allow the biscuits to brown or the flavour will be spoilt.

Bun Loaf 19th century

Bun loaf is usually classified as a plain cake. However, this version from Victoria Cust's manuscript cookery book of 1839, having more butter and sugar than the usual recipe, is moist and rich enough to have appeared on her elegant tea table. It was often eaten generously buttered.

Makes two 2 1b (900 g) loaves or an 8-inch (20-cm) cake

1 lb (450 g) plain flour
8 oz (225 g) butter
8 oz (225 g) light muscovado sugar
8 oz (225 g) currants
3 oz (75 g) candied peel, chopped
2 level teaspoons carraway seeds
1 teaspoon baking soda
½ pint (300 ml) milk
2 eggs, beaten

Pre-heat the oven to 200°C (400°F, Mark 6). Have ready two 2 lb (900 g) loaf tins or one 8-inch (20-cm) diameter cake tin, buttered and the bottoms lined with buttered paper. In a large bowl sift the flour, and rub in the butter. Add the sugar, pressing out lumps, then the currants, candied peel, and carraway seeds, and toss to mix. Make a well in the centre.

Dissolve the baking soda in the milk, and pour it into the well in the centre of the dry ingredients, then pour the eggs in, and toss the dry ingredients from the perimeter to the centre to mix, keeping everything as light as possible. Put the mixture into the prepared tin(s), level the top lightly, then turn the oven down to 170°C (325°F, Mark 3), and bake for about 1½ hours for the loaves or 2 hours for

the round cake, until a skewer inserted in the centre comes out clean.

To make individual buns or rock cakes, use a little less milk and heap the mixture in small mounds with two forks on a buttered baking sheet, and bake at 200°C (400°F, Mark 6) for 20 minutes.

Lady Abbesses 19th century

These 'biscuits' remain white. In the recipe Victoria Cust copied into her manuscript cookery book of 1839 she adds, 'put a little jam on each and some good Whipt Cream.' But jam would be gilding the lily, since they are already very sweet. They go well with soft fruits that need no sugar – raspberries, mulberries, blackberries, wild strawberries. But they are also lovely just served plain with coffee.

Makes 9

1½ oz (40 g) ground almonds
3 oz (75 g) icing sugar
¾ oz (20 g) softened butter

Pre-heat the oven to 120°C (250°F, Mark ½). Butter nine individual-sized tart tins. Whizz the ground almonds in an electric coffee grinder for a few seconds until they make an oily paste, or use a pestle and mortar, or mash in a warmed bowl with the end of a rolling pin. Put all the ingredients into a bowl, and blend together to form a dryish paste.

Press the paste firmly into the tart tins with the back of a dessertspoon, keeping the edges neat. Bake in the centre of the pre-heated oven for 45 minutes. Leave to cool, then carefully turn out. They keep well in a tin.

Stokos Early 20th century

This recipe appears in Lucy Hitchman's manuscript cookery book, which includes her 'War Time Recipes' from 1914–17, all simple and economical for a time of rationing. Stokos is a cheap (and healthy) alternative to lemonade, since some of the body is provided by cereal rather than sugar. It was a traditional harvest drink in Cheshire, and is similar to lemon barley water in its effectiveness (now medically proved) in replacing lost body fluids during illness, and of course in sweaty occupations such as harvesting. It makes an extremely pleasant and refreshing drink. 'If preferred lime juice may be used instead of lemon.'

Makes 4 pints (2.2 litres)

2 oz (50 g) fine oatmeal or oatflour
2 oz (50 g) sugar
$\frac{1}{2}$ lemon, sliced finely
$\frac{1}{4}$ teaspoon ground ginger
$\frac{1}{2}$ pint (300 ml) boiling water
$3\frac{1}{2}$ pints (2 litres) cold water

If you are using oatmeal, grind it into flour in an electric coffee grinder. In a saucepan mix the oatflour, sugar, lemon slices, ginger, and boiling water, stirring briskly to eliminate lumps, and let it stand for 10 minutes.

Transfer to a vessel (not metal) that will hold 5 pints (3 litres), then gradually add $3\frac{1}{2}$ pints (2 litres) of cold water. It is now ready for use. There's no need to strain it.

Stokos should be drunk fresh and certainly within 24 hours if not refrigerating.

Frangipan Early 20th century

Frangipan in the seventeenth century meant the perfume of red jasmine, but by the nineteenth century also meant a confection that included almonds. This Erddig recipe, written by Mrs Louisa Yorke during the First World War, has no almonds at all, but it is still a very nice pudding indeed, and was obviously a favourite since she had several versions of it. She has written 'Mrs Rogers' (her housekeeper from 1907 to 1914) next to it.

Serves 4

2 tablespoons apricot jam
peel of 1 lemon
12 fl oz (375 ml) creamy milk
2 oz (50 g) plain flour
1 oz (25 g) butter
3 eggs, separated

Pre-heat the oven to 180°C (350°F, Mark 4). Have ready a $2\frac{1}{2}$-pint (1.5-litre) ovenproof dish, well buttered. Spread the jam in the base. Simmer the lemon peel very gently in the milk, uncovered, for 30 minutes, squashing it occasionally with a wooden spoon, then allow to cool. Discard the peel, and measure the milk. Make it up to $\frac{1}{2}$ pint (300 ml) in a saucepan, add the flour and butter, and whisk continuously over a medium heat. It will soon begin to thicken – immediately lift the pan off the heat, and whisk vigorously. When the mixture is smooth, return the pan to a gentle heat, and cook, stirring continuously with a wooden spoon, for a few minutes more. Off the heat, stir in the egg yolks. Whisk the egg whites until stiff, add a good tablespoon to the mixture in the pan to lighten it, then carefully fold in the rest with a metal spoon.

Pour the mixture into the prepared dish, and bake just above the middle of the pre-heated oven for 45 minutes. It will rise like a soufflé. When removed from the oven it will sink in a few minutes, so serve at once. It needs no accompaniment, but hedonists may like to eat it with thin cream poured over.

Plum Cake Erdhig 1890 Late 19th century

Among her 'War Time Recipes', all very plain indeed, Lucy Hitchman has written out an earlier Erddig recipe for rich plum cake, probably to make as a special treat.

Makes an 8-inch (20-cm) round or a 7-inch (18-cm) square cake

6 oz (150 g) butter
6 oz (150 g) muscovado sugar
2 oz (50 g) black treacle
3 eggs
a little warm milk
8 oz (225 g) currants
8 oz (225 g) sultanas
4 oz (100 g) candied peel chopped
8 oz (225 g) plain flour
1 teaspoon mixed spice
1 teaspoon ground nutmeg
$\frac{1}{2}$ teaspoon ground cinnamon

Grease and line with greased paper a deep 8-inch (20-cm) round or 7-inch (18-cm) square cake tin. Pre-heat the oven to 220°C (425°F, Mark 7). Beat the butter until soft, add the sugar and treacle, and beat well until light and creamy. Add the eggs one by one, beating the mixture well between each, then add the milk, dried fruit, and lastly, fold in

the flour and spices. Use only enough milk to make a soft dropping consistency.

Spoon the mixture into the prepared cake tin and level the surface. Tie folded brown paper around the tin with string and place it in the middle of the pre-heated oven or just below the middle. Immediately turn the oven down to 150°C (300°F, Mark 2), and bake for $2\frac{1}{2}$ hours, or until a skewer inserted in the centre comes out clean. Leave in the tin for 20 minutes to rest, then turn out onto a rack to cool.

A nice addition is to drizzle 2 tablespoons of brandy over the cake while it is still warm. If kept in an airtight tin, 'it will keep and improve for 3–6 months'.

Chester Pudding Early 20th century

Some versions of Chester pudding are flavoured with lemon and have the whipped egg whites piled on top in a meringue. Louisa Yorke's version of this local speciality is a simple one.

Serves 4

5 oz (125 g) pastry, made with 3 oz (75 g)
    flour and $1\frac{1}{2}$ oz (40 g) fat
2 oz (50 g) butter
2 oz (50 g) caster sugar
1 oz (25 g) ground almonds
2 eggs, beaten
1 tablespoon jam

Pre-heat the oven to 200°C (400°F, Mark 6). Grease a 7-inch (18-cm) pie dish. Roll out the pastry on a floured board, and line the pie dish with it. Melt the butter and sugar in a saucepan, add the almonds, then stir in the beaten eggs. Stir the mixture over a gentle heat until it thickens. Spread the jam over the pastry in the pie dish, and pour the mixture over it. Bake for 30 minutes in the pre-heated oven.

Lucy Hitchman's version ('ground rice cheese') is also enjoyable – just substitute 2 oz (50 g) ground rice for the almonds, omit one egg, and flavour it with lemon juice. Either version can be served warm or cold.

Barley Scones Early 20th century

Barley was a staple grain in Wales, and was grown on the estate at Erddig. Barley bannocks, mixed only with milk or water, and cooked on the bakestone or griddle in Wales, Scotland, and northern England, remained until the end of the eighteenth century the staple bread in some parts. Louisa Yorke wrote down this recipe about 1920. The scones are quick to make, are delicious eaten fresh and hot with cold butter and home-made raspberry jam, but equally good cold – the texture is rather damp and cake-like. Barley scones have a distinctive earthy flavour, which goes well with mature English cheese, such as Cheshire, Cheddar, Lancashire, and Wensleydale.

> *Makes 8 small or 1 large one*
>
> *8 oz (225 g) barley flour*
> *3 oz (75 g) white flour*
> *$1\frac{1}{2}$ teaspoons baking powder*
> *a pinch of salt*
> *1 oz (25 g) butter or lard (butter tastes best)*
> *scant $\frac{1}{2}$ pint (300 ml) milk*

Pre-heat the oven to 230°C (450°F, Mark 8). Grease a large baking sheet. Sift the flours, baking powder, and salt together, and rub in the butter or lard.

Make a well in the centre, and pour the milk in, then stir round the edge of the milk, lightly incorporating the flour mixture. Turn onto a floured board, work lightly into a ball, then pat out to form a round about $\frac{3}{4}$ inch (2 cm) thick. Alternatively, break the dough into eight equal pieces, and lightly pat each of these into a small round of the same thickness. Handle the dough as little as possible.

Place the round(s) on the greased baking sheet, and bake in the top half of the pre-heated oven for 10 minutes for the small scones, or 15 to 20 minutes for the large scone. The scones will be pale, slightly crisp outside and tender within.

IRELAND

Birr Castle, Co. Offaly
Alison Rosse

Birr Castle, Co. Offaly

There has been a castle at Birr for at least 700 years. The Norman invaders, who came at the end of the twelfth century, built the first wooden castle on a mound above the river. But we can go much further back than that in the history of Birr. Seven centuries before the arrival of the Normans, St Patrick walked up the river to Brosna. He would have passed the site of the monastery soon to be founded at Birr by St Brendan, one of the great scholar-abbots of early Christian Ireland, and patron saint of Birr, who died in 571 at the remarkable age of 180!

But for an understanding of the roots of Irish eating habits, we need to go back still further, back beyond the fourth century BC, when the Celtic-speaking peoples were becoming established, to their predecessors, the pastoral nomads of the Bronze Age.

The Bronze Age tribes who herded their cattle along the Shannon basin, some of the best pasture in Europe, were still only half settled, warring with each other, raiding each other's herds and fighting over bulls, as is told in legend. Cattle were their wealth and prestige, second only in importance to their wives and children. Cattle provided them with meat, skins, milk, curds, cheese, and butter – so much butter that they preserved it for future use, as did their descendants, by burying it in the bogs

in reed baskets. Great lumps of it, stored and forgotten, are still dug up to this day, round and hard and more than 1,000 years old, imprinted with the pattern of the basket – and smelling distinctly rancid. Even today Ireland consumes more butter than any other member of the EEC.

The food eaten in the Dark Ages, and later by Ireland's chieftains, saints, and scholars is surprisingly well documented in early poetry, in historical annals, and in lives of the saints dating back to the seventh century. One food that was particularly appreciated was watercress. In ancient poetry, the mad King Sweeny, who had been turned into a bird – or at least in his madness thought he had – and flew around the country perching in trees, complaining of his sad fate, spent much of his time searching for watercress. As is well-known now, watercress is full of Vitamin C and iron, and in the days before many people were settled enough to have gardens, watercress was an important green vegetable. Its Irish name, *biolar*, derives from the same watery root as the word Birr, and today, great clumps of cress still grow vigorously at the well near the site of the old monastery at Birr, as they would have done in St Brendan's time. Sometimes, too, we still serve it at the Castle as a vegetable, lightly cooked in butter like spinach.

In early medieval times when the O'Briens were

High Kings of Ireland, their seat was at Kincora, near Killaloe, thirty miles to the west. Among the so-called 'tributes' to which they were entitled were various special foods at certain times of the year. One of these was 'the cresses of the Brosna'. The chieftains of the territory around Birr, the O'Carrolls, would have been responsible for bringing the cress from the river near Birr to the King for his feasts. Other delicacies from the territories of other chieftains included 'the venison of Naas and the fish of the Boyne'.

The O'Carrolls, chiefs of Ely O'Carroll, were a powerful and warlike clan whose territory at the time of their greatest expansion spread north to the bogs, west to the Shannon, and south into Tipperary. Their hold on this territory was only partly shaken by the Norman invasion. Their main refuge in such times of trouble were the Slieve Bloom mountains close to Birr, which had been part of their principality since the fifth century. Finn McCoul himself, the mighty legendary Irish hero, was said to have been secretly brought up in these mountains; and other legends tell of these heroes and chieftains of ancient Ireland hunting there with their wolf-hounds. From the same source we know that they ate well: large quantities of pork, many different sorts of sausages, mutton, some beef, and salmon and trout from the rivers. From their hunting expeditions, the O'Carrolls would have supplemented their diet with venison and wild boar.

These early huntsmen had a special way of cooking their quarry in a pool of water, brought to the boil using heated stones. They wrapped the meat in dried grass and flung it into the water, which was kept at boiling point by throwing in even more heated stones. This wild, and to our eyes rather masculine, method of cooking was taken until recently to be as much a legend as the size of Finn McCoul's spear, but within the last few years archaeologists have tried re-using some of the ancient cooking places where this method was employed, called *fulacht fiadh*, which may formerly have been used at festivals and other gatherings. They heated up once again the piles of large burnt stones, tossed them into the water, and when it was boiling threw in a 10 lb joint of mutton. The meat cooked perfectly, taking twenty minutes to the pound, just as it would do in a modern oven. In early times the meat would have been eaten with melted butter, and perhaps some watercress. As Eugene O'Curry, a great source of information on Irish food and manners who wrote in the last century explained, 'the *biolar* or watercress was used at feasts as a salad with meats'.

Part of the meat for the feasts appears to have been roasted: small box-like structures have been found at some of the *fulacht fiadh*, and it has been suggested that these were ovens for roasting. This may have been the start of the custom which has lasted even down to this century, that an Irish meal should consist of something roasted as well as something boiled. Hospitality on a large scale, another strong tradition, also already appears to have been part of Irish life in these ancient times. The early Irish chieftains and kings always kept a joint boiling in the cauldron on the hearth, so that no one was turned away without something to eat or drink. Another tradition, that monastic houses should always keep a fire burning, probably dates back to prehistoric times, too. There was an echo of this belief in the last century, when after the Great Famine whole villages were forced to emigrate: the moment of raking out the ashes of the hearth for the last time was one of the most significant and painful, and never to be forgotten.

Monastic food was certainly more frugal than that of the chieftains, but appears to have been healthy enough. St Brendan's 180 years were due no doubt to his sanctity, but must have owed something to his diet: trout from the river, wild herbs and berries, game trapped in the woods, and the occasional jug of mead. St Ciaran, another Celtic hermit, lived a few miles away from Birr, and according to an early account of his life, 'although he had ten doors to his cattle yard, he consumed but very little of the abundant produce of these cows. His evening meal was a small piece of barley cake and two parsnips from the garden and water from the spring well. The skins of calves constituted his clothes and it was on a pillow of stone he usually slept.'

None of the dishes of the ancient Irish heroes appear in the recipe books that I have at Birr. They only go back to the mid-seventeenth century, by which time the Parsons family had settled there. In 1620, towards the end of the reign of James I, Sir Laurence Parsons, District Attorney for the Province of Munster, one of the new English planter class, had 'acquired' Birr Castle with the town and lands around. Later Tadhg O'Carroll was to complain to the King that those lands had been in his family for upwards of 1,000 years.

Although some English families, including the Parsons, had been in Ireland since Elizabethan times, the central plains and bog lands around Birr were generally unknown to them. Contemporary English accounts describe the 'wild Irish' as dressing in skins and sleeping on the ground. Sometimes they were even compared to American Indians. In such exaggerated accounts of primitiveness, the

English usually saw only what they wanted to see. But the fear of the Irish was genuine enough: they spoke a different language, wore different clothes, and cooked different food. To the Parsons family, Birr must have seemed like a colonial outpost, an adventure.

It must have appeared a wild and ruined place to Sir Laurence, this O'Carroll stronghold, fought over and now empty: the grass growing long in the castle bawn, ivy on the walls of the old tower, the horses' hooves echoing under the gate tower, hostile eyes watching. With great energy and in tiny writing, a Parsons characteristic that continues into the twentieth century, Sir Laurence recorded his transformation of the medieval fortress at Birr into a Jacobean home. His accounts cover a frenzy of demolishing and rebuilding, clearing and replanting. It is in an aside in these records, between writing off a debt of 142 barrels of lime and buying a three-year-old bull, that he records the arrival of his wife, Lady Anne, and his children, together with one of the small sons of the Earl of Cork. They moved into the new house, built over and around the gate tower into the bawn, which is shown in a drawing in the front of the earliest cookery book I have from the Castle, compiled by Dorothy, Sir Laurence's daughter-in-law, in the mid-seventeenth century. It shows a large building in the Dutch style with many high chimneys and gables. Below it is written in Dorothy's hand 'An Excellent receipt to spend 4000 pound'.

Only a year later, in 1628, the account ends abruptly, after a note of money given to his wife before one of his journeys on circuit in Munster. He never returned, dying suddenly while he was away. Undaunted by her husband's death, Lady

126

Anne Parsons stayed on. She had a good business head, as the accounts of leases, land, cattle, and sheep bought and sold show. Life was anything but peaceful, however. Twice the Castle was besieged, once during the troubles before the Cromwellian period in 1649, and again just before the Battle of the Boyne in 1689. The O'Carrolls, and the Molloys, and Coughlans to the north, also kept a watchful eye on Birr, and although by the second siege Lady Anne herself was dead, her influence with the Irish and their apparent respect for her helped the family when the tide turned against them.

So began almost four centuries of family life in this castle by the river. Day after day, meal has followed meal: winters with woodcocks from the bog to be plucked, summers with fish to be fried and fruit to be preserved. Holidays have given housekeepers and cooks time to catch their breath, but, for almost 400 years, somebody has had to think of three meals a day. Dorothy, who came to the castle when she married Sir Laurence's son William – from this time onwards the names of Laurence and William alternated across generations – wrote her cookery book in 1666. It is said that 'the past is a foreign country', yet her recipes bring her different world surprisingly close. Many of her vegetables and herbs still grow in the garden at Birr, and her 'hartichoake pie' (see page 138), the first of her recipes that I tried, was a wonderful way to use up a particularly abundant crop of artichokes.

Dorothy, whose cookery book sheds such a beam of light into the past, was probably the second or third generation of her family to live in Ireland. She inherited many of her mother-in-law's recipes as well as the herb, vegetable and flower gardens, and the orchard her father-in-law, Sir Laurence,

had taken such trouble to plant. Her recipes, full of almonds, raisins, spices, rosewater, and cinnamon – obviously all quite easily available – go back to the cooking of Elizabethan times with their heavy, almost oriental spicing. Indeed Dorothy acknowledges that 'those that are most especially excellent, ... are marked EP, being all approved & tried by ye Lady Elizabeth Parsons in her life time'. These recipes go back to her husband's aunt, Elizabeth, wife of Sir William Parsons, the Surveyor General for Ireland. Most of the EP recipes seem to be in the mainstream of English sixteenth-century cooking. The recipe for Marrow Pudding, warming on a winter day, is very like the Lord of Devonshire's Pudding given by Lady Fettiplace, included in Hilary Spurling's book of her Elizabethan recipes (*Elinor Fettiplace's Receipt Book*, London, 1988).

At Birr, food for the family, living off the land, varied only with the seasons. The farm continued to produce sheep and 'beeves', pigs and chickens, and the garden was still full of artichokes. Pickling and preserving also followed a seasonal pattern: pickling artichoke hearts followed on from making strawberry jam and elderflower wine. Herbs, both wild and cultivated, would also have been gathered in their season for the important medicinal recipes which form almost half of the earlier cookery books.

Family meals at Birr may have always included some traditional Irish dishes, but the first firm evidence of this comes from a cookery book compiled by Alice Parsons, married to Dorothy's great-great-grandson over 100 years later. Towards the end of the eighteenth century, she scribbled one of her mapped-out table plans on the back of a piece of paper that her husband, another

Laurence, was using for genealogical notes. She put 'Potatoe Loaves' among the 'Salmon, Leg of Mutton, Soup and Tongue', a modest meal by standards of the day; and she still had to think up her 'Head', short for head or main dish, which was to be followed by 'Pancakes, Plumbs and Omlet'. Three more empty circles show where she hoped for further inspiration. Her side table so far had 'Boiled Beef' only.

Alice, born Alice Lloyd, came from a beautiful house called Gloster, built at the end of the seventeenth century, only five miles from Birr. One of three pretty sisters who sang and played the piano, her family background was much the same as that of the Parsons. Originally from Wales, although with some Irish blood, that of the O'Moores, the family had settled in the country 200 years before. It is not surprising, then, that Alice's cookery book seems more Irish than Dorothy's. When reading it I can almost feel her looking over my shoulder, harassed and slightly disorganized, but a wonderful party-giver whose plans would always turn out fun and delicious in the end. Her husband, Sir Laurence, adored her, and wrote love letters to her even from the House of Commons in London where, much to his disgust, he had to travel after the Irish Act of Union of 1800. Later, when he gave up politics, he built the gothic music room at Birr for her, which must often have been filled with music and dancing, polkas and quadrilles.

Alice's cooking was simpler than Dorothy's, with far fewer exotic spices, complicated caudels, and cures for violent illness, a reflection of the increasing peacefulness of the times. Its Irishness shows through in the recipes for pickling salmon, barm brac (see recipe on page 150) and potato barm,

'which Miss Mahan says answers extremely well'. There are several recipes for salmon, one for 'salmon done in the Sligo way', and some from her own home, including 'Beef pickled as it is done at Gloster'. The neighbours have less entirely English names, recipes coming from a Mrs Mahan and a Mrs Daley, as well as Anglo-Irish names still here today, such as Annesley, St George, and Derby. Spring water, no doubt taken from St Brendan's Well, is often mentioned.

Alice's recipes are recognizable as good old-fashioned country, even farmhouse, cooking. She pickled walnuts and cucumbers, and salted beef in large quantities as had her predecessor, Frances Parsons, whose lead cistern, 'so large it would hold the carcasses of 5 or 6 beeves', was taken possession of by her husband's troops during the siege of 1689, to be melted down for bullets. Between pickling and preserving Alice added in household hints. A note on the 'materials for making two very large shapes of jelly', which included 'a bottle of cyder, 6 eggs, the whites, 2 lemons, 1 lb brown sugar, 1 shillings worth of skinned calves feet or sheeps feet', is sandwiched between advice on how to varnish mahogany tables, and blacking for shoes.

Puddings were already important. At one point Alice lists various possible dishes under the headings 'Head Dishes', 'Side Dishes' and 'Puddings'. The puddings are by far the most numerous – only six 'Head Dishes' compared to 26 puddings, including lemon pudding, baked apple pudding, 'macerony' pudding, puffs, and pyramid of pastry. In a nineteenth-century cookery book belonging to Emma, Viscountess de Vesci, at Abbey Leix, twenty miles to the south-east of Birr in Co. Laois, there are no less than thirty-eight recipes for puddings. In the recipes I have chosen from both

Alice's and Dorothy's books, I notice that the eighteenth-century ones are almost all puddings, while the seventeenth-century ones are mainly meat dishes. Possibly Alice was not such an adventurous cook, and her meat dishes may have consisted simply of a roast chicken or joint of meat.

There is no reason, though, why Alice's food, although simple, should not have been delicious. As an example of good food that needs no complex preparation, the diary of Humphrey O'Sullivan, a school teacher in Kilkenny, who occasionally recorded the delicious meals he shared with his friend the priest in the 1830s, shows ingredients that need only a good cook to produce perfection: 'We had two fat trout that were sweet too, and substantial. One of them was as large as a small salmon. Then followed hard boiled hen eggs and bruised asparagus, swimming in butter, laid out on fresh cream and salt.' Or: 'Beef tripe swimming in butter and fresh milk, bacon with beef kidneys and white cabbage, roast duck with green peas. Scalteen [whisky boiled with sugar and butter] and port wine to drink.' Such meals had been enjoyed in Ireland since the Middle Ages, with no recourse to cookery books.

All Alice's recipes must have been well tested. Under a recipe for making jam, she writes 'not a good preserve'; then, presumably having tried it again, she writes below 'it *is* a good preserve'. Her recipe for lemon cheese (see page 153), given to her by a Mrs Bligh, is delicious, and shows the care taken in her instructions. This is typical of Alice's determination to explain everything carefully, often adding further notes at the bottom. Such sweet 'cheese' dishes, cream 'cheese', and dutch 'cheese', for all of which Alice included recipes in her book, would have replaced the cheeses which by the

eighteenth century were no longer available in Ireland, and were not to be revived until the 1970s. Just as my mother-in-law's delicious recipe for Neapolitan butter (see page 154) took the place of the cheese course at dinner parties in the 1930s, so Alice had to make up her own substitutes. The decline of cheese-making seems to have coincided with the rise of the potato, which may indeed have been a contributory factor, by reducing the need for cheese. It is not known exactly why cheese in Ireland disappeared so completely after it had been one of the staple foods up to the seventeenth century. Myrtle Allen, from Ballymaloe Country House Hotel, who has done much research on Irish food, has suggested that its decline and eventual disappearance was caused by the enormous butter export market which started to grow in the seventeenth century, taking all the surplus milk. Once this decline had begun, it quickly escalated. Cheese-makers are notoriously mysterious and secretive about their recipes, so once they have fallen into disuse, they are easily lost and gone within a generation.

Hospitality, however, continued to be part of the life of every big house in Ireland, whether it was Gaelic or Anglo-Irish, farmhouse or castle. In the remote areas of the west of Ireland, where English was, even in the eighteenth century, rarely understood, the almost aggressive medieval Irish hospitality continued to survive. A description of a chance encounter with the local chief on a remote lakeside in Mayo, written by a Mr Cuffe of Ballinrobe in the middle of that century, gives a last glimpse of this world:

There were two Cabins Thatched, opposite to one another, one was the kitchen and appartments for

the family. The other was the entertaining room
neatly strewed according to the Irish fashion with
Rushes and the upper End of the Room was a kind
of Platform raised above the ground with Boards
and two or three Blankets on each, which was the
Lodging for strangers and visitors . . ., A bottle of
Brandy was the wet before dinner, and the
Entertainment was Half a Sheep Boiled at top, Half
a sheep roasted at Bottom, broiled Fish on one side,
a great wooden bowl of Potatoes on the other, and
a heaped plate of salt in the middle. After dinner
some pretty good Claret and an enormous Bowl of
Brandy Punch of which according to the old as well
as the modern Irish Hospitality, the guests were
pressed to take their full share . . . Towards evening
the chief began to grow mellow, he call'd his Favorit
girl to sing which she did very well and was a neat
handsome jolly girl. Before he called her in, he
stipulated that they were welcome to any liberty with
her from the Girdle upwards but he would not
permit any underhand doings. A Bagpiper likewise
attended and . . . an old Irish bard came in who for
their entertainment made Verses . . . and Sung several
songs on the Virtue and great prowess of the
Ancestors of his Chief . . .

In this case the travellers' only chance of escape
was to try and get their host more drunk than they
were themselves, so that, in the early hours of the
morning, they could creep back to their boat.

Most reports of travels around rural Ireland in the
eighteenth and nineteenth century comment more
favourably on the hospitality than on the cuisine.
This, I think, does not mean that the Irish did not
know how to cook. The travellers, usually male
and therefore unlikely to talk of cookery, were
only dropping in on a society which lived less over-

civilized lives, and usually saved its best cooking
for the seasonal festivals: weddings, christenings,
and wakes. So, while the welcome traveller would
get a roasted sheep or goat, probably killed in his
honour, or a salmon fresh from the river, he would
go away never knowing about the stews, broths
and sweetmeats that took so long to prepare, and
would perhaps only be found on the table at certain
times of the year and at the important seasonal
festivals.

Alice's own hospitality followed the tradition of
the great ancient Irish houses, giving hospitality to
all comers. But by the time she was compiling her
cookery book, many of the Irish themselves had
gone from their castles and fortified homes. Most
of the lands of the O'Carrolls had passed into
other hands. Their tower houses stood ruined and
empty, with sometimes a modest farmhouse built
against the walls. Otherwise, only occasional plants,
such as the medieval parsley (*Carum petroselinum*)
or the shiny leaves of alexanders, showed evidence
of the long abandoned herb gardens.

Nevertheless, several of Alice's dishes – still cooked
today – can be connected with the ancient Irish
tradition of food linked with the pre-Christian
festivals of the Celtic year. One of her recipes is
for barm brac (see page 150), cooked for
Hallowe'en, the Christianized form of the Celtic
Samhain, the beginning of the Celtic New Year.
'Barm' was a word coming from the Irish *beorma*,
meaning a form of fermented yeast, and 'brac'
meant speckled, so a barm brac was a yeasted
cake, speckled with raisins or dried fruit. Alice also
includes recipes for making barm from potatoes,
as well as from ale and sugar. A barm brac, baked
with a sixpence, a ring, and a button hidden in it,

would also tell the future: wealth, marriage, or bachelorhood, in a tradition which probably dates back to prehistoric times. (Many countries in the Indo-European tradition, from Iran to Scandinavia, have hidden surprises in their cakes and dishes.) Another dish certainly cooked in her kitchen, though the recipe was taken for granted, and, like much traditional cooking, only written down in recent times, was colcannon (see page 162 for recipe), the meal of bacon and cabbage traditionally eaten on 1 August, the festival of Lughnasa. Though the Celtic god Lugh himself is long forgotten, his festival was remembered until recently, especially in the Slieve Bloom mountains, as a time for picnics and picking berries.

The scale of Alice's hospitality is suggested by some of the quantities in her recipes. Her recipe for making muffins uses half a gallon of water and half a gallon of barm to make a cream, which is then added to half a stone of flour. The number of muffins this produced would have kept the largest family gathering happy. Wine of different fruits was also made in huge quantities. One recipe for elderflower wine, written with the help of her younger son Laurence, brings the family alive. Laurence writes in larger and larger letters, ending with a flourish: 'This is the best Irish wine that is made and is extremely beneficial (mixed with water) for those with delicate lungs.' A few blots follow, then, 'Hurrah for shuggar'. 'Oh Lawrence, how could you spell it that way,' noted his mother below in much smaller writing.

Such was the reputation for hospitality in the Anglo-Irish house, that in the eighteenth century it was said to be much easier to get into an Irish gentleman's dining-room than to get out of it. A detailed description exists for a party given by Alice

and her husband at Birr in 1820. It must have been an especially large gathering, as the whole house is being used, and the explicit instructions for the moving of furniture, and thought given even to the candles and music stands, shows again Alice's eye for detail:

In the morning the 3rd the carpet to be taken off and the drawing rooms washed and dry rubbed ... The cook to make this day 18 dishes of pastry and to chop veal and hams for 18 dishes of sandwishes. The dairy maid to be prepared with 13 qts. of cream for the next day, for ice. The cook to make 9 dishes of jelly. The narrow tables to be laid out in the parlour, and one round one composed of two parts, and cloths laid on them and silver dishes, to be ready for the supper on the following evening, 4 decanters on each table for water, large and small glasses on each. 12 china plates piled on each table, and spoons – Dishes to hold in all 15 glasses and cups of Ice. These tables with supper on them to be brought into the large Drawing room at one o'clock at night –

Tea to be made and coffee in the orange bedchamber, and handed on trays to the company in the drawing rooms – at 9 o'clock –

Negus composed of Lemon Wine and cyder and white sugar – with water, to be brought into the large drawing room at 10 o'clock ... two fiddlers to be engaged to play quadrilles in the large drawing room ... The lamps to be well prepared and trimmed. A table in the Yellow drawing room with 8 candles for the music – Candles on Pianforte and on the Musick stand, on the shelves of which the Musick for the Evening to be placed ...

Although at Birr, and generally throughout the Irish countryside, entertaining was usually fairly relaxed and informal, in Dublin, the greater formality that was to come later in the century was already beginning to be felt. With Irish irony, the writer Maria Edgeworth, one of the first Irish novelists writing in the early nineteenth century, describes how a meal of the time was laid out by a Dublin lady trying hard to impress:

The dinner had two great faults – profusion and pretention. There was, in fact, ten times more on the table than was necessary ... there was a disparity between the entertainment and the attendants. The mistress of the house called for 'plates, clean plates!' But none did come when she did call. At last one course was fairly got through, and after a torturing half-hour, the second course appeared ... the wine-sauce for the hare was spilt ... but what was worse, there seemed little chance that the whole of this second course should ever be placed altogether rightly on the table. 'Set the seakale at this corner ... the macceroni yonder with them puddings, – ogh James! the pyramid in the middle.'

Even as early as the eighteenth century, Dublin was becoming a sophisticated and cultured city. Alice's father-in-law, Sir William, kept a small black personal account-book when he was in Dublin towards the end of that century. He carefully noted his purchases, and the range of fish, game, and vegetables that was available is very large, and impressive in its healthiness. There was plenty of fish, generally cod, whiting, oysters by the hundred, lobsters, scallops, soles, crabs, and cockles; good vegetables such as celery, and salad greens; and parsley, cabbage, parsnips, carrots, turnips, and spinach; and for fruit, lemons, and occasional oranges, the latter a treat saved up for outings to the theatre. In the months between January and April

game was clearly easy to get in the city. Sir William bought woodcock, teal, and mallard, and on 13 January 1778 a haunch of venison. Salt, and dairy products such as butter, cream, and buttermilk, and the wages for a dairymaid are listed apart.

All the food purchases were fitted in between random jottings such as 'Lost at cards', 'to the play', and 'Tavern', as well as notes on the purchase of newspapers, black silk stockings, 'to Mick for sundries for the stable', powder, 'brush to take spots out of linen', and the *Philosophical Survey of Ireland*. Sir William's jottings instantly convey the atmosphere of mid-eighteenth-century Dublin, with its coffee houses, newspapers, militant pamphlets, and intellectual discussions in elegant surroundings.

In 1806 Alice's husband had inherited the title of Earl of Rosse from his uncle, though not the fortune he had hoped would go with it. The Irish Act of Union of 1800, which had removed the Irish parliament from its seat in Dublin, and forced the Irish representatives to travel to London, had turned the Parsons and other such families back again towards England. In spite of Sir Laurence's initial awkwardness and homesickness, he and Alice had a London house by the late 1820s, and it was from there that their youngest daughter, Alicia, eloped with another Irishman, the son of Sir John Conroy, in May 1837. Although hotly pursued by her elder brother, William, she and her lover succeeded in racing him to Gretna Green, where they married. Alice and Laurence, deeply disapproving, forgave the young couple, but the marriage did not work out well. William, Lord Oxmantown, made a respectable marriage, however, at about the same time, to a Yorkshire heiress, Mary Field from Bradford, starting a new family tradition of marrying girls from England.

William became the 3rd Earl in 1841, but he was not in the usual mould of the Irish landowner. With his wife Mary's fortune he built the then biggest telescope in the world in the middle of the park at Birr. She added another floor to the now gothicized Castle, and then another wing, to accommodate the visiting scientists from all over the world. She also built on kitchens and laundries, servants' rooms, and rooms for her children and their tutors. She herself must have had great energy, for as well as producing eleven children – sadly only four of them lived to be adults – she became one of Ireland's earliest photographers. In Mary's photographs the past finally comes visually before us. Her best show beautifully composed groups of her own children as they grew up: mischievous-faced boys, buttoned into uncomfortable best clothes; and their girl cousins, neat young ladies with smooth shining hair parted in the centre, like heroines in a Brontë novel.

And so Birr began to fall into the pattern of most aristocratic mid-nineteenth-century British houses. Mary's cooking and entertaining seem to have been on a grand scale. She would have had a housekeeper, possibly English – whose ways would be more familiar to her than those of the local Irish whom she knew less well – to run the household efficiently for her, whether she and her family were in Ireland or not.

For the first time since the Parsons arrived at Birr, the kitchen was moved. Mary created an enormous basement kitchen under the new wing that she had added, with pantries and larders from which the food was hauled up in a lift. The old kitchen became the still-room, and remained so until turned back again to its former use by my mother-in-law in the 1930s, when Mary's monumental kitchen

made way for the central heating plant. The kitchen-garden, too, was enlarged, and more high-walled gardens built; greenhouses and fruit trees and newly introduced vegetables provided a constant supply of carefully grown delicacies, including grapes, figs, and asparagus. The number of gardeners employed must have been very large, and in the house, with new laundries and kitchen, the number of staff also increased greatly, and needed to be well run and organized.

It was Mary who at last gave the house a dining-room. Like everything else she did, it was on a massive scale: 40 feet long with a high ornate ceiling, huge Gothic windows, and enormous crimson curtains. The table, still *in situ*, stretches to fit twenty-two people, sitting on high baronial chairs, and the armorial oak sideboard, opposite the window, is so heavy that it could only have been made there on the spot. By Mary's time the formal dinner party had arrived, very different to Alice's informal evenings, when fiddlers had played and tables were piled with decanters and glasses, jellies and sandwiches. By the 1840s men and women processed into dinner two by two from the drawing-room, and the meal was served by footmen, each course consisting of one dish – soup or entrée or meat – as it does now. There could be very many of these courses, depending on the grandeur of the meal.

In 1853, William became one of Queen Victoria's Commissioners of the Great Exhibition. At the Exhibition Mary bought glass, silver, and china, all covered in a vine-leaf pattern, to reflect the vine leaves entwined around the cornice of her new dining-room. A menu exists for the party given four years later, in 1857, at the Castle to visiting members of the British Association for the

Advancement of Science, one of the greatest events in the town during the mid-nineteenth century. The menu, which was for a very large number of people, had little of a distinctive character. It consisted of soups and entrées: 'Turtle à l'Anglais, cucumber sauce, purée of spinach', veal with mushrooms, and many different fish dishes, including 'Sole à la Normandy, Whiting à la Mazarine, and Salmon'. Of the desserts, however, we are only told that they were of a 'recherché character'.

I have often wondered what happened at Mary's dinner parties on the nights when the sky cleared; whether the distinguished astronomers would have been allowed to leave the table, buttoning on their overcoats and picking up their top hats, to rush to the telescope, or whether they would have remained seated making polite conversation around the table laid with the Great Exhibition silver and plate. Probably under Mary's matriarchal eye they would have remained seated until the last delicious pudding was finished.

A letter from a Miss Cobbe of Newbridge in Co. Kildare, a scientifically minded young lady, describing her visit to the telescope with Lord Rosse, concludes: 'The castle and grounds are very handsome and evidently the philosopher understands the art of good living, for a better dinner I never did eat – champagne, plate, etc for 6.'

One of the reasons why nineteenth-century hospitality in Ireland was on a bigger scale than ever, was the sheer size of the families. Many people had ten or twelve children, and as they grew up and had children of their own they created vast house-parties. At the Cobbe's home, Newbridge, Co. Dublin, a shy guest asked, and was promised,

that there would be no entertainment especially for her, so was horrified on walking into the dining-room to find thirty-two people sitting down to luncheon. She turned in alarm to her hostess, who reassured her that this was only family.

But life at Birr in the mid-nineteenth century was not all grand dinner parties and lavish entertaining. The building of the telescope, which had started in 1840, was interrupted by that horrific catastrophe, the Great Famine, which to this day is still not far from the minds of the Irish. The population had grown enormously over the previous 150 years, and in many places had become totally dependent on the potato. Corn and other crops were grown, but only for export. When disease struck the potato, it led in many places to total starvation. Out of a population of eight million, four million died or emigrated. Birr, although not as badly hit as some parts of the country, was never to recover its pre-famine population of 8,000.

Many of the large country houses set up soup kitchens. In the records at Abbey Leix is a 'soup for poor people'. This simple recipe may well have been used in large quantities during the famine: 'A gallon of water, $\frac{1}{2}$ pint of split peas, 6 potatoes, 2 onions, 2 ozs rice, pepper and salt. Add this to 1 lb lean beef cut into pieces.'

Mary and William, however, tried to help the poor by giving employment. Many parts of the demesne were enhanced, and long walls were built, employing at times up to 500 people. Nevertheless, from Mary's photographs it is clear that, locally at least, only the very young, and the very poor, were thin. Food was plentiful for the comfortably off, and was eaten in large quantities. Imported foodstuffs were easily available in the town, which, in spite of the decline in population after the famine, continued to prosper. A list of tradesmen shows eight grocers, four bakers, confectioners, brewers, ironmongers, and others.

Later in the nineteenth century, and in the early twentieth century – the era of shooting parties and amateur dramatics – a book of recipes and clippings was kept by Edith Cramer the housekeeper of Mary's daughter-in-law Cassandra. As a young girl newly arrived from England, she scratched her name on a window pane in 1874. With Edith, the past comes almost into living memory. She lived on into the 1930s when my mother-in-law remembers meeting her. In the tradition of the previous books, she has medicinal hints – remedies for coughs, as usual, and also for seasickness – in her book, as well as plain, no nonsense recipes for practical nursery food, such as her recipe for Brown Pudding: 'Soak 4 ozs Brown Bread and 2 oz Oatmeal in a pint of boiling milk; when cold stir in 2 eggs well beaten and a little nutmeg and sugar. Pour into a buttered bason, boil 1 hour.'

For much of this century my mother-in-law, Anne, was responsible for running the daily life at Birr, together with Annie Shortt, who was cook-housekeeper. The partnership lasted for nearly forty years, during which they produced food that was memorable, rich, exotic, and beautiful to look at. Their floating angels (see recipe on page 152), once tasted, can never be forgotten. Annie, who died in 1987, was my last insight into the past. She had come here first, aged twelve, one of a country family of fourteen, and had started work as a kitchen-maid in the twenties, when my mother-in-law remembered her as a beautiful girl scrubbing the floors in the basement. It was under my mother-

in-law's supervision that she became a brilliant and instinctive cook.

One winter morning, looking together for a large copper pot to cook a ham, Annie and I investigated the disused Victorian kitchen together. This huge room, built on by Mary Rosse, was used from about the 1850s to the 1930s, the period of the Castle's greatest expansion. We opened the dusty, pale blue 'presses', and looked at the copper pots, all carefully wrapped in fifties' newspaper. Half-way up the stone steps, with the chosen copper pot already heavy in my hands, I turned to look back, feeling almost like Alice in Wonderland in the process of shrinking, at the table big enough to dance on, the giant-sized cupboards, and the enormous, now empty, room. It was easy to imagine it buzzing with pre-luncheon activity, everything ready to 'go in' on time: the huge pans of vegetables, the blue linoleum floor scrubbed, Annie's friends and sisters with sleeves rolled up getting ready for the roast to come out of the oven, the copper no longer put away, but gleaming on the shelves. As if she could read my mind Annie, too, looked back. 'I never could understand', she said, 'why we'd be getting the meal ready all for the one time. When I came here first, that is.'

Later she told me stories of kitchen life, recalling with delight how she and her sisters would run out on a stifling summer evening, avoiding the glances of the housekeeper and butler. I could imagine the back door banging, the giggling and running feet. Other stories were of cooking, both triumphs and disasters: the time the lobsters, brought back alive in the boot of the car from Dublin, ate the sole intended for the next meal; the time the housekeeper, after reassuring herself of the quality of the sherry supply for the marmalade, went fishing one evening, tripped on her trout rod, rolled down the moat, and broke her arm.

Although she hardly ever left Birr, Annie was able to decipher notes made by Anne on the Trans-Siberian railway, recipes from Mexican kitchens and Hungarian palaces. It was difficult for her to explain her methods to me when I first came to Birr, but later, going through my mother-in-law's instructions, drawings of how the dishes should be presented, and her library of cookery books, mostly of the 1930s, I discovered some of the secrets.

My mother-in-law's menus for dinners and lunches were in the mainstream of fashionable 1930s cooking, with much cream and white wine, and recipes from books such as Nancy Shaw's *Food for the Greedy* (1936), and *Lady Sysonby's Cook Book* (1935). In spite of Osbert Sitwell's warning in the foreword of Lady Sysonby's book, 'you will not find written in these pages the exuberant note of parvenue extravagence', the dishes given there are, to my taste, decidedly rich. All have notes and corrections in my mother-in-law's hand. Against the chocolate soufflé which Annie used to make (see recipe on page 169), my mother-in-law has written 'utterly lovely'.

Many of my mother-in-law's dinners and lunches were served to the house-parties which became a feature of Irish life in the 1930s; the train, the boat, and again the train, or possibly a chauffeur-driven car, would bring the guests over the Irish Sea and through the green countryside. Elizabeth Bowen recorded such scenes: the table laid for endless courses, the dining-room, the glass, and the silver, much the same as in the days of Mary Rosse, but the food, like the clothes, lighter and more delicate.

Puddings were now strictly for the nursery and lunch-time. Sole Mornay would be followed by veal, the meat cut into easy-to-pick-up servings, and covered in a creamy sauce. Even after the Second World War this food and the parties continued, since there was no restriction on the amount of butter and cream, and no rationing; to visitors from post-war England, it was a revelation.

In contrast to all these fashionable dishes – and indeed at any date back to Dorothy's time, the big house was proudly producing exotic imports – other food was typically Irish. There were lobsters from Galway Bay and smoked gammon from Sligo, breakfasts with soda bread – the special Irish brown bread which we still make almost every day, and teas with potato cakes and barm brac, for those who had walked the bogs all day in search of woodcock. At lunch, at least before the Second World War, there still existed the 'side-table'. On it would be the cold joint of meat or ham that might have been there at breakfast, and which would eventually find its way down to the servants' hall. The gentleman would ask the lady sitting next to him, or perhaps the lady across the table whose eye he managed to catch, if he could possibly get her something from the side-table. They might then go together to investigate, and also, as my mother-in-law explained, continue any other conversation they might not want overheard.

Yet for all the changes of transport, and hence the availability of different and more exotic ingredients in the town, and the coming of the refrigerator and deep freezer, Annie's recipes reach right back to Dorothy's in the seventeenth century. They spring mainly from good, healthy living off the land, from knowing exactly when the redcurrants should be picked, and even which fields made the cows give the best butter. Much of the food still came from the farm, and vegetables were gathered from the garden. The artichokes were, and are still, in good supply.

My husband, when he was a boy, remembers how much, even then, the household was self-providing. The children were sent on a yearly round of picking and gathering: morels and gulls eggs on the bogs in spring; and in the autumn mushrooms, and, with nanny and a pony and trap, blackberries on the slopes of the Slieve Boom. Some of these we still search for, especially the morels, so good with venison, and the sloes to make sloe gin. The game larder, too, was full all the winter with pheasant, snipe and other game, hung the exact number of days to make them just right for the table.

Now, perhaps more than ever, cooking at Birr has come full circle, as I try out Dorothy's recipes, and live as much as I can off the land, in the knowledge that woodcock and venison have no added hormones or antibiotics. Our own vegetables are grown organically. Cheese also has come back to Ireland, and in the last ten years many different varieties have become available, and are finding an international market.

Ireland must still be one of the best places in the world for the production of food. The air is less polluted, the land less over-fertilized than in many other parts of the Western world, and hopefully this will be appreciated before damage is done in a mistaken effort to catch up with the rest of Europe. At Birr the rivers, the Little Brosna and the Camcor, still produce trout and watercress, and the bogs, though sadly diminished, are still a breeding ground for woodcock and snipe, and long may they continue to be so.

Recipes

'Hartichoake' Pie 17th century

This would have been a large pie: the original recipe, from Dorothy Parsons' manuscript cookery book of 1666, uses three chickens. It is baked very dry, so the 'caudel' can be absorbed without making the pastry sag. You can make it in a deep pie dish with just a pastry top, but the method given below is for a genuine seventeenth-century raised pie, which looks exciting, and with the sugar and spice in the filling has more of the original flavour.

Serves 8 to 10

Pastry
1 lb (450 g) plain flour
1 level teaspoon salt
7 fl oz (200 ml) water
6 oz (150 g) butter

Filling
6 oz (150 g) butter, sliced
10 cooked artichoke bottoms
2 tablespoons candied orange and lemon peel
1 tablespoon sugar
10 cloves
$\frac{1}{2}$ teaspoon nutmeg, grated
$\frac{1}{2}$ teaspoon ground mace
1 cooked chicken, meat removed from bones and cut into 1 inch (2.5 cm) cubes

marrow, from 2 bones boiled for 15 minutes, sliced
1 egg yolk, beaten
salt and freshly ground black pepper

Caudel
7 fl oz (200 ml) white wine
2 egg yolks, beaten
2 tablespoons sugar

Make the pastry by sifting the flour and salt into a bowl, and making a well in the centre. Bring the water to a boil, stir in the butter until melted, and pour this into the well in the flour. Lightly mix the flour into the water and butter mixture to form a ball of pastry. Cover the bowl with a damp cloth, and leave in a warm place for 30 minutes.

Pre-heat the oven to 170°C (325°F, Mark 3). Grease a deep, loose-bottomed 7-inch (17.5-cm) cake tin. Roll out the pastry on a floured board, and use it to line the tin and make a top for the pie.

Fill the pie by placing the slices of butter on the bottom, then covering these with the artichoke bottoms. Sprinkle over half the candied peel, half the sugar, and half the spices. Arrange the chicken cubes on top, and sprinkle these with the remaining candied peel, sugar, and spices. Dip the slices of marrow into the beaten egg, and arrange these on top of the chicken. Season lightly with salt and pepper. Place the pastry top on the pie, and make a small hole in the centre of it. Bake in the pre-heated oven for 2 hours.

Just before the pie is ready, make the caudel. Place all the ingredients in a small pan over a very low heat, and stir constantly until the mixture thickens. Do not allow it to boil. When the pie is baked, remove from the oven, allow to stand in the tin for 10 minutes, then remove from the tin, and carefully pour the hot caudel through the hole in the centre of the pastry topping. Serve.

Liver Pudding 17th century

This is a combination of two recipes given in Dorothy Parsons' manuscript cookery book of 1666. One is signed 'EP', and she says it is the best recipe, but the other has more detailed instructions. It has a very interesting texture, almost like a pâté. One recipe says to place the mixture in 'oxes gutts' to boil it, while the other suggests 'butter and flour a cloth and tye the pudding up in it'. It is much easier, however, to use a pudding basin. I have served it with bread as a first course, but garnished with watercress (from St Brendan's well, of course) it can be part of a buffet – hot or cold.

Serves 10 as a starter

8 oz (225 g) pig's liver
1 oz (25 g) butter
6 oz (150 g) fresh white breadcrumbs
8 oz (225 g) shredded beef suet
$\frac{1}{2}$ pint (300 ml) double cream
1 lb (450 g) currants
3 eggs
1 tablespoon rosewater (optional)
pinch of salt

8 oz (250 g) sugar
pinch of nutmeg
$\frac{1}{2}$ oz (15 g) ground cloves
rind of 3 oranges and 3 lemons, grated

Chop the liver, and fry it lightly in the butter. Process the cooked liver, the breadcrumbs, and the suet together in a food processor, or pound them together in a mortar and pass through a sieve. Place in a bowl, and blend in about half the cream. Slowly add, stirring with a wooden spoon, the currants, eggs, rosewater (if using), salt, sugar, spices, and grated rind. Finally, blend in enough of the remaining cream to form a stiff paste (you may not need all the cream).

Place the mixture into a well greased pudding basin, but don't fill it full as the pudding will rise. Cover the basin with two layers of buttered paper or foil. Put it into a saucepan of simmering water; the water should come half-way up the side of the basin. Simmer gently for $1\frac{1}{2}$ hours.

Calf's Head Hash 17th century

This seventeenth-century recipe is extremely similar to one from Mrs Beeton's *Book of Household Management*, published nearly 200 years later. The original begins:

Take a calves head and boyle it tender, then cut it into thick bits and put it into the pan with half a pint of strong broth.

For those who cannot face the whole 'calves head', I suggest buying the veal and starting from there.

The original recipe says 'serve it up on sippets' – 'sippets' were small thick slices of bread, which had been used from medieval times to scoop up food, and help absorb gravy. It also adds 'you may fry bacon and put amongst it, which is very good, and fry some of the brains with yolks of egg for garnish', and suggests putting the calf's head in the middle of the serving dish and the hash itself around it.

Serves 6 to 8

1 lb (450 g) veal, cut into thick strips about
    2½ inch (6.5 cm) long
½ pint (300 ml) stock
1 glass white wine
1 onion stuck with cloves
1 tablespoon fresh herbs: thyme, savory, and
    parsley, finely chopped
6 shallots, finely chopped
1 tablespoon capers
4 oz (100 g) butter
3 egg yolks
1 dessertspoon vinegar
pinch of nutmeg
2 anchovy fillets, chopped
6 oysters (optional)

Put the strips of veal in a pan with the stock, the white wine, and the onion stuck with cloves. Add the herbs, the shallots, and the capers. Boil for 30 minutes. Take the pan off the heat, and stir in the butter until it melts.

Take the egg yolks, and beat them up with the vinegar, and nutmeg, then add this to the mixture in the pan. Return the pan to the heat, turn the heat down very low, and cook, stirring constantly until the mixture thickens. Add the anchovies, and oysters if desired. Serve.

Sausages 'without gutts' 17th century

This seventeenth-century recipe is very good for a simple lunch, perhaps for a large number of children, and makes a change from ordinary shop-bought sausages. I find that any mixture that is left over makes a very good stuffing for a chicken or turkey. I have used considerably fewer eggs than Dorothy Parsons did. She would make very large quantities of the meat mixture, and store it in a 'gallipot', a sort of apothecary's jar, in which, covered in clarified butter, the meat was said to keep for up to six weeks in a cool place.

Serves 10

1 lb (450 g) pork, roughly chopped
1 lb (450 g) suet, shredded or chopped
2 teaspoons grated nutmeg
1 tablespoon chopped sage
freshly ground black pepper
salt
3 whole eggs
1 egg yolk
2 oz (50 g) butter, for frying

Lightly process all the ingredients, except the eggs and butter for frying, together in a blender or food processor, or pound them together in a mortar. Beat the eggs, and blend into the meat mixture.

Shape the mixture into 10 little rolls. Heat the butter for frying in a frying pan, and fry the rolls for about 5 minutes on each side, until well browned. Serve immediately.

Fricassee 17th century

This recipe can be made up with chicken or rabbit. It is a combination of the three original seventeenth-century recipes, one of which recommends throwing in a pint of oysters. The simplest of the three, however, gives the general idea:

Take 2 rabits, quarter them and breake all the bones, clap them into a large frying pan covered with a pint of white wine, and a pint of water, a bunch of sweet herbs chopt, 2 anchoviees and some capers. Let all these simper gently an hour, then take some off the broth, beate it up with the yolke of an egg and some butter and lemon.

Serves 8

8 oz (225 g) butter
2 small chickens, each quartered to make 8 pieces in all
1 tablespoon fresh herbs: thyme, marjoram, and savory, finely chopped
2 onions, finely chopped
salt
pinch of mace
pinch of grated nutmeg
$\frac{1}{2}$ pint (300 ml) water
$\frac{1}{2}$ pint (300 ml) white wine
2 anchovy fillets, chopped (optional)
3 egg yolks
1 lemon, thinly sliced

Melt the butter in a frying pan, add the chicken pieces, the herbs, and the onions, and season with a little salt, and the spices. Fry the chicken until it is well browned on all sides, then add the water, the white wine, and the anchovys. Simmer gently for 15 minutes. Remove the pan from the heat.

In a bowl beat up the egg yolks, and add to them 6 tablespoons of liquid from the frying pan. Then add the thinly sliced lemon. Pour this into a small saucepan, place over a low heat, and stir rapidly so that it does not curdle until it thickens. Pour over the chicken in the frying pan, stir well, and place the frying pan over a high heat. Simmer rapidly for about 5 minutes, then serve piping hot with 'sippets' – small thick slices of bread.

Jumballs 17th century

There seem to be many recipes for jumballs. Over the years they occur almost as frequently as 'quaking puddings'. The jumballs from this recipe, attributed to a Mrs Jenkes, turn out like macaroons. The rosewater and caraway seeds give an unusual taste. They are best eaten the day they are made. The original recipe suggests icing them:

For ye icing a little rosewater and sugar boyled upon the fire
When you have iced them put them a little in to ye oven to dry.

Makes about 30

$1\frac{1}{2}$ lb (700 g) plain flour
1 lb (450 g) sugar
1 teaspoon ground coriander
1 teaspoon caraway seeds
6 oz (175 g) butter, softened
4 egg yolks
3 tablespoons rosewater
6 tablespoons single cream

Pre-heat the oven to 150° C (300°F, Mark 2). Grease two large baking sheets. Sift the flour, sugar, and spices together into a large bowl. Rub in the butter, then beat in the egg yolks, rosewater, and cream, and work to form a stiff paste.

Form the paste into 30 small balls, and arrange

these on the prepared baking sheets. Bake in the pre-heated oven for 30 minutes.

Almond Pudding 17th century

I have two seventeenth-century recipes for this pudding, both of which use 1½ lb ground almonds, which must have been cheaper and perhaps easier to acquire in quantity than they are now. (They were much used in gentry cookery in England in the sixteenth and seventeenth centuries.) I have cut down the quantity used. Once again, as with the liver pudding (see page 139) this was intended to be boiled in 'gutts', some sort of animal intestine, and would then have come out in a long roll to be sliced. I prefer to cook it in a pudding basin. The rosewater and the almonds give it the flavour of the very sweet Iranian cakes that are eaten at Ramadan.

Serves 6 to 8

8 oz (225 g) ground almonds
8 oz (225 g) fine white breadcrumbs
8 oz (225 g) sugar
8 oz (225 g) beef suet, shredded
pinch each of ground nutmeg, mace and cinnamon
½ pint (300 ml) single cream
3 egg yolks
3 tablespoons rosewater

Place the ground almonds, breadcrumbs, sugar, beef suet, and spices in a large bowl, and mix well together. Make a well in the centre, and pour the cream, egg yolks, and rosewater into it. Stir at the edge of the liquid, so that the dry ingredients are gradually incorporated from the sides to form a thick paste.

Place the mixture into a well greased pudding basin,

cover with two layers of foil or buttered paper tied over the top. Put in a large saucepan of simmering water; the water should come half-way up the sides of the basin. Simmer gently for 1 hour. Serve hot.

Poached Salmon with Oysters 17th century

This seventeenth-century recipe called for a 'jowle' of salmon. This was the widest bit, nearest the head. It was considered the most tasty, and when salmon were so common and easy to get, there would be no problem in using only the best cut.

Serves 8 to 10

3 lb (1.25 kg) middle cut piece of fresh salmon
1 pint (600 ml) wine vinegar
½ pint (300 ml) water
1 dessertspoon lemon juice
1 quart (1.2 litres) oysters
8 oz (225 ml) fresh shrimps

Place the salmon in a large pan. Pour over the vinegar, water, and lemon juice. Add the oysters and shrimps. Bring to the boil, cover the pan, lower the heat, and simmer gently for about 30 minutes. When the salmon flakes away from the bone, it is cooked.

Stewed Beef with 'Sippets' 17th century

This recipe was given to Dorothy Parsons by a Mrs Jenkes. It goes well with the potato pie on page 143. I use Guinness as the 'ale' or sometimes a lighter beer. In the seventeenth and eighteenth centuries, every big household brewed their own beer, and Alice Parsons in the late eighteenth century gives several recipes in her cookery book for making 'barm', which was used in brewing. One is for potato barm.

Serves 8 to 10

3 lb (1.25 kg) stewing beef, cubed
$\frac{1}{2}$ pint (300 ml) 'ale' or Guinness
$\frac{1}{2}$ pint (300 ml) red wine
1 onion, roughly chopped
1 lb (450 g) butter
$\frac{1}{2}$ lemon, thinly sliced
a pinch of mace
1 tablespoon fresh chopped herbs: rosemary, thyme, parsley
1 anchovy fillet, chopped
juice of $\frac{1}{2}$ lemon

Place the beef, 'ale' or Guinness, wine, onion, half the butter, and the lemon slices in a large heavy-bottomed pan. Bring to a boil, lower the heat, and simmer gently for 30 minutes. Add the mace, chopped herbs, and anchovy, then simmer for a further 30 minutes. Take out the beef, place in a serving dish, and keep warm.

Add the remaining butter to the juice in the pan, and stir over a low heat until melted. Stir in the lemon juice. Pour this sauce over the beef, and serve hot on 'sippets' – small thick slices of bread.

Potato Pie 17th century

This early seventeenth-century recipe comes from Dorothy Parsons' aunt, Elizabeth. The quantities are enough for a pie 7 inches (17.5cm) in diameter. It makes a good accompaniment to stews (try it with the stewed beef on page 142), and is also good for a buffet lunch. It is possible that this pie was made originally with imported sweet potatoes. True potatoes are said to have come to Ireland with Sir

Walter Raleigh. But Sir Laurence Parsons was the next occupant of his house, the Myrtle Grove in Youghall, so he could have taken them with him to Birr.

Serves 10 to 12

Pastry

1 lb (450 g) plain flour
1 level teaspoon salt
7 fl oz (200 ml) water
6 oz (150 g) butter or lard

Filling

6 oz (150 g) butter
1 dessertspoon rosewater
12 cooked peeled potatoes, cut in half
9 hard-boiled eggs, the yolks only to be used, cut in half
2 level teaspoons cinnamon
pinch of salt
1 dessertspoon candied orange and lemon peel
$\frac{1}{2}$ lemon, thinly sliced
1 dessertspoon raisins

Caudel

$\frac{1}{2}$ pint (300 ml) white wine
2 egg yolks, beaten
1 tablespoon sugar

Make the pastry by sifting together the flour and salt into a bowl, and making a well in the centre. Bring the water to a boil, stir in the butter until melted, and then pour this into the well in the flour. Lightly mix the flour into the liquid to form a ball of pastry. Cover the bowl with a damp cloth, and leave in a warm place for 30 minutes.

Pre-heat the oven to 170°C (325°F, Mark 3). Grease

a deep, loose-bottomed 7-inch (17.5cm) cake tin. Roll out the pastry on a floured board, and use it to line the tin and to make a top for the pie.

For the pie filling, first mix the butter with the rosewater, chill, then take half of it, slice very thinly, and lay on the bottom of the pie. Then fill the pie carefully with the halved potatoes and egg yolks, and sprinkle over the spices, salt, peel, lemon slices, and raisins. Slice the rest of the butter and lay it on the top. Put on the pastry top, making a small hole in the centre. Bake for 2 hours in the pre-heated oven.

Just before the pie is ready, make the caudel. Place all the ingredients in a small pan over a very low heat, and stir constantly until the mixture thickens. Do not allow it to boil. When the pie is baked, remove from the oven, allow to stand in the tin for 10 minutes, then turn out of the tin, and carefully pour the hot caudel through the hole in the centre of the pastry topping. Serve.

Roast Hare 'with a pudding in ye belly'
17th century

This recipe from Dorothy Parsons' manuscript cookery book, was given to her by her aunt, Elizabeth.

Serves 4 to 6

1 young hare
8 oz (225 g) shredded suet
4 oz (100 g) fresh white breadcrumbs
1 teaspoon nutmeg
1 tablespoon fresh thyme and marjoram, finely chopped
pinch of salt
3 eggs, beaten

6 tablespoons single cream

Sauce

6 anchovy fillets, finely chopped
4 tablespoons claret or other red wine
8 oz (225 g) butter, diced

Pre-heat the oven to 180°C (350°F, Mark 4). Remove the innards from the hare, and wash it thoroughly. Dry with kitchen paper, and set aside. Mix together the suet, breadcrumbs, nutmeg, herbs, salt, eggs, and cream to make a stuffing, and spoon this into the body cavity of the hare. Roast the hare in the pre-heated oven for 1½ to 2 hours.

Make a sauce by heating the chopped anchovies in the wine, without boiling, for about 5 minutes. Then stir in the butter until it melts and is well blended. Serve hot, poured over the carved meat.

Colcannon Traditional

This traditional dish was eaten at Hallowe'en, sometimes, like barm brac, with a ring or button hidden in the middle. It was also eaten at the midsummer festival of Lughnasa, and probably dates back to very early times. Though I have found no recipe for it in the archives at Birr, it must certainly have been eaten there. The ingredients are variable; leeks can be substituted for shallots or scallions. Sometimes parsnips are added. The name comes from *cal ceann fhionn*, white cabbage, but kale can also be used.

The traditional way of cooking it was in a huge heavy pan with a thick lid over an open fire. From the seventeenth century onwards, all the vegetables were often cooked together, with the potatoes on the bottom.

Serves 8

1 medium head of cabbage
6 shallots or 3 leeks
7 fl oz (200 ml) milk
8 potatoes, cooked and mashed
salt and freshly ground black pepper
4 oz (100 g) butter, melted

Cut the cabbage into four, and remove the hard
parts and outer leaves. Chop the rest finely, and
cook until tender. Clean and chop the shallots or
leeks, and cook in the milk for about 5 minutes.
Add them, with the milk, to the mashed potatoes,
and beat until fluffy. Then add the cooked cabbage
and continue to beat. This can be done in a blender,
but be careful not to over-process. Season to taste.

Serve piled onto a plate with a well in the middle
into which the melted butter is poured.

Two Mushroom Recipes 18th to 19th century

These recipes, from Alice Parsons' manuscript
cookery book, date from the late eighteenth and
early nineteenth centuries. They make good starters
if served on toast, but can also be a good
accompaniment to a meal. They should only be
made with freshly picked mushrooms from the
fields. The all-year-round hygienic supermarket
variety do not have the same flavour or texture. I
have used them as an accompaniment to roast
venison (see recipe on page 146), using the morels
which grow in the woods near Birr in early spring.
They would also make a satisfying light meal
served with the 'curious salad' combination
suggested on page 146.

Serves 4

'To Frigassee Mushrooms'

wild mushrooms, freshly picked, enough to fill a
    2-pint (1.2 litre) bowl
milk and water, to wash the mushrooms
salt
$\frac{1}{2}$ pint (300 ml) single cream
1 bay leaf
a blade of mace or a pinch of powdered mace
4 oz (100 g) butter, sliced
1 egg yolk, beaten

Pick over the mushrooms, then wash them in milk
and water, and rub with a little salt. Place them in
a pan with the cream, bay leaf, and mace, and stew
gently for about 7 minutes. Stir in the egg yolk and
butter, until the butter melts and the mixture
thickens. Serve immediately.

'To Stew Mushrooms'

wild mushrooms, freshly picked, enough to fill a
    2-pint (1.2 litre) bowl
milk and water, to wash the mushrooms
$\frac{1}{4}$ pint (150 ml) milk
$\frac{1}{4}$ pint (150 ml) water
salt
1 bay leaf
a blade of mace or a pinch of powdered mace
1 small glass white wine
1 tablespoon flour
2 oz (50 g) butter

Pick over the mushrooms, then wash them in some
milk and water. Place in a pan with the $\frac{1}{4}$ pint (150
ml) milk, the $\frac{1}{4}$ pint (150 ml) water, salt to taste,
the bay leaf, and the mace. Stew gently for about
7 minutes. Then pour off the liquor, stir in the

wine, the flour, and the butter, and cook gently, stirring all the time, until the mixture thickens slightly. Serve immediately.

'Curious Salads' Traditional

It is still not known exactly what plant the shamrock was, except that it had three leaves. In 1728 William Moffet wrote of the 'curious salads' of the Irish, which included the shamrock, as well as watercress, sorrel, and nettles. In the papers of Lord Orrery, a relative of Dorothy Parsons, it is shown that 'sallett' was served along with the ribs of beef and racks of lamb at his sophisticated table in Castlemartyr, Co. Cork, in 1679. In times of famine the English were appalled to see that the starving Irish had their mouths stained green from eating grass – but they may well have known better than the English which plants could be eaten in their season, and where to find them in the fields and woods. At the seaside, seaweeds were also eaten. Carragheen moss (*Gigartina stellata* and *Chondrus crispus*) was used in puddings as a gelling agent and as a thickening in soups. Dulse (*Palmaria palmata*) was also eaten raw, and I have included it in the salad.

To make a traditional Irish salad gather together the following (all of which can be readily found in the summer months):

> morels
> dulse
> watercress
> chickweed
> young dandelion leaves
> common sorrel
> wood sorrel (*a possible candidate for shamrock*)
> salad burnet

> alexanders
> wild garlic

Leave the morels soaking overnight in salty water to remove any slugs, then rinse, slice, and set aside. Soak the dulse in a cupful of water for about 5 minutes, squeeze it dry, and slice it in strips. Pick out clean young leaves or bunches of leaves from the other plants. Wash them, and dry gently in a cloth. Tear the larger ones into smaller pieces. Place all the ingredients in a large salad bowl, and toss the salad in an oil and vinegar dressing.

Fry the sliced morels lightly in butter and sprinkle on top of the salad. Serve.

Roast Venison with Morel Sauce 20th century

This is my own recipe for cooking fallow deer from the woods. I also use the morel sauce with other game, woodcock or wild duck. If it is a good year for morels I slice up the extra ones, toss them lightly in butter, cool, then freeze them.

> Serves 8 to 10
>
> 7 lb (3 kg) haunch of venison
> oil and red wine for marinating
> 1 tablespoon chopped fresh herbs: thyme, rosemary, marjoram
> 8 oz (225 g) honey
> 4 oz (100 g) butter
> 1 tablespoon plain flour
> 2 oz (50 g) morels, finely chopped
> ½ pint (300 ml) red wine

Marinate the haunch of venison by pouring over equal quantities of oil and wine to cover, and sprinkling in the chopped herbs. Leave for up to 24 hours if possible.

Pre-heat the oven to 200°C (400°F, Mark 6). Remove the venison from the marinade, and wipe dry. Blend together the honey and butter, and rub it all over the venison. Place the venison in a roasting tin, and place in the pre-heated oven for 30 minutes, basting every 10 minutes. Reduce the heat to 150°C (300°F, Mark 2), and cook for a further 1¾ hours, basting regularly. The honey and butter should make a blackened crust over the roast which will seal in the juices. Allow the meat to stand for 15 minutes before carving.

Make a sauce, by pouring the fat and juices from the roasting pan into a small pan. Add the flour, morels, and red wine, and stir over a low heat until the mixture thickens slightly. Serve poured over the carved meat.

Watercress Soup 20th century

Watercress grows at Birr all the year round. According to early Irish literature, it was much sought after, especially in winter, and known for its healing powers. If you cannot get enough watercress, you can add lettuce, and if sorrel is in season, some of that too.

Serves 6 to 8

8 oz (225 g) watercress
12 oz (325 g) potatoes
1½ oz (40 g) butter
2½ pints (1.5 litres) chicken stock
salt and freshly ground black pepper
4 tablespoons single cream

Wash the watercress and chop roughly, leaving a few leaves whole on one side for decoration. Peel and chop the potatoes. Melt the butter in a saucepan, add the watercress, and cook over a low

heat until it is soft. Add the potatoes, mix well, and pour on the stock. Bring to the boil, season with salt and pepper to taste, and simmer for about 30 minutes until the potatoes are soft. Drain off some of the liquid so that you can mash the potatoes, or put it all in a blender. Pour back the liquid, and reheat the soup, adding the cream just before serving. Garnish with watercress.

White Soup Early 19th century

This recipe comes from Alice Parsons' manuscript cookery book. I can imagine it being ladled out of the huge china tureens which are still here at Birr. Alice measured the vegetables in plates and half plates: 'Half a plateful of young onions, the same of turnips, half that quantity of carrots ...'

Serves 10 to 12

1 lb (450 g) butter, plus 2 oz (50 g) to add later
8 oz (225 g) onions, chopped
8 oz (225 g) turnips, chopped
4 oz (100 g) carrots, chopped
2 medium lettuces, chopped
4 pints (2.2 litres) good chicken stock
1 tablespoon fresh chervil, finely chopped
pinch of nutmeg
pinch of mace
pinch of white pepper
2 to 3 egg yolks
1 pint (600 ml) double cream

Put the 1 lb (450 g) butter in a large pan over a low heat. When it is melted and sizzling gently, add the prepared vegetables, and let them stew slowly in the butter until just tender. Then drain off any surplus fat, pour in the stock, and simmer gently for 30 minutes. Stir in the chervil, the remaining 2 oz (50 g) butter, the spices, and the pepper.

Beat the egg yolks and cream together in a bowl, and just before serving pour this into the hot soup, stirring constantly over a low heat until the soup thickens slightly. Do not let it boil or it will curdle. Serve immediately.

Boiled Ham 20th century

From very early times there are references in Irish literature to sausages and ham. Killing pigs must have been an on-going part of life at Birr. Dorothy Parsons gives two seventeenth-century recipes for pig meat – 'to collar a pig', and 'to souce a pig'. Both of them are forms of preserving with salt and herbs. Alice Parsons also gives recipes for preserving or 'pickling' ham and bacon, using very large quantities of saltpetre, and one sees why the large lead cisterns were needed. There is also a Victorian recipe in the archive for curing a 15 lb (6.5 kg) ham. It is rubbed in 1 lb bay salt, 2 lb of common salt, 4 oz saltpetre, and, the next day, 1 lb hot treacle. Fortunately I can now buy the ham already 'cured', and it is not usually necessary these days to soak it, as was done when it used to become very salty in the curing. Boiled ham or bacon was often served with a roast chicken in the Irish tradition of something boiled and something roast.

Serves 20

1 large ham, 15–20 lb
1 pint (600 ml) cider
1 bunch watercress (optional)
4 oz (100 g) brown sugar

Put the ham in a large pan. Pour in enough water to cover the ham and the cider. Bring to the boil, and let it simmer slowly for about 4 hours. You may need to add more water. In the last 30 minutes add the watercress.

Take the ham out of the pan, and let it cool. Pre-heat the oven to 190° C (375° F, Mark 5). Remove the watercress from the pan, and chop roughly. When the ham is cool, take off the rind, rub the brown sugar into it, and place in the pre-heated oven for 30 minutes so that the sugar hardens. Place on a serving dish, and garnish with the chopped watercress.

Gingerbread 18th century

This recipe appears in eighteenth-century handwriting at the back of Dorothy Parsons' manuscript cookery book. I have halved the original quantities of the ingredients.

Makes about 30 biscuits

$1\frac{1}{2}$ lb (700 g) flour
1 oz (25 g) powdered ginger
pinch of grated nutmeg
8 oz (225 g) sugar
8 oz (225 g) butter
grated rind of $\frac{1}{2}$ lemon
$\frac{1}{4}$ pint (150 ml) treacle
$\frac{1}{2}$ pint (300 ml) cream

Pre-heat the oven to 150°C (300°F, Mark 2). Grease two large baking sheets. Sift the flour and spices into a large bowl, mix in the sugar, then rub in the butter until the mixture resembles fine breadcrumbs. Stir in the grated lemon rind.

Put the treacle and cream in a pan over a low heat,

and stir until well blended. Add to the mixture in the bowl, and mix thoroughly to form a stiff paste. Roll this out on a floured board until about $\frac{1}{16}$ inch (1.5 mm) thick. Cut into rounds $2\frac{1}{2}$ inches (6 cm) in diameter. Lift these with a palette knife onto the prepared baking sheets, and bake in the pre-eated oven for 30 minutes. Turn out onto a rack to cool.

Gooseberry Pudding 19th century

'There were a prodigous number of dishes round the desert, which at once pleased the eye and pallate' was the opinion of a young girl describing a ball given at Tullamore, the neighbouring town to Birr, in the early nineteenth century. One of those dishes could have been Alice Parsons' gooseberry pudding. They might have also used her recipe for making 'a very large jelly' for the centrepiece: 'There was a mighty pretty thing which was a hunt in jelly, the ground green for grass and the hounds in their propre colors ... swans made of blancmange swiming. I can't tell what it was that they were swiming in, but it was directly like water ...'

> Serves 6 to 8
>
> 2 lb (900 g) gooseberries, topped and tailed
> 1½ lb (700 g) sugar
> 1 small glass sweet white wine
> 4 egg yolks, beaten
> 3 oz (75 g) plain biscuits, such as 'Marie' biscuits
> 8 oz (225 g) butter

Pre-heat the oven to 150°C (300°F, Mark 2). Grease a large ovenproof dish. Boil the gooseberries until soft with the sugar, pulp them in a blender, place in a bowl, and stir in the glass of sweet white wine,

and the egg yolks. Pound up the biscuits and add them to the other ingredients. Beat the butter until soft, then blend well into the mixture. Turn into the prepared dish, and bake in the pre-heated oven for 1 hour.

If you wish, you can at the last minute beat up 3 egg whites with 4 oz (100 g) sugar until stiff, place this on the top, and bake 15 minutes longer for a meringue topping.

Peripatetic Pudding 19th century

This is a Victorian pudding from Mary Rosse's housekeeper's book. I am not sure why this is called peripatetic pudding, but I imagine it could be one of the puddings ending Mary Rosse's meals in her new dining room, with the astronomers by this stage anxious to go out and study the heavens through Lord Rosse's gigantic telescope. It is easy to make and very good.

> Serves 4 to 6
>
> six large slices of sponge cake
> 3 oz (75 g) sugar
> 8 oz (450 g) butter
> 8 oz (450 g) marmalade
> 4 eggs
> 1 tablespoon sherry

Pre-heat the oven to 180°C (350°F, Mark 4). Lightly butter a medium-sized baking dish, and line it with the slices of sponge cake. Mix the remaining ingredients together well, pour over the sponge cake in the baking dish, and bake for 1 hour, until golden brown and crisp on top. Serve hot.

Irish Breads Traditional

These two breads were traditionally made in Irish homes for breakfast. The recipe for spotted dick, sometimes known as spotted dog, comes from Chrissie Maguire.

Spotted Dick

12 oz (325 g) flour
pinch of salt
2 teaspoons bicarbonate of soda
2 oz (50 g) margarine
4 oz (100 g) sugar
12 oz (325 g) raisins
$\frac{3}{4}$ pint (450 ml) sour milk
1 egg, beaten

Pre-heat the oven to 230°C (450°F, Mark 7). Grease a baking sheet.

Sift the flour, salt, and bicarbonate of soda together into a large bowl. Rub in the margarine until the mixture resembles fine breadcrumbs. Stir in the sugar and raisins. Make a well in the centre, pour in the milk and egg, and mix in gradually, taking the dry ingredients in from the sides, to form a stiff dough.

Turn onto a floured board, and knead lightly. Pat into a round cake about 2 inches (5 cm) thick. Using a knife, mark with a cross, and place on the prepared baking sheet. Bake in the pre-heated oven for 45 minutes. Turn out immediately onto a rack to cool.

Soda Bread

1 lb 8 oz (700 g) wholemeal flour
1 teaspoon bicarbonate of soda
pinch of salt
1 pint (600 ml) sour milk

Pre-heat the oven to 190°C (375°F, Mark 5). Grease a baking sheet. Sift together the flour, bicarbonate of soda, and salt into a large bowl. Make a well in the centre, and pour in the milk. Mix in gradually, incorporating the dry ingredients from the sides into the milk to form a stiff dough.

Turn onto a floured board, and knead lightly. Pat into a round about 2 inches (5 cm) thick, and place on the prepared baking sheet. Using a knife, mark with a cross, and bake in the pre-heated oven for 35 to 45 minutes. Turn out immediately onto a rack to cool.

Barm Brac Traditional

Barm brac is a cake traditionally made for Hallowe'en, the Celtic New Year and festival of Samhain. Rings for marriage, buttons for bachelorhood, and other trinkets are hidden in it to tell the future. Alice Parsons had two eighteenth-century recipes for it, but I feel it better to give this modern variation.

1 lb (450 g) flour
pinch of nutmeg
pinch of salt
2 oz (50 g) butter
$\frac{1}{2}$ oz (15 g) yeast
2 oz (50 g) brown sugar
$\frac{1}{2}$ pint (300 ml) milk
2 eggs, beaten
8 oz (225 g) raisins
8 oz (225 g) sultanas
4 oz (100 g) mixed peel

Pre-heat the oven to 200°C (400°F, Mark 6). Grease a deep 8-inch (20-cm) loose-bottomed cake tin. Sift together the flour, nutmeg and salt in a large bowl, and rub in the butter. Cream the yeast with a teaspoonful of the sugar in a little tepid water. Mix the remaining sugar with the flour mixture. Add the milk and beaten eggs to the yeast, keeping aside a little of the egg to glaze the bread. Beat the liquid into the dry ingredients until the batter is stiff but elastic, then fold in the dried fruit and peel. Turn into the prepared cake tin, cover with a cloth and leave in a warm place to rise for 1 hour.

Bake in the pre-heated oven for 1 hour. Turn out immediately onto a rack to cool.

Ratafia Ice 18th century

This recipe was given to Alice Parsons by Mrs George St George of Tyrone House in Galway. It is very creamy and can be made in an ice cream machine; otherwise it needs stirring up twice during the freezing. It could be served with wafers or a caramel sauce.

The ice house was a feature of many eighteenth- and nineteenth-century 'big houses'. It was often like a covered cave in the ground with a deep stone-lined well to house the ice, with which it was filled in winter, packed in with clean straw. There was an ice house at Birr, where ice was collected from the lake, and this is Alice's method of freezing:

Have your ice pounded very small and mixed with as much salt as Ice in a bucket with holes in the bottom to let the water off, then put in your freezing pot in which is your cream, cover it and keep it twirling round as fast as possible by the handle until it grows thick, then blend your cream with your spatula and when thick enough for a spoon to stand in it (if you chuse it a hard Ice) fill your moulds with

it, cover and bury them in a fresh ice prepared as above. . .

Serves 8 to 10

4 oz (120 g) ground almonds
2 tablespoons sugar
2 tablespoons water
2 pints (1.2 litres) double cream

Put the ground almonds in a small pan with the sugar. Gradually stir in the water until just moist, then add $\frac{1}{3}$ pint (200 ml) of the cream. Heat gradually, stirring, until just about to boil, then simmer over a very low heat for 2 minutes. Take off the heat and put in the fridge to get quite cold, then stir in the rest of the cream.

Pour into an ice cream machine, and follow the manufacturer's instructions for freezing. If you haven't got an ice cream machine, pour into a metal bowl or other container, and place in the freezer or freezing compartment of a refrigerator, set at its lowest setting, for 1 hour. Remove, and beat to break up any ice crystals that have formed. Return to the freezer for a further $1\frac{1}{2}$ hours, then remove, beat again, and return to the freezer for 3 to 4 hours. It is now ready to serve.

Chocolate Soufflé 20th century

This is a recipe from *Good Sweets* by Ambrose Heath (1937), which was used regularly by my mother-in-law, Anne. Against it in her copy of the book she has written 'utterly lovely', and it is indeed delicious, but, like many of her 1930s recipes, very rich.

Serves 6

2 oz (50 g) chocolate

1 tablespoon milk

2 oz (50 g) caster sugar

2 oz (50 g) fine white breadcrumbs

2 egg yolks, beaten

3 teaspoons rum

$\frac{1}{4}$ pint (150 ml) double cream, whipped

Put the chocolate into a pan with the milk over a low heat, and stir until the chocolate melts. Stir in the caster sugar, and the breadcrumbs. Mix thoroughly, and add the egg yolks and rum. Remove from the heat, and beat well together until nearly cold, then fold in the whipped cream.

Spoon the mixture into a large serving dish, or into individual ramekins, and chill for 3 to 4 hours in the refrigerator before serving.

Eggs in Potatoes 20th century

This is from my mother-in-law Anne's manuscript cookery book.

Serves 6

6 large potatoes

6 eggs

8 oz (225 g) butter

Worcester sauce

Heat the oven to 190°C (375°F, Mark 5), and bake the potatoes in their jackets until nicely soft (about 1 hour). Remove from the oven, and place on a baking sheet. Cut a slice off the top of each, and scoop out a dessertspoon of potato. Put this in a bowl, mash it with a little of the butter and leave on one side.

Put a large knob of butter and a dash of Worcester sauce into the scooped-out hollow on the top of each potato, then crack in an egg. Pipe some of the

reserved mashed potato around each egg, then return the potatoes to the hot oven, and bake for 5 minutes until the eggs are set. Serve immediately.

Potato Cakes Traditional

These are traditionally served for tea or supper in Ireland. The ingredients are flexible; milk can be used instead of butter. They are a good way of using up left-over mashed potato.

Makes 16

1 lb (450 g) mashed potato

2 oz (50 g) plain flour

pinch of salt

1 oz (25 g) butter

1 egg, beaten

butter or bacon fat for frying

Put all the ingredients together in a bowl, and mix well to form a stiff dough. Turn out onto a floured surface, and roll into two circles, about $\frac{1}{2}$ inch (1.2 cm) thick. Cut each circle into eight triangles.

Heat the butter or bacon fat in a frying pan until sizzling, add the triangles of potato cake, and fry for about 3 minutes on each side, until well browned. Serve hot.

Birr Floating Angels 20th century

I think this is an adaptation of a recipe in *Lady Sysonby's Cook Book* (1935) called Caramel Soufflé, but this is the way it was done by Annie Shortt (cook-housekeeper at Birr). It was used only for special occasions, such as going back to school requests, as it is a heart-stopper when it comes to turning it out, and the spun-sugar is not easy.

Serves 6 to 8

Caramel

4 oz (100 g) sugar
2 tablespoons water
1 egg yolk

Meringue

4 to 5 egg whites
4 oz (100 g) caster sugar

Make the caramel by heating together the sugar and water until it turns brown and treacly. Pour half of this caramel into the bottom of a 1½-pint (900 ml) pudding basin, and leave the rest on one side in the pan.

Beat the egg whites until stiff, then fold in the caster sugar, a tablespoon at a time, and beat again until stiff. Spoon this meringue into the pudding basin on top of the caramel. Cover the basin with two layers of foil or grease proof paper, fastened securely on, and lower into a large pan of boiling water, so that the water comes half-way up the sides of the basin. Put the lid on the pan, turn the heat down *very* low, and leave to simmer very gently for 2 hours.

When the pudding has been cooking for about 1¾ hours, take the pan of remaining caramel, add the egg yolk, place over a low heat, and cook slowly, stirring, for 10 minutes. Leave somewhere warm.

When the pudding is ready, turn out of the basin onto a warm plate. Put the basin back in the water, boil very hard so that you can pull out the strings of the spun-sugar caramel sitting at the bottom, and drape them over the, hopefully, upright pudding. Then take the warm caramel sauce, stir, and pour around the pudding. Serve at once.

Lobster Birr Castle 20th century

This 1930s recipe, from my mother-in-law Anne's manuscript cookery book, is very rich and luxurious (the truffles would have been available in Dublin in the 1930s). It can be served in a pastry case, or in scallop shells. It can also be used to fill pancakes. Dublin Bay prawns can be used instead of lobster, and it is very good even without the truffle.

Serves 6 to 8

12 oz (325 g) lobster meat, cut into ½-inch
   (1.2 cm) pieces
2 oz (50 g) butter, melted
1 truffle, chopped
6 mushrooms, chopped
pinch of salt and cayenne pepper
1 small glass dry sherry
2 egg yolks
½ pint (300 ml) cream

Place the lobster meat in a saucepan with the melted butter. Add the chopped truffle, chopped mushrooms, salt, and cayenne pepper. Cover the saucepan and simmer for 5 minutes. Add the sherry and cook for 3 minutes more.

Beat the egg yolks and cream together, add to the lobster mixture and shake over the heat until the mixture thickens, about 2 minutes. Do not stir, and serve immediately or it will curdle.

Lemon cheese 19th century

This early nineteenth-century dish would have been an addition to the final course of a dinner. I usually serve this as part of the cheese course, and with a salad. It is not really very sweet. A tablespoon of brandy can be added to the mixture:

Some think a tablespoonful of brandy put into the cream and let to stand an hour before the whipping with the other ingredients makes it whip better and grow thick sooner.

You will need two muslin cloths for hanging it up in.

> 3 pints (1.7 litres) double cream
> 1 tablespoon sugar
> grated rind and juice of 1 lemon

Whip all the ingredients together, and place on a large sheet of muslin. Tie up to form a bundle, and hang over a bowl to drain for 24 hours.

Turn the mixture into a small sieve, and wrap it, in the sieve, in another large sheet of muslin. Tie up the muslin, and again hang over the basin to drain for a further 4 to 5 hours. Take down, turn the 'cheese' into a dish, and serve.

Neapolitan Butter 20th century

This savoury was often served instead of a cheese course by my mother-in-law, Anne, at her dinner parties. Until about ten years ago it was very hard to find any Irish cheese, and there are many substitute recipes in the archive at Birr. Although there is now a great revival of Irish cheese-making, this is a useful alternative.

> Serves 10 to 12

> 1½ lb (700 g) butter
> 6 anchovy fillets, mashed
> 3 oz (75 g) Cheddar cheese, grated

> 1 tablespoon chopped parsley
> 1 teaspoon lemon juice
> 1 oz (25 g) softened butter, for piping

Soften the butter, and three portions of 8 oz (225 g) each. Blend one portion with the mashed anchovy, one portion with the grated cheese, and the third portion with the chopped parsley and lemon juice.

Form these flavoured butter portions into similar sized rectangles, place on a dish next to each other with the anchovy-flavoured portion sandwiched in the middle. Decorate the top with soft piped butter, and serve with cream crackers and other cheese biscuits.

Potted Lobster 19th century

This Victorian recipe was copied into the housekeeper's book in the late nineteenth century. It could also be done with crab meat.

> Serves 4 to 6

> 2 lobsters
> 10 oz (275 g) butter
> pinch of cayenne pepper
> pinch of ground mace

Cook the lobsters in boiling water for 20 to 25 minutes. (In the original recipe they were almost certainly cut up alive.) Then remove the meat, including the coral, and cook it slowly in 6 oz (150 g) of the butter in a small pan, with the cayenne pepper and mace, for 5 minutes, until the butter is well blended in. Turn the mixture into a blender, and process to a smooth paste, or pound in a mortar.

Press the mixture into individual pots or ramekins.

Melt the remaining butter in a pan over a low
heat, and pour a layer of it over the lobster mixture
in each pot. Leave to cool until the butter is set,
then serve with brown bread.

Poires Ranovolo 20th century

This is an adaptation of a recipe from *Lady
Sysonby's Cook Book* (1935) which was used
regularly by my mother-in-law, Anne, at Birr in the
1930s.

> Serves 8
>
> 2 oz (50 g) plain chocolate, grated
> $\frac{1}{2}$ pint (300 ml) whipped cream
> 8 pears, peeled, halved and blanched (you could
>   use tinned pear halves)
> 6 egg yolks
> 2 oz (50 g) sugar
> 1 tablespoon sweet sherry

Mix the grated chocolate with the whipped cream,
first setting aside 2 heaped tablespoons of cream
for the topping. Spread the chocolate and cream
mixture on the bottom of a flan dish. Lay the
blanched pears (drained of all juice) on top of the
cream.

Beat up the egg yolks with the sugar, and add the
sherry. Beat until thick and light-coloured. Lastly
mix in the 2 heaped tablespoons of whipped cream
that you have set aside, and pour this mixture over
the pears. Chill in the refrigerator for at least 3 to
4 hours before serving.

Bibliography

Castle Hill

Manuscripts

Fortescue MSS in the Devon Record Office (DRO 1262/M)

Plans of Castle Hill in 1804 in Sir John Soane's Museum

Courtenay MSS in the Devon Record Office (DRO 1508/M)

Richard Supple Dinner Book, Brooke of Oakley MSS vol 30, in the Northamptonshire Record Office

Books

Acton, A. *Modern Cookery*, London 1845

Adams, S. & S. *The Complete Servant*, London 1825 (reprinted 1989)

Bouquet, M. *Family, Servants and Visitors: the Farm Household in Nineteenth and Twentieth Century Devon*, Norwich 1985

Bradley, R. *The Country Housewife and Lady's Director*, London 1727 (reprinted 1980)

Carter, C. *The Complete Practical Cook*, London 1730 (reprinted 1984)

Digby, Sir Kenelm *The Closet of the Eminently Learned Sir Kenelme Digby, Kt., Opened*, London 1669 (new edition 1910)

Ellis, W. *The Country Housewife's Family Companion*, London 1750

Farley, J. *The London Art of Cookery*, London 1783

Fortescue, Hugh, 4th Earl *A Chronicle of Castle Hill*, London 1929

Fortescue, Sir Seymour *Looking Back*, London 1920

Fortescue, Lady Winifred *Beauty for Ashes*, London 1948

Glasse, H. *The Art of Cookery Made Plain and Easy*, London 1747 (reprinted 1983)

Heal, F. *Hospitality in Early Modern England*, Oxford 1990

Kenney, Herbert, A. *Common-sense Cookery*, London 1894

Kitchener, W. *Apicius Redivivus: or, The Cook's Oracle*, London 1817

M.W. *The Queens Closet Opened*, London 1655 (reprinted 1984)

Morgan, J. & Richards, A. *A Paradise out of a Common Field*, London 1990

Nott, J. *The Cook's and Confectioner's Dictionary*, London 1726 (reprinted 1980)

Piscator *Fish, how to Dress and how to Serve*, London 1843

Raffald, E. *The Experienced English Housekeeper*, Manchester 1769 (reprinted 1970)

Glamis Castle

Manuscripts

Strathmore Papers *Vols 238, 241, 244 and 245*. The recipes used have been drawn from the Strathmore Papers, *Vols 243 and 245*; also from *The Recipe Book of Lady Clerk of Tillypronie*, compiled between 1841 and 1901 but published posthumously in 1909; also from the recipe collection of Hon. Mountstuart Elphinstone, by kind permission of Lord Elphinstone.

Books

Brown, Catherine *From Broth to Bannocks*, Glasgow 1990

Lady Castlehill's Receipt Book: original recipes from a collection made in 1712 by Martha Lockhart, the Lady Castlehill, ed. with intro. by H. Whyte, Glasgow 1976

Hamilton, Lord Frederick *The Days before Yesterday*, London 1937

Hope, Annette *A Caledonian Feast*, Edinburgh 1987

Kay, Billy & Maclean, Cailean *Knee Deep in Claret; a Celebration of Scotland and Wine*, Edinburgh 1983

Marshall, Rosalind *The Days of Duchess Anne: Life in the Household of the Duchess of Hamilton, 1656–1716*, New York 1973

McNeill, F. Marian *The Scots Kitchen*, Glasgow & London 1929

——*The Scots Cellar*, Edinburgh 1956

Reid, John *The Scots Gard'ner*, Edinburgh 1683 (reprinted with an intro. by Annette Hope, Edinburgh 1988)

Scottish History Society *The Ochtertyre House Booke*, Edinburgh 1907

Erddig Hall

Manuscripts

Manuscript cookery books:

c. 1684	Clwyd Record Office	D/E/1203
c. 1765	Clwyd Record Office	D/E/2551(a)
2 books of Victoria Cust, aft. Mrs Yorke, 1837 & later		
2 books of Mrs Louisa Yorke, early 20th century		D/E/2794
2 books of Miss Lucy Hitchman, early 20th century		

Other manuscripts examined at Clwyd Record Office are noted at the appropriate points in the text. Manuscript material for which no CRO number is given has already been published in one or more of the books listed below (*see* Cust, Palmer, Waterson).

Books

Cust, A.L. (Mrs Wherry) *Chronicles of Erthig on the Dyke*, 2 vols, London 1914

Glasse, H. *The Art of Cookery*, London 1747 (reprinted 1983)

Myddelton, W.M., (Ed.), *Chirk Castle Accounts A.D. 1666–1753*, Manchester 1931

Palmer, A.N. *History of the Thirteen Country Townships of the Old Parish of Wrexham . . . and Erddig*, Wrexham 1903

Palmer, A.N. & Owen, E. *A History of Ancient Land Tenures in North Wales and the Marches*, 2nd edn, Wrexham 1910

Pettitt, E.L., comp. *Clwyd Archives Cookbook*, Clwyd Record Office, Hawarden 1980

Roberts, E. 'Everyday life in the homes of the gentry', pp. 39–78, *Class, Community and Culture in Tudor Wales*, J. Gwynfor Jones (Ed.), Cardiff 1989

Waterson, M. *The Servants' Hall: a Domestic History of Erddig*, London 1980

Birr Castle

Manuscripts

The archives at Birr have been the main source, especially MSS A/17 (*c.* 1670) and E/13A (*c.* 1800).

Books

Briggs, R. *The English Art of Cookery According to Present Practice*, Dublin 1791

Fitzgibbon, T. *Irish Traditional Food*, London 1983

Foster, R.F. *Modern Ireland, 1600–1972*, London 1988

Bibliography

Lucas, A.T. 'Irish Food Before the Potato', *Gwerin*,
3, pt.2 (1960), pp.8–43 (The extensive scholarly
bibliography at the end has been the mainstay
for my background reading)

McCormick, M. *Irish Country Cooking*, Bath 1988

O'Curry, E. *Manners and Customs of the Ancient
Irish*, Dublin 1873

Spurling, H. *Elinor Fettiplace's Receipt Book*,
London 1983

Acknowledgements

I am grateful to Lady Margaret Fortescue for information about Castle Hill and permission to use the Fortescue MSS in the Devon Record Office. My thanks, too, to the Archivist and staff of the Devon Record Office and Christopher Tongue of the Northamptonshire Record Office. Sally Jaine was a great help with the recipes and Wendy Baker with the typing. Caroline Davidson gave advice.
Tom Jaine

I am grateful to Mary, Countess of Strathmore DL. for permission to use the Strathmore Papers; also to Mrs Joan Auld, their archivist, and the National Library of Scotland, who made it possible for me to work from them in Edinburgh. I would like to thank Lord and Lady Elphinstone of Drumkilbo in Perthshire for generously lending me the Hon. Mountstuart Elphinstone's typed collection of recipes.
Annette Hope

I would like to thank Mr Geoffrey Veysey and Mss Elizabeth Pettitt and Fiona Wilkinson-Buckley of Clwyd Record Office, Hawarden, for easing the task of examining many documents for Jennifer Stead and me. Mr Robert Dillon, Administrator of Erddig Hall, kindly sent me helpful information about the house and its contents; and I am also indebted to Mr Lindsay Evans of Wrexham who first drew my attention to the Welsh Bards of the Nobility, and to Thomas Pennant's description of Evan Lloyd at Cwm Bychan.
C. Anne Wilson

I am grateful to all the friends and family in Birr who helped in trying out the receipts and eating them, and those who explained traditional Irish food, especially Margaret Hogan and Chrissie Maguire. I am also grateful to Myrtle Allen of Ballymalloe House for all her help, and to Anthony Malcomson, who catalogued the Birr Castle Archives, without which my research would not have been possible.
Alison Rosse

Index

*Numbers in **bold** refer to recipes*